George Orwell the

C000109864

Also available from Continuum

Graham Greene Michael G. Brennan

London Narratives Lawrence Phillips

The Postwar British Literature Handbook edited by Katharine Cockin and
Jago Morrison

George Orwell the Essayist

Literature, Politics and the Periodical Culture

Peter Marks

continuum

Continuum International Publishing Group
The Tower Building   80 Maiden Lane
11 York Road   Suite 704
London SE1 7NX   New York NY 10038

www.continuumbooks.com

© Peter Marks 2011

British Library Cataloguing-in-Publication Data
A catalogue record for this book is available from the British Library.

ISBN: 978-1-4411-4873-5 (hardcover)
       978-1-4411-2584-2 (paperback)

Library of Congress Cataloging-in-Publication Data
Marks, Peter, 1958-
  George Orwell the essayist : literature, politics and the periodical culture / Peter Marks.
      p. cm.
  Includes bibliographical references.
  ISBN 978-1-4411-4873-5
  1. Orwell, George, 1903-1950–Criticism and interpretation. 2. English essays–20th century–History and criticism. 3. Politics and literature–Great Britain–History–20th century. I. Title.
  PR6029.R8Z734 2011
  824'.912–dc23
                                                    2011016498

Typeset by Newgen Imaging Systems Pvt Ltd, Chennai, India
Printed and bound in India

Contents

Acknowledgements   vi

Introduction: Orwell, the Essay and the Periodical Culture   1

Chapter 1 From Blair to Orwell: Finding a Voice (1928–36)   18

Chapter 2 The Radicalized Orwell: From Spanish to Global
          Conflict (1937–9)   49

Chapter 3 Orwell in Wartime: Socialism, Patriotism and
          Cultural Threat (1940–5)   83

Chapter 4 Orwell and the Uncertain Future (1946–50)   134

Chapter 5 The Posthumous Orwell and the Afterlife of the Essays   187

Bibliography   203

Index   209

Acknowledgements

The journey to the completion of this book began long ago. I wish to acknowledge with immense gratitude the input of Professor Cairns Craig and Professor Sir Bernard Crick at the start of that journey. As I wrote once before, then-Dr Craig's deft use of the intellectual carrot and stick stopped me making an ass of myself. Professor Crick's humane encouragement over too long a time was crucial in my finishing this project. My sincere regret is that he did not live long enough to see this book published.

I also need – as all students of Orwell now need – to thank profoundly Professor Peter Davison, Ian Angus and Sheila Davison for their monumental and breathtakingly detailed edition, *The Complete Works of George Orwell*. Others have already sung its praises, but I wish to add my voice as well. As readers will see from the first pages, the *Complete Works* is omnipresent. Every time I opened one of the 20 volumes – and I opened them countless times – I learned something.

All errors are my own.

To the many friends and colleagues and family members who have suffered my rehearsal of the arguments contained here, apologies. Those closest to me have endured the most, so I acknowledge the love and patience of Ella Watson Marks, who will get her father back in reasonable condition. To Jo, whose tenderness and solicitude match her fortitude and forbearance, endless thanks. This one's for you.

A note on references: *The Complete Works of George Orwell* is listed as *CO* in references, with the appropriate Roman numeral designating the particular volume.

Introduction:

Orwell, the Essay and the Periodical Culture

Reading the obituaries of his friend George Orwell, the writer and commentator Malcolm Muggeridge observed with cleared-eyed cynicism that he could understand how 'the legend of a human being is created' (Coppard and Crick, p. 271). At the time of his death Orwell was a well-considered writer chiefly famous for the crystalline brilliance of his political allegory *Animal Farm* (1945). *Nineteen Eighty-Four* had been published in Britain and in the United States six months before Orwell died in January 1950, and was receiving highly enthusiastic reviews. It had already sold over 70,000 copies and been selected by the Book-of-the-Month Club in America. Despite these portents, Muggeridge could never have guessed that of all his literary contemporaries Orwell would survive best into the twenty-first century, surpassing in influence, prestige and public awareness the likes of W. H. Auden, Graham Greene, Christopher Isherwood and Evelyn Waugh. Orwell would enter the cultural footnotes of Britain, read as an acute and authoritative interpreter of England and Englishness (Scruton, 2006). Some judge him one of the pre-eminent English prose stylists of the last century, while a less controversial evaluation would place him comfortably among the greatest political writers of the modern era. Probably he is the most widely read author of political fiction of the last hundred years and almost certainly the most referenced and recognized, even by those who have never opened *Animal Farm* or *Nineteen Eighty-Four.*

All this is well known. His essays, which this book examines at length, are appreciated individually but have been less fully or extensively considered. Yet essays made up a substantial part of Orwell's literary output, contributing significantly to his cultural and political development while transmitting his observations and arguments to a varied and vivid assortment of readers. They also helped fashion the posthumous image of Orwell as a broad-ranging public intellectual able to examine with a fresh and attentive intelligence an array of subjects: the political and cultural forces at work in totalitarian societies; seaside postcards; the qualities that make Charles Dickens 'worth stealing'; the potential future under the atom bomb; the sociological implications of common toads; the decline of political language and the complex allure of Gandhi. Their impact has been felt in surprising areas, the cultural theorist

During seeing Orwell's essays on popular culture as important to the
_____s of cultural studies as an academic field (During, p. 35). The *OED* cites
'You and the Atom Bomb' as the first instance of the term 'cold war', while
the writer and academic David Lodge has used 'A Hanging' to analyse salient distinctions between fiction and non-fiction. Orwell's essays are a staple
of composition courses at American universities. British Prime Minister John
Major quoted from 'The Lion and the Unicorn' in painting a cloying portrait
of Britain's virtues, and 'Politics and the English Language' was used as a reference point for a book on political discourse in the United States in the run-
up to the election of Barack Obama. Scores of Orwell's essays entertain and
provoke long after the initial circumstances that prompted them have passed,
anthologies regularly bringing together different gatherings for appreciative
international audiences. 'A Hanging', 'Shooting an Elephant', 'Boys' Weeklies',
'Politics and the English Language' and 'Why I Write' are recognized as classics of the form. Not that the essays are universally lauded. Salman Rushdie
reads 'Inside the Whale' as 'advocating ideas that can only be of service to our
masters' (Rushdie, p. 97), and academic Scott Lucas accuses 'The Lion and the
Unicorn' of being 'a vehicle for cultural nationalism that knew no complexity'
(Lucas, p. 21). Some critics read *Nineteen Eighty-Four* as the work of a writer
doomed by ill-health recording his existential despair and the rejection of
socialist principles. But in fact his essays provide substantial counterevidence,
revealing an engaged, argumentative figure, a perceptive cultural analyst
arguing against political quietism and continuing to champion Socialism as
he understood it.

Tracking Orwell's development through his essays highlights his inquisitive,
often combative intelligence, his keenness to contribute on contentious issues
and his unaffected curiosity about popular culture. This approach also shows
how, for all his assertiveness, he was capable of changing his views radically.
So, for example, in a July 1939 review article published in the journal *The
Adelphi* he labels the British and French empires 'a far vaster injustice' than
Fascism (*CO, XI*, p. 360). Yet in 'My Country Right or Left', published in *Folios
of New Writing* in autumn 1940, he recalls a dream on the eve of the war which
convinced him 'that I was patriotic at heart, would not sabotage or act against
my own side, would support the war, would fight in it if it were possible' (*CO,
XII*, p. 271). The confident expression of views in his famously lucid prose did
not inoculate him from errors of judgement or from the need to reconsider
those views. Orwell was responsive to new conditions, and the essay supplied
him with a versatile medium through which to broadcast opinions and, where
appropriate, his subsequent revisions. His essays also enjoyed an 'afterlife',
becoming integral to the posthumous assessment of Orwell as a great prose
stylist and a perceptive cultural commentator. And as Rushdie's assertion
shows, they also furnished critics with material to expose perceived blind spots
and biases. This study assesses the essay's significance to his larger literary

achievement, arguing that collectively these short, seemingly ephemeral pieces are central to his literary, political and cultural achievement. The vast number of essays he wrote precludes consideration of them all. But this book argues that we understand the complexities, subtleties, contradictions and evolution in Orwell's writing and thinking better by understanding his essays.

His place among the first rank of essayists needs explaining at this intro-ductory stage if only because in the twenty-first century that status seems unproblematic. As early as 1969 the influential American critic Irving Howe was calling Orwell 'the greatest English essayist since Hazlitt, maybe since Dr Johnson' (Howe, p. 98), and John Hammond declared in 1982 that in 'vol-ume, range and intellectual depth his essays are unrivalled in this century'. Hammond adds that in pieces such as 'A Hanging' and 'Charles Dickens' Orwell 'made a lasting contribution to English literature and moreover enlarged the horizons of the English essay in a significant and dynamic way' (Hammond, p. 226). Graham Good devotes a chapter to Orwell's essays in his extensive study of the form, observing that Orwell 'can be seen as revising the tradition of the political essay', a line 'which runs from Swift through Hazlitt' (Good, p. 174). More recently, Claire de Obaldia readily locates Orwell in the 'great tradition' that includes the founding figures of the genre such as Michel de Montaigne and Francis Bacon alongside an international elite stretching over several centuries: Saint-Beuve, Renan, Roland Barthes, Addison, Steele, Dr Johnson, Charles Lamb, Virginia Woolf, T. S. Eliot, Ralph Waldo Emerson, Benn, Mann, Unamuno, Ortega, Jorge Luis Borges and others (de Obaldia, p. 2). Commentators and critics repeatedly compare the quality of his essays favourably against Orwell's other work. His first major biographer, the British political scientist Bernard Crick, judges that the essays 'may well constitute his lasting claim to greatness as a writer' (Crick, p. vii). From a literary perspective the American critical titan Harold Bloom, introducing analyses of *Nineteen Eighty-Four*, declares bluntly that 'Orwell, aesthetically considered, is a far bet- ter essayist than a writer' (Bloom, p. 1). Unless he is damning with faint praise, Bloom's statement counts as a considerable recommendation. John Rodden, the most diligent and informative observer of Orwell's reputation, questions whether Orwell's literary status 'can bear the weight of esteem and signifi-cance which successive generations have bestowed upon him'. But he is willing to make an exception 'perhaps in the essay form, where his compelling ethos so strongly appeals' (Rodden, p. x). Even when doubts arise about the quality of works as talismanic as *Animal Farm* and *Ninety Eighty-Four*, then, Orwell's essays still get praised.

For all this acclaim, Orwell died having published only two volumes of essays: *Inside the Whale and Other Essays* (1940) and *Critical Essays* (1946). And even this brief list overstates the truth, for *Critical Essays* contained two of the three essays from *Inside the Whale*. If we add to these volumes his pamphlet essay for democratic socialism, 'The Lion and The Unicorn' (1941), his contributions to wartime volumes such *The Betrayal of the Left* (1941) and *Victory or Vested Interest?* (1942), the long essay *The English People* (1947) – which he dismissed himself as a 'silly little' book – and the occasional reprint of his essays in other collections, fewer than 20 essays out of well over 100 that he had had published were available to the general public during his lifetime. Many subsequently famous pieces including 'Politics and the English Language', 'A Hanging', 'Bookshop Memories', 'Decline of the English Murder', 'Reflections on Gandhi' and 'Why I Write' were not included in these volumes, and were unknown to most people in 1950. The collections themselves achieved only limited sales: *Inside the Whale*'s print run was 1,000 copies; the two impressions of *Critical Essays* totalled less than 9,000, while its American version, *Dickens, Dali and Others: Essays in Popular Culture*, ran to 5,000 (Fenwick pp. 90, 245–6). *The Lion and the Unicorn*, printed in book form, was more successful, but only 10,000 copies were published (ibid., pp. 91–2), and when Orwell died it was nearly a decade out of print. The possibility at the beginning of 1950 that he might be considered an essayist worth placing alongside Montaigne, Dr Johnson, Emerson and T. S. Eliot would have seemed absurd.

Where were the other essays that would elevate Orwell into the exalted company of Montaigne and Bacon? His introductory 'Note' in *Critical Essays* supplies an answer:

> Most of these essays have appeared in print before, and several of them more than once. 'Charles Dickens' and 'Boy's Weeklies' appeared in my book *Inside the Whale*. 'Boy's Weeklies' also appeared in *Horizon*, as did 'Wells, Hitler and the World State', 'The Art of Donald McGill', 'Rudyard Kipling', 'W.B. Yeats' and 'Raffles and Miss Blandish'. The last-named essay also appeared in the New York monthly magazine, *Politics*. A shortened version of 'The Art of Donald McGill' appeared in the *Strand Magazine*. 'Arthur Koestler' was written for *Focus*, but will probably not have appeared before this book is published. 'In Defence of P.G. Wodehouse' appeared in *The Windmill*. 'Benefit of Clergy' made a sort of phantom appearance in the *Saturday Book* for 1944. The book was in print when its publishers, Messrs Hutchinsons, decided that this essay must be suppressed on grounds of obscenity. It was accordingly cut out of each copy, although for technical reasons it was impossible to remove its title from the table of contents. To the other periodicals which have allowed me to reprint my contributions, the usual acknowledgements are due. (*CO, XVIII*, p. 106)

Orwell's essays almost always appeared first in literary and political periodicals. Some of these journals were almost unknown except to their subscribers, while most had circulations lower than 5,000. Today, only literary scholars (and few of them) are likely to have heard of *Focus* or *The Windmill*, and to these can be added dozens of short-lived or relatively poorly subscribed journals such as *Gangrel, Now, New English Weekly, The Highway* and *Fortnightly Review*. Other journals that published his essays – *The Adelphi, Horizon* and *Partisan Review* are prime examples – had a substantial reputation while they lasted, but even so their actual readerships were surprisingly small, *Horizon's* never exceeding 10,000. Cumulatively, though, these periodicals were crucial to the intellectual and critical vigour of the 1930s and 1940s. Orwell wrote for dozens of them – the index of serials in the *Complete Orwell* runs to four pages (*CO,* *XX,* pp. 550–3) – but in the posthumous collections that appeared before *The Collected Essays, Journalism and Letters of George Orwell* in 1968 the journal origins of these pieces were ignored, obscuring the crucial role those periodicals played in Orwell's literary development. This study resituates Orwell's essays in the periodical culture in which they first appeared, presenting the first sustained account of their importance to what and how he wrote, as well as to the development of his ideas and reputation.

Countless writers, famous and obscure, benefited from the changing and interactive world of periodicals, some of which lasted only a handful of issues, others which survived for decades. Together these journals published essays and poems, literary and social criticism, manifestoes, short stories, reviews and editorials; some of them printed avant-garde art. They promoted new critical and creative work, nurtured talent and provided platforms for established writers. Some aligned with literary, artistic and political movements and parties, others fiercely proclaimed their independence. Journals presented writers with attentive and informed audiences and readers with work of sometimes astounding quality and originality (and with much that was mediocre and forgettable). Many journals were fleeting affairs dependent on the enthusiasm of a few staff and the fickle support of subscribers. But without them most of Orwell's essays would not have been written, never mind published. The same holds true for many other writers. The collective importance of periodicals to the production and reception of new material cultural debate over several centuries has been incalculable. When Orwell was writing they seeded literary movements, responded to tumultuous national and global events, provided forums for any number of cultural and political debates, evaluated literary trends and innovations, and attempted to shape the cultural and sometimes even the political future. Many of the speculations proved false, many of the attempts to influence failed, but this should be expected; periodicals operated in 'real time', providing invaluable evidence of positions and trends as they developed, not as they reconstituted and were later represented. This holds true for Orwell, too, as well as for other periodical writers. Discovering changes or apparent inconsistencies in his views (as this study does) hardly exposes him as a fraud, toppling him like the statue of a deposed tyrant. Seen in context, his essays offer a fine-grained record of the changes and reappraisals in his literary and political thinking. Close examination of them shows Orwell to be opinionated and perceptive, but not infallible.

Studies of George Orwell's work are often founded upon a particular perception or portrait of the man, on the grounds that defining this idiosyncratic figure facilitates an understanding of his writing. The approach adopted here gives context at least equal weighting with biography (the two aspects clearly are linked), but a definitional problem also remains in the essay form itself. Definitions that attempt to encompass all types of essays tend towards a perplexing vagueness, while those aiming to render the essay's essential qualities prove inadequate for the variety of pieces which are labelled or which label themselves as essays. The problem is long standing, Samuel Johnson's *Dictionary* of 1755 describing the essay as 'a loose sally of the mind, an irregular, undigested piece, not a regular and orderly performance' (Johnson, p. 167). This explanation prompts more questions than it answers. A modern *Dictionary of Literary Terms* shows few advances:

> essay (F *essai* 'attempt') A composition, usually in prose (Pope's *Moral Essays* in verse are an exception), which may be of only a few hundred words (like Bacon's *Essays*) or of book length (like Locke's *Essay Concerning Human Understanding*) and which discusses, formally or informally, a topic or a variety of topics. It is one of the most flexible and adaptable of all literary forms. (Cuddon, pp. 306–7)

After the heavily qualified first sentence, the observation in the second seems unnecessary.

One response to these difficulties involves returning to Frenchman Michel de Montaigne, who coined the label *Essais* for his collection of short discursive pieces published in 1580. Montaigne named a new genre, set down some of its main elements and created a benchmark for quality. In the introductory 'Note to the Reader' he also makes what a recent editor of his essays declares 'a revolutionary decision' by stating: 'I myself am the subject of my book'. M. A. Screech argues that '[i]n the history of the known world only a handful of authors had ever broken the taboo against writing primarily about oneself, as an ordinary man' (Screech, p. xv). Montaigne acknowledges the dangers in this position:

> If my design had been to seek the favour of the world I would have decked myself out better and presented myself in a studied gait. Here I want to be seen in my simple, natural, everyday fashion, without striving or artifice: for it is my own self that I am painting. Here, drawn from life, you will read of my defects and my native form so far as respect for social convention allows. (ibid., p. lix)

He understands that in putting himself centre stage he invites very personal criticism. His essays utilize ancient wisdom – Montaigne was impressively learned – but ultimately they display his sensibilities, his judgement. If he remains the father figure of the essay, Francis Bacon seems his obvious heir in England. The first edition of Bacon's essays, published 17 years after Montaigne's, acknowledges debts both in the title and within the text. As Montaigne had done in France, Bacon set a high benchmark in England. Yet Montaigne's educated discursiveness and conversational tone find little parallel in Francis Bacon's aphoristic, didactic essays. If Montaigne wants to discuss, Bacon yearns to direct. These early essayists provided different models, suggesting the prospect of development for later writers exploiting the essay's potential. From the outset, the form was versatile, malleable and responsive.

This protean quality frustrates some scholars. Hugh Walker in 1915 attempts to categorize essays relative to an ideal, distinguishing two groups: 'essays par excellence', as well as those 'compositions to which custom has assigned the name, but which agree only in being comparatively short . . . and in being more or less incomplete . . . [Such] essays do not strictly belong to a separate literary form: the historical essay is an incomplete history' (Walker, p. 3). In contrast to these incomplete versions of other genres or forms, essays par excellence 'under no circumstances expand into treatises: they are complete in themselves'. Yet incompleteness cannot be excluded from this understanding of the essay. Walker admits that, especially in his early writings, Bacon uses the essay in its definitional sense, literally and precisely as an 'attempt' at a subject. He implies that incompleteness constituted a kind of adolescent phase that Bacon eventually outgrew, although he accepts that in Bacon's early essays 'the connexions (sic) are not worked out and expressed, but are implicit and can be supplied by the intelligence of an alert reader' (ibid., p. 18). Incompleteness cannot be ignored, and as we will find it has a positive aspect, activating reader participation.

Another traditional scholar, Marie Hamilton Law, tries to impose a form of quality control, contending that 'highest type of all, the one that is most certainly to be classed as pure literature among the fine arts is the personal or the familiar essay' (Law, pp. 7–8). She underlines the subjectivity of the familiar essay: 'personality is its keynote . . . The familiar essay conveys the moods, the fantasies and whims, the chance reflections and random observations of the essayist' (ibid., p. 8). Writers such as Montaigne, Sir Thomas Browne and Abraham Cowley are lauded as early exemplars of the highest form of essay, with Charles Lamb the carrier of the torch. Law contrasts this ideal with the periodical essay, which she argues has an 'ulterior purpose: to bring news "foreign and domestic", to afford entertainment, and to bring about a reform in morals, manners and taste' (ibid., pp. 8–9). As with Walker, she classifies essays into two classes:

> those writings which possess some distinction of thought and manner and central qualities of permanence and those that are merely topical, ephemeral, journalistic, or technical . . . and treatises which burden our current

periodicals, both popular and learned, and which flourish today and tomorrow are cast into the oven. (ibid., p. 7)

Where Walker tries to impose completeness as the defining term, Law employs the medium in which the essay is published.

As most of Orwell's essays appeared in journals, Law's argument requires some response, but the idea of completeness deserves fuller consideration, as it raises questions about what the essay might be, what it does, and its relation to readers. One provocative argument gets made by the literary critic and theorist Georg Lukács in 'On the Nature and Form of the Essay', written as an introduction to his 1910 essay collection, *Soul and Form*. Lukács asks: 'what is an essay? What is its intended form of expression, and what are the ways and means whereby this expression is accomplished?' (Lukács, pp. 1–2). He treats the essay as an inherently critical form, and considers 'the essential, the value-determining thing about it is not the verdict (as is the case with the system) but the process of judging' (ibid., p. 18). A more polemical argument along these lines can be found in Theodor Adorno's 'The Essay as Form' (1958). Adorno challenges what he describes as the denigration and censure of the essay by the German academic establishment, placing the essay form in opposition to the 'petty completeness' of science. He suggests that the essay functions as a 'critique of the system . . . accentuating the fragmentary, the partial rather than the total' (Adorno, p. 157). As with Lukács, Adorno celebrates incompleteness as inherently critical; a recognition of the tentativeness of knowledge. He calls the essay the 'critical form par excellence', one that carries out a 'critique of ideology' (ibid., p. 166).

Anglo-American critics have considered the essay's effect on readers. Stanley Fish sees Francis Bacon's primary concern not in mature presentation but 'with the experience that form provides' (Fish, p. 81). Fish views Bacon's aphorisms as essentially heuristic, calling on the sceptical intelligence of the reader. This has a salutary effect, for though

> the content of aphorisms is not necessarily more true than the content of methodical writing . . . it minimizes the possibility that the mind . . . will take the coherence of an artful discourse for the larger coherence of objective truth. (ibid., p. 87)

A similar case can be made about Montaigne. Richard Sayce observes that Montaigne's revisions of his essays constitute a fundamental feature, for

> Montaigne rereads what he has written earlier and in the rereading is stimulated to new reflections which sometimes go beyond their point of departure, enlarging, qualifying, setting off on a tangent, even contradicting. (Sayce, p. 12)

While for some authors the establishment of the 'definitive' version of a particular essay is important, with 'Montaigne this scarcely makes sense because each stage has equal validity, each contributes something to the moving figure' (ibid., p. 9). The extent of this revision becomes clear in the acknowledgement by J. M. Robertson, introducing E. J. Trechmann's 1927 translation of the essays, that at his death in 1592, Montaigne left a copy of the latest edition 'with numerous corrections, and additions written on the margins' (Robertson, in Montaigne, 1927, p. xiv). These corrections and additions are more than mere tinkerings, if, as John O'Neill contends in his study of Montaigne, the essay constitutes 'an experiment in the community of truth, and not a packaging of knowledge ruled by definitions and operations' (O'Neill, p. 9). O'Neill's assessment has obvious similarities with Fish's reading of Bacon. O'Neill also recognizes, as Walker did of Bacon's early essays, that Montaigne' essays 'are unwelcome to the passive reader. They require that the reader share in the author's activity'. Given the rhetoric of active readers, communities of truth and the upsetting of rules, O'Neill not surprisingly reads the essay as 'a political instrument inasmuch as it liberates the writer and the reader from the domination of conventional standards of clarity and communication' (ibid.).

The 500-year-old form initiated by Montaigne is more than a plucky survivor. Rather than a deficiency, incompleteness shapes as a crucial activating force. Carl Klaus describes the essay elegantly as 'a means of thinking on paper', while Graham Good comments that the essay's knowledge 'is organised artistically rather than scientifically or logically. The essay's open-minded approach to experience is balanced by aesthetic pattern and closure' (Good, pp. 14–15). He situates reading in one of the cultural contexts where the form flourished, suggesting that the 'empirical and individualistic quality of English culture and the early dominance of bourgeois values were obviously very hospitable to the essay' (ibid., p.viii). From the position of late-twentieth-century feminism Ruth-Ellen Boetcher Joeres and Elizabeth Mittman stress a similar point, that the essay 'emerges from a patriarchal European/white origin' (Joeres and Mittmann, p. 12). But they add that while we might expect that the form was antagonistic to other perspectives, in fact it is active and flexible: 'Essays stress process over product' (ibid., p. 20). And they ask usefully: 'What happens when we add the reader as a factor in the process of essay production and think of the essay as a dialogue, as initiating discussion, as inviting reaction, response?' (ibid., p. 18). For them, as for many other scholars of the essay, the form is inherently interactive.

What should be obvious is that no particular model of the essay encompasses the range of writing that labels itself or might be labelled an essay. The derivation of the term 'essay' from the French for 'attempt' allows the form a great deal of freedom from the burden of proof required of a thesis or a book. Incompleteness liberates the essay from the necessities of sequence and structure, so that essayists can move rapidly and dexterously to the meat of the topic. They can make provisional, contentious and speculative observations,

comments and statements liberated from the need to fully justify and substantiate. For a polemicist like Orwell the essay could provide a vital tool for communicating unorthodox or provocative opinions that might not stand up to
sustained scrutiny, but which could activate responses and reactions. Its small
canvas provided the rhetorical space for his vivid arguments, and over time
essays allowed him to develop and employ a variegated palate. The personal
voice central to many (although not all) essays advertised and simultaneously
helped cultivate Orwell's own take on the world, reflecting the changes, subtleties, variety, bias and occasional contradictions of that voice. Because no topic
is prohibited, essays can roam freely across all terrain, restricted only by the
inquisitiveness of the essayist.

Given that most of Orwell's essays first appeared in journals, an analysis of
them based primarily on the writings of Montaigne or Bacon is inadequate. The
establishment of the periodical in the late-seventeenth- and early-eighteenth
century marks the birth of the periodical essay, a development allowing essayists to comment upon the social, political and cultural events of the moment
to relatively defined and self-selecting audiences. A brief history of the British
periodical helps situate and explain the periodical culture in which Orwell's
essays appeared. The first number of *The Tatler* appeared in 1709, providing a
marker both for the establishment of the periodical as an active element in the
literary and social environment and of the periodical essay as a literary form.
Along with its successor *The Spectator*, *The Tatler* essentially was a journal of
moral reform and so for the most part eschewed politics for cultural concerns
(Bond, pp. 67–8). But increasingly, eighteenth-century periodicals tended to
attach themselves to a particular political party, if not indeed to be purpose-
built for the job. They inevitably attacked the positions of opponents as well as
defending and broadcasting those of their own party. Hugh Walker notes 'the
warfare between Smollett in "The Briton" and Wilkes in "The North Briton"'
(Walker, p. 155). Periodicals flourished not simply as discrete organs, then,
but as elements in a broad and active environment of argument and counter-
argument. The periodical essay developed within this realm of cultural and
political interpretation and contestation.

The German social philosopher Jürgen Habermas has attempted to con-
ceptualize this wider context, and while his ideas have been productively challenged they offer an instructive reference point. In *The Structural Transformation
of the Public Sphere*, Habermas postulates the existence of a 'public sphere'
mediating between the state and the individual. In the ideal form, individuals within this sphere are able to 'confer in an unrestricted fashion – that is,
with the guarantee of freedom of assembly and association, and the freedom
to express and to publish their opinions' (Habermas, 1974, p. 49). Habermas
uses this model to analyse the history of modern public debate, seeing a public
sphere developing first in Britain at the turn of the eighteenth century and
soon after in France and Germany. Although he detects national differences,

essentially the bourgeois public sphere emerges from the fundamental challenge to established monarchical authority: 'The bourgeois were private persons; as such they did not "rule" . . . instead, they undercut the principle upon which the existing rule was based' (Habermas, 1989, p. 28).

The emerging bourgeoisie demanded that power be open to 'rational-critical public debate'. Centres for this new form of social discussion were the rapidly-increasing number of coffee houses and the journals that arose from those sites, which themselves became 'centers of criticism – literary at first, then also political' (ibid., p. 32). Habermas develops the link between coffee houses and periodicals, arguing that rather than merely providing an outlet for debate the activities associated with the coffee houses modify the basis of that debate. Members of the bourgeoisie

> almost immediately laid claim to the officially regulated 'intellectual newspapers' for use against the public authority itself. In those journals, and in the moralistic and critical journals, they debated that public authority on the general rules of social intercourse. (Habermas, 1974, p. 52)

This process expanded the number of constituent debaters to include

> all private people, persons who – insofar as they were propertied and educated – as readers, listeners and spectators could avail themselves via the market of the objects that were the subject of discussion. (Habermas, 1989, p. 37)

The classical bourgeois public sphere, Habermas contends, declines from the highpoint of the eighteenth century, the expansion of the public sphere beyond the boundaries of that group in the nineteenth century undercutting the critical–rational debate he takes as the key feature of the bourgeois public sphere. Habermas asserts that with the

> diffusion of press and propaganda, the public body expands beyond the bounds of the bourgeoisie . . . [consequently] losing the coherence created by bourgeois institutions and a relatively high standard of education. (Habermas, 1974, p. 54)

He suggests that the development of the mass commercial press in the nineteenth century constituted the 'transformation of the journalism of conviction to one of commerce', with a resulting deterioration in public debate (Habermas, 1974, p. 53).

The relevance of the concept of the public sphere to the analysis of Orwell's essays lies in a model that places the periodical and the periodical essay within the context of public discussion and contestation. The model is problematic, especially in its restriction of critical–rational debate to a certain class. Some commentators argue that Habermas fails to account for the exclusivity of his bourgeois public sphere, a space that kept out (by definition) other classes, as well as women. Mary Ryan, for example, praises women 'who have long been banished from the formal public sphere and polite political discourse' (Ryan, p. 285), while Terry Eagleton argues that while *The Tatler* and *The Spectator* were organs of social, moral and political criticism, the main impulse of the bourgeoisie in the period was 'one of class consolidation'. For Eagleton this marks the highpoint of the classic bourgeois public sphere, where 'the ferocious contention of essayists and pamphleteers took place in the gradual crystallisation of an increasingly self-confident ruling bloc in England, which defined the limits of the acceptably sayable' (Eagleton, p. 12). Although Eagleton emphasizes the self-legitimating limits of bourgeois 'rationality', he recognizes that with the formulating of broad public opinion, '[d]iscourse becomes a political force' (ibid., p. 13). For him the late eighteenth- and early nineteenth century also sees the formation of what he terms a 'counter-public sphere': 'a whole oppositional network of journals, clubs, pamphlets, debates and institutions [invading] the dominant consensus' (ibid., p. 36). The periodical press plays a key role in an arena that is 'much less of a bland consensus than of ferocious contention' (ibid., p. 37). By the mid-nineteenth century, Eagleton suggests, the potentially explosive nature of these political and intellectual upheavals threatens the dominant political order. Mark Morrisson observes that criticisms of Habermas

> point out the problem of uncritically accepting the principle of open access to the bourgeois public sphere. . . . but they also show that the bourgeois public sphere was not *the* public sphere; there were alternative public spheres even during the eighteenth century. (Morrisson, p. 9)

The ranks of periodicals were extended in the late nineteenth century with the development of the 'little magazine'. These spurned the political in favour of the aesthetic, incorporating what Frederick Hoffman and others have described as a

> rebellion against the traditional modes of expression and the wish to experiment with novel (and sometimes unintelligible) forms; and a desire to overcome the commercial or material difficulties which are caused by the introduction of any writing whose merits have not been proved. (Hoffman et al., pp. 4–5)

This leaning toward the aesthetic did not preclude little magazines from advocacy, Christopher Kent noting that as their numbers increased in the twentieth century some journals became 'manifestoes for literary and artistic movements, often urgently proclaiming the advent of one ism or another – futurism, imagism, vorticism, cubism: modernism, in short' (Kent, p. xxii). He assesses the increasing stridency and dogmatism of the little magazine in the early years of the twentieth century as paralleling 'a wider trend in English public life as home rulers, feminists, Tories, and Laborites all adopted a more militant and confrontationalist style' (ibid.). For Janet Lyon, the manifesto itself functions as a disruptive or eruptive challenge, rejecting

> the neutralizing discursive forces of the public sphere, which always and everywhere move to subordinate a sectional group's specific demands to a shifting but nevertheless hegemonic formula of 'universal good.' Universal good, the manifesto suggests, looks very different to those who have limited or ineffectual access to the coffeehouse and its class-marked discourse. (Lyon, p. 32)

The public sphere's capacity to exclude as well as to incorporate needs to be taken into account.

One of the obvious groups who remained largely excluded while Orwell was writing were working class authors. Christopher Hilliard comments that

> When Valentine Ackland sifted through poetry submissions to *Left Review* [1934-8] early in the journal's life, she was depressed to find that most originated in Oxford Cambridge, Chelsea, and Bloomsbury, their authors 'time-servers, toadies . . . desperately imitating Auden and Day-Lewis'. (Hilliard, p. 133)

Left Review, in fact, presented itself as a champion of the working class, at certain points staging competitions to encourage working class writing. Pamela Fox dismisses these as part of 'a transparent form of slumming, announcing an all-too-earnest wishes to "proletarianize" themselves and the world' (Fox, p. 53). Attempts were made to start up working class journals, such as *Poetry and the People* (see Marks, 2009, pp. 641–6), but these were rare and meagre efforts that struggled to gain any real purchase. The basic requirements of establishing journals (including premises, presses, staff, paper, an ample supply of quality writing, distribution networks and a large enough group of potential readers) were difficult enough to achieve for those with sufficient money, connections and time to contemplate the venture. Keeping the journal afloat once it had been launched added enormous new strains. Little wonder that few working class ventures took off and that the middle class monopolized the editors of, and contributors to, periodicals and magazines. Orwell's sometimes tense but often friendly relationships with some of those who exercised control over sections of the periodical culture would prove crucial to his literary development. His middle-class background and Eton education repeatedly promoted connections unavailable to a working class equivalent. In some ways an outsider, he could at times gained privileged access to the restricted public sphere.

It is instructive to see the periodical culture in Britain of the 1930s in relation to that of the 1920s and what had gone before. One reading of the link between the decades would trace a movement away from the aesthetics-dominated world of the 1920s and earlier to a more politically-engaged environment in the 1930s. There is something to be said for the bold simplicity of that narrative, but the reality was more complex and provisional. For one thing there was a substantial overlap or flow-through so that many of the important journals of the 1920s (*The Criterion, The Adelphi, Time and Tide, The New Statesman* among them) continued to thrive into the 1930s, adding to the general periodical mix. Peter Brooker and Andrew Thacker note that in the 1920s 'one definite response' by journals to the previous decade 'was a refusal of dogma, exemplified by the many "isms" that dominated the pre-war cultural field' (Brooker and Thacker, p. 456). The writer and scholar Malcolm Bradbury makes a similar claim, proposing a rough distinction between the experimental and risky little magazine and the more eclectic literary review, adding that 'very crudely you could say that the period before the First World War in Britain is largely the period of the little magazine, and the period after the First World War is the period of the literary review' (Gortschacher, pp. 280–1). Not all journals matched Bradbury's scheme, and Cyril Connolly, who unlike Bradbury was both a writer and an editor of a literary periodical (*Horizon*), makes a distinction between 'dynamic' and 'eclectic' journals. Attitude determines this distinction rather the period in which they are produced, Connolly considering that the dynamic journals

> have a shorter life and it is around them that glamour and nostalgia crystallise. If they go on too long they become eclectic although the reverse process is very unusual. Eclectic magazines are also of their time but they cannot ignore the past or resist good writing from opposing camps. (Connolly, 1964, p. 414)

Orwell's essays appeared in journals that attempted to engage with as wide a public as possible, rather than in those that spoke gnomically to a highly selective coterie.

The period in which Orwell wrote favoured this more eclectic and publicly active approach. 'As events in [1930s] Europe took on an ever more ominous tone,' Muriel Mellown observes, 'the emphasis inevitably shifted to the pressing political issues – disarmament, isolationism, pacifism, the rise of the Nazi Party, the war in Spain' (Mellown, p. 446). She claims that 'the decade of the thirties produced arguably the most valuable magazines of the century, all of them betokening in some way the drift to the political left' (ibid., p. xx).

New Statesman and Nation editor of the time Kingsley Martin makes a similar assertion:

> In some ways, the [nineteen] thirties were the great age of the weeklies. All the young writers who wished to make a reputation as literary figures or even as budding politicians looked to the weeklies as the natural place in which they could establish themselves. (Martin, 1968, p. 12)

From a more objective standpoint Stephen Koss argues in his mammoth study *The Rise and Fall of the Political Press in Britain* that while newspapers in the twentieth century sloughed off their politically partisan skins, 'the journals of opinion – the *New Statesman*, the *Spectator* . . . *Time and Tide* . . . Claud Cockburn's *The Week* . . . appropriated many of the critical functions of the political press' (Koss, pp. 497–8). These statements need to be tempered by noting the relatively small circulations of many journals, but it seems clear that cumulatively periodicals, journals and reviews played a substantial and often forgotten role in the cultural and political discourse of the time.

Not all the 1930s periodicals were politically inclined. Geoffrey Grigson's *New Verse* (launched in 1933), John Lehmann's *New Writing* (1936) and Connolly's *Horizon* (1940) all explicitly dissociated themselves from political allegiances; initially, at least. Brooker and Thacker comment that the very titles of new journals in the 1930s tell 'a complex, faceted and changing story':

> On the one hand, *Experiment, Venture, New Verse, New Writing, Twentieth Century Verse* and *Contemporary Poetry and Prose* declared an emphasis on 'newness', and the modernity of the present moment. On the other, *Cambridge Left, Left Review*, and *Poetry and the People* advertised an overtly radical and progressive politics. Together they suggested a combined awareness not simply of 'now' but of this moment in time, going forward in response to a specific call for commitment and action. (Brooker and Thacker, p. 592)

This narrative continued to change into the 1940s. Nearly all the journals listed above had wound up by 1940, replaced over time by new periodicals and reviews such as *Horizon, Polemic, Windmill, Politics and Letters* and *Gangrel* – to name only a few of those in which Orwell's essays would be published. The public sphere, or some version of it, continued to be replenished and reconfigured as cultural and political forces emerged during the Second World War and into the postwar period. The overt political engagement of the 1930s would be replaced by a more sceptical or even apolitical attitude among many writers. Yet the aesthetic experiments of High Modernism were under critical scrutiny. The 1940s, opening to the cacophony of full-blown European war and ending with the horrendous prospect of global annihilation, created new pressures and novel opportunities to which periodicals and those who wrote for them responded.

Taking the long view, Orwell's friend, the writer and editor Richard Rees, argued for the significance of four periodicals in Orwell's career:

> *The Adelphi* . . . helped him to get a start; *Horizon*, by publishing among other essays by him, *The Art of Donald McGill* and *Boys' Weeklies*, helped to establish him among the best-known essayists of his day; *Partisan Review* made him known in America, through his 'Letters from London' during the war, as a leading spokesman of English Left intellectuals; and after the war, the brilliant but short-lived *Polemic* was to publish several of his later and more sombre politico-literary essays on the degradation of language, the interaction of politics and literature, and the prospects of literature under totalitarianism. (Rees, pp. 75–6)

While a vivid snapshot of how some journals functioned during Orwell's career, Rees' comment suggests an almost sequential and even intentional process in Orwell's association with these journals, whereas the reality was appreciably more varied and ad hoc. His essays and articles appeared in dozens of journals: the highbrow *Horizon* and the obscure *Gangrel*; the slightly leftist *New English Weekly* as well as the more radical *New Leader* (organ of the Independent Labour Party); *Time and Tide*; the aesthetically inclined *New Writing* and the more political and philosophical *Polemic*; *Left News*, journal of the Left Book Club, and the influential American periodical *Partisan Review*, along with many others. Understanding the diversity of these journals and their places within a larger developing periodical culture helps illuminate essays usually considered without reference to their provenance. Many periodicals had reasonably distinct audiences that Orwell was aware of in advance, sometimes using this knowledge for polemical impact. His provocative argument on the Spanish Civil War, 'Spilling the Spanish Beans', for example, published in the *New English Weekly*, derives in part from the belief that in Britain there has been a 'quite deliberate conspiracy (I could give detailed instances) to prevent the Spanish situation from being understood' (*CO, XI*, p. 46). Orwell's expectation that the politically sympathetic audience of *New English Weekly* might need convincing that they had been duped feeds into the strategies he adopts. As with many essays, knowing the audience Orwell was addressing prompts a richer awareness of the type of argument he makes.

Reconsidering Orwell's essays within the periodical context in which they first appeared also provides a useful corrective to misreadings based on a belief that because those pieces were produced by someone now considered one of the major modern political writers they received substantial attention when published. In most instances this was not the case – indeed what would become one of Orwell's most famous essays, 'A Hanging', was published before he took the pseudonym 'George Orwell'. During the 1930s he remained a relatively minor figure, and this remained true until the publication of *Animal Farm* less than five years before he died. For most of his career before that he had virtually no international profile, and even through the late 1940s he was at best a respected figure. Knowing his posthumous status, Rees understates the importance of the periodical culture generally in nurturing, transmitting and at times prompting Orwell's ideas, assessments and arguments. We risk misreading his essays if we think they initially came freighted with that immense reputation. Resituating his essays in their original contexts helps us better understand the dynamic forces at work in the periodical culture and how these influenced what Orwell wrote on and why he wrote what he did. This approach helps trace Orwell's development as an essayist and as a writer more generally; beginning, where he began, in Paris.

Chapter 1

From Blair to Orwell: Finding a Voice (1928–36)

For a writer acclaimed as both a master of English prose and a perceptive commentator on 'Englishness', it is slightly disorienting to find George Orwell first appearing in print as a professional writer in French. The Paris-based newspaper *Monde* published 'La Censure en Angleterre' on 6 October 1928 by 'E.-A. Blair', that hyphen giving the stodgy Eric Arthur Blair some Gallic panache. Blair had left the Indian Imperial Police the previous year and was now resident in Paris, attempting unsuccessfully to establish himself as a fiction writer while toiling at low-status jobs. Some of his experiences were later worked up as *Down and Out in Paris and London* (1933), where he first adopted the pseudonym 'George Orwell'. In October 1928 that book and name were unimagined and unimaginable. During this stay (he lived in the French capital until late 1929) Blair produced two novels and several short stories he thought worth sending to a London literary agent, L. I. Bailey (Crick, pp. 192–6). Nothing of this apprentice work survives. 'La Censure en Angleterre' does, and it is instructive that Blair's first professional writing appeared in a journal, as would everything he had accepted until *Down and Out in Paris and London*.

Monde also published Blair's short study of the novelist John Galsworthy in March 1929, while another French journal, *Le Progrès Civique*, ran several articles on conditions in Britain: on unemployment; a day in the life of a tramp; beggars in London. It also printed his article on the British Empire in Burma. Amid these brief pieces, all in French, 'A Farthing Newspaper' appeared in the British magazine *G. K.'s Weekly*. There, the author's name was shorn of its hyphen, replaced by the stolidly British 'E.A. Blair'. Peter Davison notes that 'correspondence survives from two other French journals, which tell of Orwell's attempts to place his work' (*CO, X*, p. 113). This amounted to some poetry and an essay on the contemporary English novel, but either this work was not published or it has not been traced. These pieces did not amount to many words (Blair's literary energies were mostly spent on writing and revising the novels) but they were published. For an aspiring writer, desperate for validation and the vicarious immortality offered by print, that can be enough.

'La Censure en Angleterre' is short and undistinguished, but publication in a new radical paper set up by French intellectual Henri Barbusse warrants attention. Barbusse had established *Monde* for progressive commentary, Marxist-oriented but independent (Guessler, 1976). Not to be confused with the daily newspaper *Le Monde*, *Monde* had international connections: its governing board included Albert Einstein, Maxim Gorki and Upton Sinclair; its first issue on 9 June 1928 boasted 150 'collaborators' including Romain Rolland and Sherwood Anderson. In time, *Monde* would become significant enough to be attacked at the Congress of Revolutionary Writers at Kharkov late in 1930, one of the period's most influential gatherings of leftist writers. Its importance far outweighs Blair's short contributions, but they reveal an appreciation that journals were potential outlets for his work. He would repeatedly return to the broad concerns expressed in these contributions (the hypocrisies of British culture, writers interested in social conditions, the situation of the marginal) throughout his career, and this article functions as a representative example of early work.

As its title indicates, it presents *Monde* readers with an account of censorship in England, beginning with unsubtle directness: 'The present state of affairs regarding censorship in England is as follows' (*CO, X*, p. 117). This abrupt opening assumes that *Monde*'s French readership had minimal knowledge of current English censorship, although it later refers to the suppression of James Joyce's *Ulysses* and Radclyffe Hall's *The Well of Loneliness* as pertinent English examples with international recognition. Blair explains what he takes as extraordinary and illogical censorship to be a function of 'prudery' invigorated by that 'strange English puritanism, which has no objection to dirt, but which fears sexuality and detests beauty' (ibid., p. 118). Clearly capable of detecting hypocrisy, Blair's rapid run through the history of English literary censorship situates it within a larger argument about social norms.

The functional prose style and a series of rather lumbering questions – including 'What conclusions can we draw?' towards the end – signal a pedestrian approach and the absence of enlivening personal insights and perspectives that might energize the piece. French readers could learn about English censorship, but nothing much about the writer's views. From the position of Blair's subsequent career modern readers would note his sociological explanation for censorship, the observed split between the British public and intellectuals about what might be offensive, and a characteristic concern: 'Why is the sense of decency so different at different times and with different people?' (ibid.). But at this point Blair himself had no sense that 'decency' would come to be recognized as a defining concern of 'Orwell'. The relative absence of a personal voice categorizes 'La Censure en Angleterre' as an article rather than an essay, the complex and engaging intersection of individual perspective and astute observation being largely absent. The same might be said of other early pieces, although they do display a small catalogue of interests that Blair would consider throughout his literary career.

While in Paris, Blair made literary contact back in Britain with several periodicals, and *G. K.'s Weekly* published 'A Farthing Newspaper'. G. K. Chesteron, a leading Catholic and conservative writer, had established the weekly in 1925 and it bore the fingerprints of its creator. Where Blair's work in French journals addressed and introduced British topics to French readers, here he reverses the viewpoint by discussing a French newspaper, *Ami du Peuple*, for the benefit of a British audience. It sells for 'ten centimes, or rather less than a farthing a copy', an extremely cheap newspaper selling in substantial numbers to a mass audience. The article prosecutes the case that a similar paper might, or even should, be produced in Britain. This appears complimentary to *Ami du Peuple*, whose proprietors want 'to make war on the great trusts, to fight for the lower cost of living, and above all to combat the powerful newspapers which are strangling free speech in France' (*CO*, X, p. 119). But Blair reveals that *Ami du Peuple* is run by industrial capitalists, promotes a politically anti-radical and anti-Socialist line, and 'brings us nearer to the day when the newspaper will simply be a sheet of advertisements and propaganda, with a little well-censored news to sugar the pill' (ibid., p. 120). While 'A Farthing Newspaper' suggests that nothing like this exists at present in Britain, there is a clear expectation that something similar might be produced with corresponding effects. Blair's outsider knowledge here provides fresh understanding, a viewpoint he will continue to adopt.

Blair also cultivated an association with *The New Adelphi* while in Paris. A September 1929 letter to editor Max Plowman made a plaintive request:

> Dear Sir,
>   During August I sent you an article describing a day in a casual ward. As a month has now gone by, I should be glad to hear from you about it. I have no other copy of the article, & I want to submit it elsewhere if it is of no use to you –
>   Yours faithfully,
>   E.A. Blair (*CO, X*, p. 148)

Plowman wrote accepting the piece and Blair replied that Plowman could 'have the article on the terms mentioned by you. If there are any further communications, will you address to 3 Queen Street Southwold Suffolk' (ibid.). Blair was returning to his parents after failing for a year and three quarters to become a fiction writer, all he had to show being articles in *Monde, Le Progrès Civique* and *G. K.'s Weekly*. Periodicals would sustain his literary ambitions for the next three years, suggesting that journal editors at least thought his work worth printing. The thin link to *The New Adelphi* offered hope.

It would be possible to write off the early articles as the ephemera any young writer works through in the opening stages of a still-tentative literary career.

Certainly they provide no substantive evidence that their author would become one of the most regarded writers of his generation. But they do show that from the beginning Blair incorporated his knowledge and experience directly into his work, and they display his awareness of periodicals as potential publication sites. Summing up this early writing Crick suggests convincingly that it is

> closer to his mature style than were his early novels. It seems as if he then regarded his journalistic style as merely workmanlike and still strove to achieve a 'literary style'. It took him some years to discover that he already possessed something much finer than what he thought he was seeking. (Crick, p. 192)

These pieces are competent, with occasionally compelling phrases or observations, but more often they are efficiently direct rather than illuminating or arresting. We could understand these limitations as functions of the journals in which the articles appeared, except that Blair would later craft deft essays in similar circumstances. The deficiency at this stage lies with the writer, not the medium. D. J. Taylor categorizes the work for *G. K.'s Weekly* and *Monde* suggestively as 'what a modern commissioning editor would call "think pieces": miniature essays which move forward from the original subject to make wider historical observations' (Taylor, p. 95). But these pieces conspicuously lack a personal voice or sense of a writer actively 'thinking on paper'.

Blair returned to a Britain that was politically transformed from the one he had left, a nation standing at the beginning of a long period of dislocation. A Labour government under Ramsay MacDonald had been elected in May 1929 only months before the Wall Street Crash that heralded the Great Depression. Almost immediately global economic forces overwhelmed the new cabinet, unemployment rising to three million by 1931. The Labour government would be replaced that year by a National coalition headed by MacDonald (who had resigned from his own party) but dominated by Conservatives. The turmoil in the national economy reflected an international disaster that was creating a treacherous new landscape in which political influences previously held in check were surfacing. The brilliant poet W. H. Auden, four years younger than Blair but already the iconic new voice of the decade, captured the foreboding in the ominous lines of 'Consider this and in our time' (1930)

> Seekers after happiness, all who follow
> The convulsions of your simple wish,
> It is later than you think (Auden, p. 47)

The climate of unease with which the 1930s began would continue to worsen. Personally, the period between when Blair left Paris and the publication of *Down and Out in Paris and London* was one of relative failure. He often stayed with his parents in Southwold, working at various pieces of writing including

what would become *Down and Out*, a work that suffered repeated rejection and
was substantially revised several times over those years. Apart from these literary efforts, he led a fairly haphazard and indolent life, picking hops in Kent,
tramping in London and the South East of England, living in rough accommodation in London, working occasionally as a tutor, and teaching at The
Hawthorns, a small private school for boys in Middlesex.

His main connection to the literary world in the early 1930s was through *The
New Adelphi*, the name *The Adelphi* adopted during a spell (1927–30) as a quarterly. It was one of the established journals in a flourishing periodical culture
that rode the financial difficulties of the times. In fact, the 1930s would see a
range of new journals appear that enlivened cultural discussion and debate:
Alfred Orage's *New English Weekly* (1932–49); F. R. Leavis's *Scrutiny* (1953), the
most influential British journal of literary studies; the short-lived radical university journal *Cambridge Left* (1933–4); the more broad-based and influential *Left
Review* (1934–8); *the European Quarterly* (1933–4), which attempted to establish
cultural links between Britain and Europe; Geoffrey Grigson's authoritative *New
Verse* (1933–9); John Lehmann's *New Writing* (1936–9); the surrealist *Contemporary
Poetry and Prose* (1936–7). These and other new journals, along with existing periodicals, sustained an active forum for debate on cultural and political events,
prospects and fears. Indeed, they provided an essential vehicle for these debates:
some, such as *Left Review*, were initiated to promote radical literary positions.
Periodicals like *New Writing* tried to eschew political activism, while others (*New
Verse* among them) consciously distanced themselves from politics, as much as
was possible in a decade tangled in political issues, competing ideologies and
calamitous events. The productive diversity of the journals within this environment allowed scores of writers to present their work to expectant audiences, supplying them with myriad responses to contemporary circumstances.

Blair's choice of *The New Adelphi* is intriguing, for he told the journal staffer
Jack Common that while in Burma he subscribed to it but was never

> a loyal supporter of the [John Middleton] Murry crusades and outlook.
> Often the magazine disgusted him. Then he'd prop it against a tree and fire
> at it till the copy was a ruin. (Crick, p. 205)

Whatever the truth of this rather macho tale, *The Adelphi* of the early 1920s
when Blair was in Burma was substantially different from that at the end
of the decade, and it continued to develop in the 1930s. John Middleton
Murry had begun the periodical in 1923, later claiming that he instigated it
to promote the ideas of his charismatic friend D. H. Lawrence. But Michael
Whitworth argues that Murry's statements about *The Adelphi*'s genesis 'are
inconsistent, and early readers may not have perceived the magazine so
simply' (Whitworth, p. 376) as a vehicle for Lawrence's views. Murry's
sometimes meandering search for spiritual, philosophical and political

enlightenment meant that the early *Adelphi* at times was dominated by his and Lawrence's enthusiasms, while also publishing Katherine Mansfield – Murry's wife – Edmund Blunden, Walter De la Mare, T. S. Eliot and Dorothy Richardson, along with others now long forgotten. For the most part it rejected the fashionable difficulties presented by Modernists such as James Joyce and Virginia Woolf, consciously addressing the informed general public. By October 1930 it reverted to its original name and monthly format, and while Murry was still influential, the journal was edited by Max Plowman and then Richard Rees. This new incarnation carried Plowman's statement that

> to feel deeply and to mean sincerely may not be enough to save a man from sententiousness and sentimentality; but without the desire and the will to face life in such a spirit the journey towards individual truth and understanding cannot even be begun. (Plowman, p. 2)

Plowman and Rees would move the journal substantially to the political Left, close to the radical Independent Labour Party (ILP). They both proved beneficial to Blair over the long term, Plowman befriending and supporting him until his own death in 1941. Rees, another Old Etonian (although not a scholarship boy like Blair), became a close friend and eventually the co-executor of Orwell's will. As the result of a private income Rees was also a good friend to *The Adelphi*:

> Rees took full financial responsibility for the journal from its resumption as a monthly in 1930. In the first few years it sold fewer than 4,500 copies per month. The total extent of Rees's subsidy is not recorded. The surviving correspondence records certain ad hoc payments: for example, £250 in June 1932 to save the printer, Aldred, from having his printing machines seized. In June 1934, Murry requested a subsidy of £700 from Rees for the coming year, and in March 1935 confirmed that the journal was losing about that sum annually, though he hoped to reduce the loss to £550. Rees took the view that it needed £900 a year. (Whitworth, p. 382)

This account beautifully catches the difficulties for most literary journals of the time, even those financially underpinned, as *The Adelphi* was by Rees. Circulations remained relatively small for most journals, losses were an expected part of the economic calculations, and the practicalities of printing and distribution could be overwhelming. Cyril Connolly argues that 'Magazines required two animators: an editor and a backer (or angel)' (Connolly, p. 427). For a good deal of the 1930s Rees played both parts.

Despite the pressures, *The Adelphi* was one of the age's most enduring periodicals. It did more for Blair than simply publish his essays and reviews, giving

him access to an engaged and loosely aligned group of writers and intellectuals who, according to Edouard Roditi, were

> rather confused, more distrustful of traditional beliefs than yet converted to
> any new beliefs. Some of us had some knowledge of Marxist literature; oth-
> ers, some acquaintance with Freudian theory, others again, some knowledge
> of DADA and Surrealism. But nothing had jelled yet in our minds, so that we
> could discuss new ideas quite freely as none of us had adopted a firm stand
> on anything, although some of us were already moving towards the ideology
> of the Independent Labour Party. (Crick, p. 205)

This suggests something half-baked and skittish, but also indicates the eclectic network of people to whom Blair gained access. To these could be added
worker-writers such as Jack Common, who would become a longtime friend
after initially being suspicious of Blair's public school mannerisms. Blair's positions on many issues were still evolving in the early 1930s. Presenting himself
to some *Adelphi* staff as a 'Tory anarchist' (ibid.), Blair possibly was motivated
by his inveterate desire to provoke, but the label also indicates his simultaneously complex and underdeveloped thinking at the time.

Blair's initial contributions to *The New Adelphi* were reviews, the first – on
Lewis Mumford's study of Herman Melville – appearing in the March–May
issue of 1930. He observes that Mumford's 'declared aim is to expound, criticize and – unpleasant but necessary word – interpret.' Accepting that interpreting the writer can be justified, Blair argues that the interpretation of
the writing, when done 'with sufficient thoroughness' will 'cause art itself to
disappear' (*CO, X*, p. 182). He judges that 'when Mr. Mumford is interpreting Melville himself . . . he is excellent; but he goes on to interpret Melville's
poetry, and therein he is not so successful' (ibid.). Commenting on Mumford's
reading of *Moby Dick*, Blair states that 'it were much better to have discoursed
on the form, which is the stuff of poetry, and left the "meaning" alone' (ibid.,
p. 183). His own literary criticism would generally examine broad cultural
and political questions rather than engaging in fine-grained textual analysis.
Michael Shelden suggests that this review is 'the first published piece in which
the distinctive voice of Orwell emerges', adding that 'after all the struggles
of Paris . . . he sounds like a real writer' (Shelden, 1991, p. 150). Perhaps, but
there is some overreaching here, as in the description of Melville as a 'man
who felt more vividly than common men, just as a kestrel sees more vividly than
a mole' (*CO, X*, p. 183), a construction that strains for effect without explaining much. Nevertheless, Shelden's detection of a distinctive voice in the review
does reflect how much of that voice develops and is fashioned in reviews, essays
and non-fiction generally.

Blair's reviews for *The Adelphi* were his only published work in 1930. A letter
to Plowman in October indicates that the article accepted late in 1929 still

needed revision. 'If you want that done,' Blair writes, 'perhaps you will send it to me, & I will attend to it. But if you find that after all you cannot use the article, I should like it back, as I might be able to send it elsewhere' (*CO*, *X*, p. 189). Blair's career might have been very different had Plowman not replied positively. *The Adelphi* published Eric Blair's 'The Spike' in April 1931, 20 months after Plowman had first indicated it had been accepted. It sketches a few days at one of the many tramps' hostels – or 'spikes' – dotted through Britain. The raw material revisits Blair's writing for *Le Progrès Civique*, but with the essential difference that the more engaged and vivid portrayal derives from the first-person perspective adopted. Blair's French articles on unemployment and tramps attempted a level of objectivity, providing information for a French readership. 'The Spike' supplies a lively, impressionistic first-hand portrait of the daily squalor, monotony and humiliation of a tramp's life for *The Adelphi*'s predominantly middle-class British audience.

This glimpse of an otherwise unrecognized world begins matter-of-factly by establishing a communal anonymity:

> It was late afternoon. Forty-nine of us, forty-eight men and one woman, lay on the green waiting for the spike to open. We were too tired to talk much. We just sprawled out exhaustedly, with home-made cigarettes sticking out of our scrubby faces. Overhead the chestnut branches were covered with blossom, and beyond that the great woolly clouds floated almost motionless in a clear sky. Littered on the grass, we seemed dingy, urban riff-raff. We defiled the scene, like sardine-tins and paper bags on the seashore. (*CO*, *X*, p. 197)

The blend of scuffed realism and lyricism suggests something closer to Orwell's mature style, while somewhat overplaying the contrast between the blossoms and the urban riff-raff. It sets up a central tension with *Adelphi* readers between their interest and their potential repulsion. The collective identity of the sprawling group conceals another dynamic, for 'The Spike's' narrator clearly has literary abilities that set him apart. He further reveals himself as new to the tramp's life by accepting the advice of 'the old hands' to bury contraband outside the spike for fear of punishment. The group enters the 'gloomy, chilly, limewashed place, consisting only of a bathroom and dining room and about a hundred narrow stones cells' (ibid., p. 198) to be greeted by the Tramp Major who administers the spike, 'a gruff soldierly man of forty, who gave the tramps no more ceremony than sheep at the dipping pond'. This conjures up a sub-Dickensian environment without Dickens' humorous caricatures. The narrator's subtle rhetorical disengagement from 'the tramps' who regularly are treated like sheep maintains the essay's social hierarchy, while the group identity allows him to indulge rather ostentatiously in working class idiom: 'When you came to be searched [by the Tramp Major] he fair held you upside down and shook you' (ibid.). This formulation does not represent the phrasing of the average *Adelphi* reader, nor of an Old Etonian. And his shared status gets tested to breaking point when the Tramp Major inspects him:

> 'You are a gentleman?'
>   'I suppose so', I said.
>   He gave me another hard look. 'Well, that's too bloody bad luck, guv'nor', he said, 'that's bloody bad luck, that is.' And thereafter he took it into his head to treat me with compassion, even with a kind of respect. (ibid.)

This exchange exposes his anomalous position in the spike's regime, simultaneously registering that observations are from someone more outside than inside that culture. His horror at the grimy bathroom underscores his marginality: 'It was a disgusting sight . . . All the indecent secrets of our underwear were exposed' (ibid.). Where real tramps would ignore the filth, the narrator's metaphorically thin skin proves acutely sensitive. The following morning he goes to wash in a communal tub of water: 'I gave one glance at the black scum on top of the water, and decided to go dirty for the day' (ibid., p. 199). The account he presents to *Adelphi* readers remains that of an empathetic observer never truly part of the environment.

Yet as an eyewitness he proves particularly informative for an audience with no experience of these conditions. The physical space gets described in detail, daily rituals are depicted, a picture mixing squalor, low level mistreatment and dull routine. The narrator's expectations of 'a sound night's rest', for example, are destroyed by the cold, and his horror at the early morning medical inspection is palpable:

> We stood shivering naked to the waist in two long ranks in the passage. The filtered light, bluish and cold, lighted us up with unmerciful clarity. No one can imagine, unless he has seen such a thing, what pot-bellied, degenerate curs we looked. (ibid.)

This combination of detail, disgust and empathy also provides brief portraits of some tramps, playing off their individuality against institutionally imposed anonymity. And the narrator emphasizes that the sheer boredom of the time spent there 'is the worst of all the tramp's evils, worse than hunger and discomfort, worse even than the constant feeling of being socially disgraced' (ibid., p. 200). This insight sets off a contentious thought that '[o]nly an educated man, who has consolations within himself, can endure confinement. Tramps, unlettered types as nearly all of them are, face their poverty with blank resourceless minds' (ibid., pp. 200–1). The hypothesis cannot be tested, and might well be false, but it indicates the narrator's separation from the established tramps.

Entrenched social distinctions determine that the Tramp Major picks the narrator 'for the most coveted of all jobs in the spike, the job of helping in the workhouse kitchen' (ibid., p. 201). This involves no real work and nets him a huge meal at the workhouse table, after which he is required to throw away five dustbins of 'good food'. When he returns to the spike he engages in conversation with a 'rather superior tramp' only on the road for six months, who 'had literary tastes, too, and carried one of Scott's novels in all his wanderings' (ibid.). But when the narrator tells him about the wasted food, the superior tramp agrees with the practice: 'You don't want to have any pity on these tramps – scum they are. You don't want to judge them by the same standards as men like you and me' (ibid., p. 202). As the narrator recognizes, his interlocutor's 'body might be in the spike, but his spirit soared away, in the pure aether of the middle classes' (ibid.). The narrator implicitly rejects the suggestion that the tramps are scum unworthy of pity, but the interchange contributes to the multilayered reading of the tramps and their conditions. The superior tramp's unsympathetic view matched that of most people, although perhaps not the average *Adelphi* reader.

The essay ends with tramps leaving their confinement via a series of disengagement rituals. But there remains a final small semi-comic scene when Scotty, 'a little hairy tramp with a bastard accent sired by cockney out of Glasgow' (ibid., p. 198), catches up with the departing narrator. Scotty had had his tobacco impounded, and the narrator had given him some of his own. ' "I owe you some fags," ' Scotty declares: ' "One good turn deserves another – here y'are." And he put four sodden, debauched, loathely cigarettes into my hand' (ibid., p. 203). The massive disjunction between Scotty's honourable motives and the narrator's appalled thoughts provides a comic finale to the essay that also neatly repositions the narrator outside the tramps' codes and ultimately their lives. The overloading of hyperbolic adjectives perhaps gently mocks the narrator's delicate sensibility, the cigarettes functioning as an unwelcome souvenir for the adventurous traveller. 'The Spike' itself portrays a world of social deprivation that might partially repel *Adelphi* readers, but the essay aims to generate a countervailing political and moral sympathy for an otherwise invisible underclass.

Blair uses the first person pronoun substantially for the first time in this essay, even if that 'I' stands somewhat aloof, part participant, part observer, communicating to the *Adelphi* audience. For all that, 'The Spike' ignores any substantive political analysis of the causes that produce this subgroup, or any real investigation of the ways in which their lives might be enhanced or the political situation changed. It remains a portrait of lives unknown to *Adelphi* readers, but since periodical audiences are self-selecting, Blair could assume that the essay would interest them given their likely political inclinations and the tenor of the journal. This was the case with many journals, so that writers could tailor their work to a known readership. The vivid, if limited, depiction of a way of life seen from a personal perspective, and the implicit social critique qualify 'The Spike' as more than an article, as an essay proper. Blair finds his feet very quickly in this form, and although 'The Spike' can on occasions be overwritten (in what ways can cigarettes really be understood as 'debauched'?) it marks a step up and forward from Blair's articles. Plowman recognized qualities that made it worth publishing in one of the more respected journals in Britain, and in accepting 'The Spike' he executed the gate-keeping role periodicals performed for literature generally, weeding out the substandard and promoting new talent.

Blair was strengthening links with *The Adelphi*, and in a January 1931 letter to 'Mr Plowman' sent from London, he promises to send another article so that Plowman 'can have a look at it. I didn't in any case suppose that you could use it yet awhile, but I thought that if you like it you might like to keep it by you' (*CO*, X, p. 195). Plowman thought the article publishable without the lengthy delays that retarded 'The Spike'. Set in Burma, its title baldly announces the topic: 'A Hanging.' As with 'The Spike', 'A Hanging' matched the political concerns and literary approach of *The Adelphi*, and in August 1931 it slipped unheralded into the journal's pages. Although it would be reprinted in the obscure journal *The New Savoy* 15 years after appearing in *The Adelphi*, the essay now considered a classic would otherwise not be reprinted in its author's lifetime.

A far more deftly constructed and stylistically refined work than 'The Spike', 'A Hanging' also more readily conforms to the standard definition of the essay, and would be included in the first posthumous collection in 1950. ('The Spike', by contrast, failed to get reprinted before the four-volume set of 1968.) Yet the connections and distinctions between the two pieces deserve teasing out, for they indicate the diversity that enlivens the essay form and that frustrates those scholars wishing to impose tight generic boundaries. Both essays consider worlds that Blair had experienced. Both present themselves as accounts of real events and situations depicted by a first person narrator who functions within the situation but who in significant ways remains sufficiently detached to recognize aspects or implications that other figures apparently do not. As well as descriptions of setting, character and action, they both offer the narrator's assessments at different moments within the narrative. The fact that they are constructed around narratives, not simply observations, requires the construction of a narrative voice, in both cases that of the eyewitness. But the 'I' in each case performs a different function. In 'The Spike' the narrator describes the situation and makes assessments, but 'A Hanging' rests less on the mere vivid description of events than on the recognition by the narrator of an ethical and political conundrum. 'The Spike' substantially takes a sociological approach, 'A Hanging' adding a crucial philosophical component.

'A Hanging' could be read as a skillfully crafted short story in the style of Somerset Maugham, a writer Orwell would later claim as 'the modern writer who has influenced me the most' (*CO, XII*, p. 148). Certainly it shares with the short story such attributes as narrative coherence and the vivid description of character and place, as well as the exploration of ethical puzzles and paradoxes and a telling conclusion. For many critics, the fact that Orwell saw a hanging (or might have seen one) salvages the essay from fictional status, Jeffrey Meyers, for example, stating categorically that it and the later piece 'Shooting an Elephant' are 'autobiographical, confessional pieces, the result of intense psychological soul-searching, showing Orwell mastering the experience and conquering his sense of failure, shame and guilt' (Meyers, 2000, p. 69). Other biographers are more circumspect, Shelden noting that 'everything about the sketch . . . suggests that it is based on a real experience' (Shelden, 1991, p. 113), with the term 'sketch' hinting at experience at least reworked for aesthetic effect. Bernard Crick, even in the revised edition of his biography, declares himself 'still skeptical that Orwell had witnessed a hanging' (Crick, p. 589), while D. J. Taylor also remains uncertain, describing 'A Hanging' and 'Shooting an Elephant' as 'figurative snapshots' (Taylor, p. 80).

Its status as fact, fiction or confluence of the two does not disqualify it as an essay. Claudia de Obaldia argues that lines between fact and fiction are inadequate boundary markers, for 'if great essays are not fictional as such, examples where in one way or another "imaginative recreation" implies "fiction" are rife' (de Obaldia, p. 11). She points to Montaigne's use of true stories in his essays, or instances where readers are invited 'to imagine a man in this or that situation' and to the English periodical essays in *The Tatler*, where Joseph Addison and Richard Steele 'introduced characters supposed to represent the main sectors of English society' (ibid., p. 12). Graham Good notes that Hazlitt's essays 'recurrently weave threads of fiction in to the web of truth' (Good, p. 85). 'A Hanging' provides an intriguing instance where later readers of the essay, more knowledgeable about the writer's life than its initial audience, might incorporate this into their reading. *Adelphi* readers did not have any biographical information about its author against which to test its truth content. In any case, for them the author was 'Eric A. Blair'.

Coming only months after 'The Spike' – which begins: 'It was late afternoon' and ends with sodden cigarettes – 'A Hanging' faintly echoes of its predecessor, beginning: 'It was in Burma, a sodden morning of the rains.' Attending the hanging of a Hindu prisoner for an unspecified crime, the narrator, presumably a colonial official (he includes himself as one of 'the rest of us, magistrates and the like'; *CO, X*, p. 208) observes the condemned man avoid a puddle on his path to the gallows. This unconscious but undeniable signal of an innate will to live triggers a revelation in the narrator, for 'till that moment I had never realised what it means to destroy a healthy, conscious man' (ibid., p. 208). Despite this personal illumination the institutional commands are carried out and the man is hanged, the incident drowned by social ritual: 'We all drank together, native and European alike, quite amicably. The dead man was a hundred yards away' (ibid., p. 210). No matter the callous performances of the witnesses, the narrator's flash of insight represents his recognition of the condemned man's right to exist. Despite his pivotal importance in structuring

and interpreting events, however, he does not see the actual hanging. The execution gets depicted as a magic trick – the man vanishes, and the institutional
distance from which the narrator observes the dead body partly neutralizes
the horror of the situation. Tellingly, the creature that responds 'humanely' to
the execution is a stray dog. Initially it intrudes into the procession towards the
gallows, licking the condemned man in a natural confirmation of his essential humanity. This act prefigures the narrator's revelation. Figured as 'half
Airedale, half pariah', the dog embodies colonizer and colonized, providing a
point of critique outside the narrator's own. Indeed, the narrator and the dog
are physically linked, a fact only recognized in passing once the man has been
executed. Then the narrator reveals:

> I let go of the dog, and it galloped immediately to the back of the gallows;
> but when it got there it stopped short, barked, and then retreated into a
> corner of the yard, where it stood among the weeds, looking timorously out
> at us. We went round the gallows to inspect the prisoner's body. He was dan-
> gling with his toes pointed straight downwards, very slowly revolving as dead
> as a stone. (ibid., p. 209)

The dog's fearful reaction once it sees the dead body, as though understanding the ghastly forces at work, plays against the temporary disengagement of
the narrator and others, reinforcing the dehumanizing act carried out. The
dog soon departs the scene, supposedly 'conscious of having misbehaved,'
(ibid., p. 210) but it has performed a crucial act by recoiling at the destruction
of a healthy, conscious man, something the narrator temporarily disregards.
Understanding the dog's profoundly symbolic significance challenges readings of 'A Hanging' founded simply on it being an autobiographical account.
Precisely what the essay conveys remains ambiguous, for although the narrator's abhorrence at the execution returns, and the crude joking and drinking
that follow expose his guilt, the concluding lines indicate his compromised
position: 'We all had a drink together, native and European alike, quite amicably. The dead man was a hundred yards away' (ibid., p. 210). The ending
generates a variety of possible judgements, depending on the reader's assessment of the narrator, the imperial power at work, and the morality of hanging.
The rhetorical pull of the piece drags the reader towards a condemnation
of hanging, but the essay's unemotional, stilted final images hint that institutional power can override the moral argument against execution. In these
circumstances those involved must live with their guilt and their complicity,
while those who benefit from imperialism (*Adelphi* readers, for instance) share
some small portion of culpability. The fact that the narrator is part of the
ruling power accentuates the corrosive effect of imperialism. Simultaneously,
given the massive power imbalances in play, his momentary empathy with the
condemned man has more emotive and ethical resonance across barriers of

race and ethnicity. Because the narrator connects the workings of empire and *Adelphi* readers, 'A Hanging' personalizes the imperial reality for those readers. The essay could survive without the specific setting as a condemnation of hanging, but would lose much of its particular substance and moral energy.

Accepting 'A Hanging' as an essay, it should be admitted that it has an ambiguous generic status, having elements that suggest a short story, or, in Shelden's terms, a sketch: a strong, coherent narrative, a degree of scene setting and dialogue. For those like Meyers who believe that Orwell saw a hanging (and shot an elephant) it remains a revealing piece of confessional autobiography. But the crafted symbolism of the dog calls the purely autobiographical reading into question, and while 'A Hanging' might work as a short story, the extended musings by the narrator on the morality of hanging and the humanity of the hanged man are so intrusive as to destabilize it were it presented as purely fiction. Stansky and Abrahams label it a 'brief, stylized essay' (Stansky and Abrahams, p. 162), usefully capturing how Blair adapts the essay form by incorporating elements from fiction while maintaining a plausible facticity. We can read it for the essential but complex moral situation that it depicts without needing to accept it as a definitive account of Blair's own experience. Given its manifest qualities as an essay it is worth remembering Blair's severe problems working into shape the material that would become *Down and Out in Paris and London*. He had completed a first draft in October 1930, but it would not be published until January 1933. As 'A Hanging' demonstrates, though, by 1931 Blair already could produce a compelling, subtle essay in lucid prose. Against this we need to remember that in the little-over 4,000 copies of *The Adelphi*, 'A Hanging' remained the work of a writer barely known even to the journal's readers.

Blair would continue reviewing for *The Adelphi* over the next few years, using his real name in the journal until August 1935, by which time 'George Orwell' already had *Down and Out* (1933) *Burmese Days* (1934) and *A Clergyman's Daughter* (1935) to his pseudonym. During this period *The Adelphi* had also developed politically, announcing its affiliation with the ILP in October 1932. A socialist party once loosely associated with the Labour Party (it disaffiliated in 1932) the ILP had several members of the parliament in the early 1930s and saw itself as a ginger group working for radical reforms. John Newsinger, in his study of Orwell's politics, suggests that *The Adelphi* 'was to become the ILP's unofficial theoretical journal' (Newsinger, p. 22) and Elgin Mellown notes that in October 1932 'Rees announced that the *Adelphi* would henceforth express the views of the I.L.P., and reflect a Marxist attitude' (Mellown, p. 13). *Adelphi* contributions repeatedly dealt with the intersections between literature and politics, C. Day Lewis's 'The Poet and Revolution' (September 1932) spiritedly calling writers to involve themselves directly in the struggle for Communism. Murry's 'Communism and Art: or, Bolshevism and Ballyhoo' was also representative, Murry arguing for 'creative', 'imaginative' Communism against the 'negative and reductive' Communism of the Bolsheviks (Murry, 1933, pp. 266–8). He encases his preferred type of Communism in quasi-mystical jargon, writing that in 'the formation of the revolutionary [Communist] nucleus, the dynamic relation between man and man, and man and the living universe, feels towards its own recreation' (ibid., p. 270). This zany blend of mysticism and activism hardly seems likely to foment mass rebellion, but the articles indicate the political circles Blair inhabited, as well as the way that journals generally could reformulate themselves.

Blair developed associations outside *The Adelphi*, with *The New Statesman and Nation* publishing his article 'Hop Picking' on 17 October 1931. The merger of *The New Statesman* and *The Nation* had only recently occurred, signalling another type of reformulation. *The New Statesman* had been set up in 1913 as a vehicle for the Fabian Society, and as competition for Alfred Orage's socialist-inclined *New Age* and the Liberal journal *The Nation*. The details of the subsequent decades are largely irrelevant here, but by 1922 *New Age* had folded and *The Nation* had merged with Middleton Murry's *The Athenaeum* (a forerunner to *The Adelphi*). These changes reflected the financial difficulties of keeping such papers economically viable, Whitworth recording that *The Athenaeum* sold 'between 3,000 and 3,500 copies per week', while *The Nation* before amalgamating with it 'sold about 6,000 per week; in 1916 *The New Statesman* sold an average of 6,000 per issue, and it maintained sales of between 6,000 and 10,000 in the early 1920s' (Whitworth, pp. 367–8). By the beginning of the 1930s, however, *The New Statesman* under its troubled editor Clifford Smith had run aground, leading John Maynard Keynes (one of *The Nation*'s backers) and others to orchestrate a merger of the two weeklies. This entailed replacing Smith with a new editor, the energetic young Kingsley Martin. The merger would prove a great success, Adrian Smith stating that it 'was the most obvious platform for those willing to take on the herculean task of reviving democratic socialism in Britain' (Smith, p. 245).

'Hop Picking' had simpler aims. Drawing from Blair's 'Hop-Picking Diary' (*CO*, *X*, pp. 212–26, 228–30) the article presents a brief account of his time hop picking from August to October 1931. As with 'The Spike', Blair makes clear that he is new to the experience, and much of the article explains the process of hop picking and the general conditions under which hop pickers work to the weekly's readers. Primarily an informative article for *New Statesman and Nation* readers with little first-hand knowledge of manual labour, 'Hop Picking' seems closer to the work Blair had published in France. One difference from that earlier work is that he makes his own position central to the perspective and tone of the piece, in contrast to the experienced workers who accept the long hours and abysmal pay as though the job was a rural escape from urban drudgery: 'For as a matter of act,' Blair states, 'hop-picking is far from being a holiday, and as far as wages go, no worse employment exists.' He exposes the 'starvation wages' and rules that reduce the hop-picker 'practically to a slave' (ibid.,

p. 234). The facts might suggest an approach akin to 'The Spike', but despite the undoubted exploitation, the overriding tone is one of amused bewilderment. Blair acknowledges that there are positive aspects to the job, declaring that the activity 'in the category of things that are great fun when they are over'. And despite not fully understanding why the same workers return each season, he recognizes that 'there is no difficulty in getting people to do the work so perhaps one ought not to complain too loudly about the conditions in the hop-fields' (ibid., p. 235). The relatively small space the *New Statesman and Nation* set aside for such articles, compared to the more extended format of *The Adelphi*, restricts the length and focus of 'Hop Picking'. Blair engages in some political critique, ending the article by commenting that 'a hop-picker us appreciable worse off than a sandwich man' (ibid.), but essentially the piece accepts that the hop-pickers do not feel exploited. Rather than the appalled figure in 'The Spike', bringing back a detailed and highly personalized account of a desperate underclass, the narrator here provides a colourful snapshot of a group who, while exploited, do not feel oppressed and despised – or politically rebellious. The article also registers Blair's connection with one of the most influential papers of the decade. Those cordial relations did not last.

In terms of published work 1932 was an almost barren year for Blair, a few reviews for *The Adelphi*, an unsigned review for *New English Weekly* and another short article for the *New Statesman and Nation* titled 'Common Lodging Houses' apart. This piece is another of Blair's informative articles based on investigations of the night-shelters administered by the London County Council (LCC). Where 'The Spike' had provided a vivid and engaging account of tramp life, the purpose here simply is to inform *New Statesman and Nation* readers about the houses themselves. Like 'Hop Picking', its brevity and focus conform to the paper's restrictions about length, but the colour and energy of that article are replaced by unadorned documentary. The personal pronoun disappears and there are no illuminating thumbnail portraits of the house inhabitants. There are occasional rhetorical flourishes, so that a loading house kitchen gets presented as a 'murky, troglodytic cave', but predominantly the prose remains functional. More than most early pieces the article presents a specific argument, Blair challenging the 'dismal uselessness' of the legislation governing the lodging houses, arguing that they should not be sexually segregated, and that the lodgers should be protected from 'various swindles which the proprietors and managers are now able to practise on them' (*CO, X*, p. 267). Perhaps because of this more argumentative approach the article provoked a response from a Theodore Fyfe, an architect who had worked on the construction of some of the LCC lodging houses, and who disputed Blair's blanket assessment of them (ibid., n. 1). Blair dismissed the letter as a 'very feeble attack' and 'not worth answering' (ibid., p. 277), but the article and Fyfe's riposte indicate in a small way the potentially interactive relationship between periodical authors and readers.

Apart from these few published pieces Blair's main employment was teaching at The Hawthorns. Victor Gollancz had agreed to publish what in July 1932 Blair suggested might be called *The Lady Poverty* (a title Gollancz sensibly rejected) but which came out as *Down and Out in Paris and London*. Blair had also suggested the uninspired 'Kenneth Miles' or the faintly ludicrous 'H. Lewis Allways' as possible pseudonyms, but plumped for 'George Orwell'. As well as working on polishing this work up for publication and developing *Burmese Days*, Blair continued to associate with *The Adelphi* and its staff, his friendships with Richard Rees, Jack Common and Max Plowman deepening when he moved to London in 1934. He occasionally contributed reviews and what at best could be described as mundane poetry that the journal also published during 1933 and 1934. *Down and Out in Paris and London* was published and then, in the United States so was, *Burmese Days* (1934). Worried about legal issues his British publisher Victor Gollancz did not publish it until June 1935. The long apprenticeship in writing full-length works was over, although what were now 'George Orwell' first books enjoyed only small successes. He remained largely unrecognized, and for several years he also remained 'Eric Blair' in reviews and poetry published in *The Adelphi* and the *New English Weekly*. These journals, and others he was fostering links with, maintained an important connection to the literary world, and continued to be the site where he was most regularly visible.

In the broader context political developments nationally and internationally threatened to impinge on the consciousness and work of all writers, invigorating or constraining literary and critical work depending on what attitude the individual took. The rise of Fascism and the tumultuous if uncertain developments within the Soviet Union marked only two of the more obvious dilemmas that rippled across Europe. The internal situation in Britain was dire enough, and *The Adelphi*'s move to the Left was one response. The short-lived university journal *Cambridge Left* offered another, carrying John Cornford's provocative essay 'Left?' which argued that it was imperative for the writer to 'actively participate in the revolutionary struggles of society if he is not going to collapse into the super-subjectivity of the older writers (Joyce, Eliot, Pound). He must emphatically deny the contradiction between art and life.' Cornford perceives in the younger generation 'the beginnings of a politically-conscious revolutionary literature for the first time in the history of English culture' (Cornford, p. 25). But *Cambridge Left* fell in the autumn of 1934, the torch of radical literary endeavour being picked up by *Left Review*, one of the most energetic left-wing journals of the mid-1930s. It began in October 1934, stressing (erroneously as it happens) that 'a second world war [is] oppressively near'. The first issue carried a Writer's International (British Section) statement claiming 'a crisis of ideas in the capitalist world to-day not less considerable than the crisis in economics' signalled by the decadence of English literature that reflects 'the collapse of a culture' (Writers' International Statement, p. 37). The journal aimed to set up 'an association of revolutionary writers' linked by their opposition to Fascism, support for the working class, opposition to imperialist war and support for the Soviet Union. I have argued elsewhere (Marks, 1997) that attempts to impose a narrow political line or aesthetic policy (most obviously, the Soviet-backed Socialist Realism) were resisted by some *Left Review* writers such as Stephen Spender and Lewis Grassic Gibbon, and Orwell would angrily refuse to contribute to a *Left Review* questionnaire on the Spanish Civil War in 1937. But *Left Review* remained an active and assertive presence in the periodical culture until its demise in 1938.

Journals started in the 1930s or already established displayed the array of approaches to interaction of politics and literature (including disengagement) different formats and publication frequencies partly determining their attitudes. A weekly such as *Time and Tide*, for example, while it contained a regular book section, 'Men and Books' – an odd title for a journal that had begun in the 1920s as a feminist periodical – directed its attention more towards weekly political events. Something of the same can be said of *The New Statesman and Nation*, which included its book section at the rear. *The Modern Scot*, by contrast, linked left-wing politics with a revival of Scottish nationalism. Even *Scrutiny* proclaimed in its first editorial that it would not be a purely literary review. But 'what is meant', the editorial asks itself,

> by that hint of a generous interest in 'modern affairs' at large . . . Well, the devotion to [politics] at the party level, is, no doubt, somewhat necessary. But something else is necessary – and prior: a play of the free intelligence upon the underlying issues. (Unsigned, 1932, 'Scrutiny: A Manifesto', p. 2)

New Verse confidently advertised its independence from politics, its first January 1933 number declaring it aligned 'to no literary or politico-literary cabal' (Grigson, p. 2). Yet by October 1934 it published the first batch of replies to 'An Enquiry' of poets, which had asked such questions as 'Do you intend your poetry to be useful to yourself or others?' and 'Do you take your stand with any political or politico-economic party or creed?' Twenty-two poets replied to this out of the 40 asked, almost half of them either rejecting the question or answering that they did not advocate a political creed or party. That the question was asked at all highlights how in the 1930s political matters could not be evaded easily.

Down and Out in Paris and London and *Burmese Days* largely suited this politically-concerned environment. Because this study focuses on Orwell's essays and the importance of periodicals, it leaves aside detailed analyses of full-length works. But clearly Orwell's books and essays complement each other in some ways; substantially in the case of 'The Spike', parts of which Blair reworked into chapters 27 and 35 of *Down and Out in Paris and London*. There the events take place in two different spikes, suggesting the manipulation of reality in one or other piece, or both. The intersection between periodicals and books was more general and yet direct, the consequence of the vital reviewing that journals carried out. Reviews can make and destroy reputations, heralding the arrival of exciting new talent or stifling that talent by tough criticism or with-holding attention. *Down and Out* generally received appreciative reviews for the work of a new writer, an unsigned notice (still the norm in many journals) in the *Times Literary Supplement* describing it as 'a vivid picture of an apparently mad world' (Meyers, 1975, p. 42), another short one in *Nation* judging it an 'interesting and rather painful document' more 'vivid' and 'absorbing' than fictional accounts of the same material (ibid., p. 45). It was also reviewed in journals to which Eric Blair had contributed, C. Day-Lewis giving it a brief positive review in *The Adelphi*, describing it as a 'tour of the under-world', and claiming that 'the body of active reformers in his country would inevitably be increased by the numbers of readers of this book' (ibid., p. 42). More encouraging still was W. H. Davies' review in the *New Statesman and Nation*. Davies had written the classic *Autobiography of a Supertramp* (1908) so his declaration that 'this is the kind of book I like to read' was recommendation enough. He praised the book as 'packed with unique and strange information. It is all true to life, from beginning to end' (ibid., p. 44). These reviews seemed to vindicate Blair's efforts to become a writer. Periodicals previously had given him the only outlet for his work, the consolation that he could write publishable material; now they validated him.

Burmese Days probes the fears, racism, pretensions and dissimulations of a group of imperial officials and traders in a remote Burmese town, and clearly has affinities in terms of setting, mood and subject matter with 'A Hanging'. It also was reasonably well-received. Writing in the *New Statesman and Nation* Cyril Connolly recognized its shortcomings but still considered it an 'admirable novel', recommending it 'to anyone who enjoys a spate of efficient indignation, graphic description, excellent narrative, excitement and irony tempered with vitriol' (cited in Crick, p. 265). It was listed as one of *The New Statesman and Nation*'s 'Best Books of 1935' (as was Enid Bagnold's *National Velvet*). While Connolly correctly detects an economic aspect to *Burmese Days*, the novel's power and interest derives from its investigation of moral failings. Connolly perhaps was responding to contemporary non-fiction studies that examined the economic foundations of imperialism such as John Strachey's *The Coming Struggle for Power* (1932), which located imperialism within the context of monopoly capitalism and Fascism, or Ralph Fox's *The Colonial Policy of British Imperialism* (1933), where Fox argues that the

> whole character of our own labour movement has been determined by the exploitation of our own colonial peoples, and the issue of the struggle of the British working class . . . cannot be considered apart from the liberation of the peoples of the Empire. (Fox, p. 11)

Orwell would move closer to this bold statement of imperialism's economic basis later in the decade, but *Burmese Days* focused on morality. An unsigned *Times Literary Supplement* noted 'traces of power' in Orwell's writing, before suggesting that a little less gall 'would have carried more conviction' and pointing out perceived inaccuracies (Meyers, 1975, p. 52). These and other notices – from the enthusiastic to the slightly dismissive – fit the normal pattern of reviews, indicating not only the different attitudes of reviewers but to some extent the different positions of the journals in which the reviews appear. Naturally, reviewers present themselves as independent critical judges, but it is likely that in many cases editors employ reviewers whose opinions they value, perhaps on the basis of shared assumptions.

A Clergyman's Daughter, which Orwell would later essentially disown as a failed experiment, received less appreciative notices. The tale of Dorothy Hare's descent from oppressed clergyman's daughter to traumatized and drifting soul, the novel incorporates elements from his earlier articles and from *Down and Out* (Dorothy spends time hop picking and then as a vagrant around Trafalgar Square) while attempting Joycean effects borrowed from the Nighttown episode of *Ulysses*. V. S. Pritchett, already an up-and-coming writer and critic, allows in the *Spectator* that 'Orwell's case is a sound one' but laments that a pivotal scene 'has unfortunately been written in a "stunt" Joyce fashion which utterly ruins the effect' (Meyers, 1975, p. 60). Peter Quennell in the *New Statesman and Nation* rated it 'ambitious yet not entirely successful' (ibid., p. 61), and L. P. Hartley claimed in the *Observer* that while the novel's thesis was 'neither new nor convincing', still 'its merits lie in its treatment, which is sure and bold, and in the dialogue, which is always appropriate, and often brilliant' (ibid., p. 59). As a forthright reviewer himself and given his own scathing sense of the novel, Orwell might have expected these types of notices. Overall, they were not calamitous, and the novel sold reasonably well.

George Orwell was now establishing himself as a writer, living in London and working part-time in a bookshop run by ILP supporters, Francis and Myfanwy Westrope, while Eric Blair still made regular appearances reviewing for *The Adelphi* as late as December 1934. An unsigned review in March 1935 signalled the transition to his pseudonym, and his reviews for the *New English Weekly* and *The Adelphi* in August 1935 were both listed as by George Orwell, although he still used his real name in correspondence with friends, agents and editors. The death of Rudyard Kipling in 1936 led to him writing a short, appreciative notice for the *New English Weekly*, a periodical that considered broad political, literary and social developments. Orwell had reviewed for the *New English Weekly* since 1932 (initially as Eric A. Blair), the year the brilliant veteran editor Alfred Orage had set it up to promote the ideas of Social Credit, a movement based on radical and contentious economic reform. In a 1933 letter Orwell mentions the *New English Weekly*, stating that he had read 'nothing, I think except periodicals, all of which depresses me beyond words'. He then comments that 'as a monetary scheme Social Credit is probably sound, but its promoters seem to think that they are going to take the main weapon out of the hands of the governing classes without a fight, which is an illusion' (*CO, X,* p. 317). 'Rudyard Kipling' was both his first piece beyond a review for the *New English Weekly* and one of his first published works outside his books to carry the name George Orwell.

His assessment of Kipling splits formally into three paragraphs: the first recognizes Kipling's enormous popularity and impact, the second questions his attitude to imperialism, and the third, which acknowledges that in the 1930s Kipling was seen as 'a kind of enemy, a man of perverted and alien genius', ends almost nostalgically: 'now that he is dead, I for one cannot help wishing that I could offer some kind of tribute . . . to the storyteller who was so important to my childhood' (*CO, X,* p. 410). That revealingly personal note echoes one in the first section where Orwell admits that 'I worshipped Kipling at thirteen, loathed him at seventeen, enjoyed him at twenty, despised him at twenty-five, and now again rather admire him' (ibid., p. 409). While the mature Orwell recognizes in Kipling's writing 'the vulgarity of his prose style', he nevertheless praises Kipling's 'supreme' construction and economy, and writes that even though his bad verse is 'a byword for badness' it stays with the reader. This memorability is itself laudable in that 'it needs a streak of genius even to become a byword' (ibid., p. 410). To admire with reservations is still to admire, and by recognizing Kipling's faults while still acknowledging his genius, Orwell goes part way to undercutting criticism of Kipling's work.

The second section considers a 'much more distasteful' aspect of Kipling's life, 'the imperialism to which he chose to lend his genius' (ibid.). 'Lending' suggests a temporary transaction that might leave intact Kipling's underlying genius, and Orwell goes on to defend Kipling's choice, arguing that '[t]he imperialism of the eighties and nineties was sentimental, ignorant and dangerous, but it was not entirely despicable' (ibid.). For whom, one might ask. As with 'A Hanging' and *Burmese Days,* Orwell's is an Anglo-centric viewpoint, concentrating on the Empire and the situation of the imperial ruler rather than imperialism proper and the position of subject peoples. He reinforces his defence of Kipling by continuing that

> the picture then called up by the word 'empire' was a picture of overworked officials and frontier skirmishes, not of Lord Beaverbrook and Australian butter. It was still possible to be an imperialist and a gentleman, and of Kipling's *personal* decency there can be no doubt. (ibid.)

Orwell often uses 'decency' to indicate the qualities of the common English people. Here it transmits more class-based connotations, implying in the language of the private club, that Kipling remained a 'decent chap'.

Not all obituaries were as forgiving. Rebecca West in *The New Statesman and Nation* characterized Kipling as

a man, loving everything in life but reality, [who] spent his days loathing intellectuals as soft and craven theorists, and yet himself never has the courage to face a single fact that disproved the fairytales he had invented about the world in his youth. (West, p. 112)

Other contemporary interpretations were less appreciative, Mulk Raj Anand – author of the highly regarded novel *Coolie* (1936), which deals with India's 'Untouchables' – arguing in *Left Review* that 'in the work of Rudyard Kipling and his numerous imitators, we hear the clarion call of an aggressive British imperialism, the counterpart in fiction of the brutal deeds wrought by the armies of monopoly-capitalism' (Anand, p. 617). Where Orwell contends that Kipling loaned his genius to the empire, Anand accuses Kipling of fully accepting and promoting imperialist tenets, creating what he labels 'Kipling's dogma: a doctrinaire racial theory that a white man is superior to ten natives any day, and that the British Empire is the holiest kingdom of God on earth' (ibid.). Clearly, Orwell's take on Kipling was not held unanimously, other journals supplying strident criticism.

By the time the Rudyard Kipling notice appeared Orwell had embarked on the transformative trip to the north of England, collecting material for what would be his most controversial and successful book to that point, *The Road to Wigan Pier* (1937). But 1936 itself was a productive year in other ways, with his novel *Keep the Aspidistra Flying* published in Britain (though none of his books between *A Clergyman's Daughter* and *Animal Farm* were published in the United States during his lifetime). Again it received mixed reviews, William Plomer describing it in the *Spectator* as 'bitter almost throughout and often crude' (Meyers, 1975, p. 65) and Cyril Connolly in the *New Statesman and Nation* judging that it was 'written in clear and violent language' that 'at times seems too emphatic and far-fetched' (ibid., p. 67). Richard Rees in *The Adelphi* was more complimentary, mentioning 'a consistent seriousness and a real vigour which make him a more promising novelist than many whose observation is subtler and sharper' (ibid., p. 69). Something of a subtext lurks in this review, for the novel satirizes a literary journal called *Antichrist* which resembles *The Adelphi* and whose well-meaning if naïve editor, Ravelston, seems a portrait of Rees. The novel's protagonist, the aspiring writer Gordon Comstock, has obvious associations with Orwell himself, and the novel reveals the importance of literary journals to aspiring writers. Comstock's literary world is shot through with periodicals; he has a poem turned down by *Primrose Quarterly*, but receives a cheque from *Californian Review* for a poem he has forgotten about (*CO, IV*, p. 169); the *Times Literary Supplement* has written of his 'exceptional promise' (ibid., p. 32); Ravelston publishes his poems in *Antichrist* and gives him books to review. *Antichrist* is described as

> a middle- to high-brow monthly, Socialist in a vehement but ill-defined way. In general it gave the impression of being edited by an ardent Nonconfomist who had transferred his allegiance from God to Marx, and in doing so had got mixed up with a gang of *vers libre* poets. (ibid., p. 88)

Rees's continued support of Orwell suggests that he took this acidic mocking with good grace.

A more demanding editor prompted what would come to be considered a major essay: 'Shooting an Elephant'. John Lehmann had worked, sometimes tensely, at Leonard and Virginia Woolf's Hogarth Press before branching out on his own, creating *New Writing* at the beginning of 1936. It carried a Manifesto, but where other journals brashly declared political allegiances, *New Writing*'s policy was understated:

> NEW WRITING will appear twice yearly, and will be devoted to imaginative writing, mainly of young authors. It does not intend to concern itself with literary theory, or the criticism of contemporaries.
>
> NEW WRITING aims at providing an outlet for those prose writers, among others, whose work is too unorthodox in length or style to be suitable for established monthly and quarterly magazines.
>
> NEW WRITING is first and foremost interested in literature, and though it does not intend to open its pages to writers of reactionary or Fascist sentiments, it is independent of any political party.
>
> NEW WRITING also hopes to represent the work of writers from colonial and foreign countries. (Lehmann, 1936, p. v)

The manifesto worked to distinguish *New Writing* from established journals that promoted literary theory or criticism (*The Criterion* and *Scrutiny*), emphasized political allegiances (the defunct *Cambridge Left* and *Left Review*) or published poetry (*New Verse*). Françoise Bort claims that this manifesto 'reads more as an anti-manifesto' and that its 'neutral tones paradoxically convey the most daring policy of the magazine: to give an age group the lead over purely aesthetic tendencies or politically aligned groups'. Bort continues that Lehmann's memoirs 'tell how he perceived *New Writing* as a space for novelty, where the spirit of the new generation could at last produce its own self-image' (Bort, p. 672). Lehmann saw the journal filling a silence in the public sphere by presenting fiction ignored by journals that promoted late modernism or politically aligned work. His claim to *New Writing*'s political independence did not go unchallenged, though, Samuel Hynes quoting a *Daily Worker* review that sees the journal as highlighting the polarization of political positions. A *Criterion* critic argues from the opposite standpoint that 'The fact that the editor finds it necessary to inform us of his comparative impartiality shows that he is aware of what might be said. That is that *New Writing* is not concerned first with literature, but with left-wing propaganda' (Hynes, p. 198). Connolly would call Lehmann undoubtedly 'the outstanding British editor of the period, capable of selecting poetry, fiction, reportage and reviews – provided they were left-wing', adding that Lehmann 'enabled England to take the lead in what was later to be called "la literature engagée"' (Connolly, 1973, p. 425). Hynes comments that the reviewers were right in that 'it was political and it was consistently left-wing' but that 'Lehmann was not being disingenuous when he claimed that his magazine would be literary' (Hynes, p. 198). When Lehmann contacted Orwell in 1936, though, he was merely another struggling young editor commissioning material. *New Writing* was unusual in several ways: it came out only twice a year, and because of backing by major publishing houses it 'came to the reader in a surprisingly luxurious format of 200 pages' and at the rather expensive price of six shillings (Bort, p. 673); Penguin books at the same time sold for six pence. This size allowed for lengthier material than would ordinarily be possible to include in a literary review, satisfying Lehmann's wish to concentrate on prose rather than on poetry. Bort comments that *New Writing*'s 'list of contributors' emphasized not

> their education or literary background, but . . . their experience of the world and their competence as observers of contemporary changes. Thus George Orwell appears in one number as 'a government official in Burma' and 'a volunteer in Spain, where he was wounded.(ibid., p. 674)

Lehmann wrote to Orwell in early 1936 asking for suitable new work, and received a guarded reply:

> I am writing a book at present and the only other thing I have in mind is a sketch (it would be about 2000 – 3000 words), describing the shooting of an elephant. It all came back to me very vividly the other day & I would like to write about it, but it may be quite out of your line. I mean it might be too lowbrow for your paper & I doubt whether there is anything anti-Fascist in the shooting of an elephant! Of course you can't say in advance if you would like it, but perhaps you could say tentatively whether it is at all likely to be in your line or not. If not, then I won't write it . . . I am sorry to be so vague but without seeing a copy of 'New Writing' I can't tell what sort of stuff it uses. (*CO, X*, p. 483)

John Hammond comments that 'it seems incredible that one of the most celebrated essays of modern times was first mooted with such apparent casualness' (Hammond, p. 214), but he writes with a hindsight neither Orwell nor Lehmann possessed. What Hammond reads as apparent casualness was understandable caution; Orwell's reply highlights the mutually tentative relationships between journals and authors, especially when the journal is new and the author largely unknown. Even so, Orwell fitted the *New Writing*'s brief to promote young fiction writers of unorthodox material. Lehmann quickly sent him a copy of the first issue, receiving the speedy reply that Orwell had read it 'with great interest' and that he 'liked [Christopher] Isherwood's story extremely'; Isherwood later incorporated this piece, 'The Nowaks', into the novel *Goodbye To Berlin* (1939). Orwell declared it 'a splendid thing that there should be at any rate one periodical which has room for long-short stories', and included 'Shooting an Elephant', repeating that 'whether it is quite in your line I am not certain. If not, perhaps I might be able to do something more suitable for some later issue of "New Writing"'. Lehmann accepted the essay, which opened the second number of the journal, one that also included work by the Trinidadian writer Alfred Mendes and Mulk Raj Anand's 'The Barber's Trade Union'. The opportunity prompted by Lehmann proved crucial to the writing of 'Shooting an Elephant', which Orwell composed quickly between his letters to Lehmann on 27 May and 12 June. Remarkably, in that same period he also got married to Eileen O'Shaughnessy.

The narrator of 'A Hanging' primarily acts as a spectator, observing rather than acting decisively, but his equivalent in 'Shooting an Elephant' functions far more centrally. Again, a low-ranking imperial official, the narrator here is rendered as complex and troubled, someone whose consciousness is central to the psychological interrogation that occurs and whose colonial position determines the minor political dilemma he confronts. As with 'A Hanging', 'Shooting an Elephant' begins by locating the narrator within the colonial setting, but in this instance the geographical detail dovetails into personal statement:

> In Moulmein, in Lower Burma, I was hated by large numbers of people – the only time in my life that I was important enough for this to happen to me . . . As a police officer I was an obvious target and was baited whenever it seemed safe to do so. (*CO, X*, p. 501)

The contrast with 'A Hanging' is crucial, with power flowing not out from the imperial centre, but back from the colonized on to the colonizer. Opposition between powerful group and ineffectual individual gets established immediately, and reverberates through the narrative. Where the situation for the condemned man in the earlier essay had been terminal and dire, here the official with putative power feels oppressed, driven by uncontrollable and malicious forces. His own antagonism to the system he ostensibly represents complicates his position: 'Theoretically – and secretly, of course – I was all for the Burmese and all against their oppressors, the British' (ibid.), evading the reality of his Britishness. From the outset ambiguities and paradoxes are set up: the narrator presents himself as an anti-British Briton, an anti-Empire imperialist, the possessor and symbol of massive institutional power put upon by those over whom he has nominal authority. None of these political or ideological aspects are raised in any significant way in 'A Hanging', which directs its focus primarily to moral questions. In 'Shooting and Elephant' the dynamics, motivations and conflicts within imperialism are central.

Despite the statement of secret motivations, the narrator's condemnation of imperialism remains oddly equivocal, for he states that he 'did not even know that the British empire is dying, still less did I know that it is a great deal better than the younger empires that are going to supplant it' (ibid.). The confused sense of time is revealing, for while he plausibly confesses not to have known that the British Empire was dying during his time in Burma, the claim not to know of something that at the time of writing still had not happened makes no sense. These ambiguities and inconsistencies threaten the narrator's position as a credible eyewitness. Paradoxically, his standing gets bolstered by openly expressed racist and sadistic leanings: he portrays the native population as laughing 'hideously', of possessing 'sneering little yellow faces', of being 'evil spirited little beasts' (ibid., pp. 501–2). He admits that 'seeing the dirty work of Empire at close quarters' oppressed him 'with an intolerable sense of guilt . . . I was young and ill-educated and had to think out my problems in the utter silence that is imposed on every Englishman in the East' (ibid., p. 501). This disclosure leads to the confession that 'the greatest joy in the world would be to drive a bayonet into a Buddhist priest's guts. Feelings like this are the normal by-products of imperialism; ask any Anglo-Indian, if you catch him off duty' (ibid., p. 502). This shocking admission reinforces the attack on imperialism by acknowledging the brutalizing effect on its functionaries. More subtly, the narrator's disarmingly honest revelations present him as a credible guide.

The construction of a self-aware and brutally honest figure precedes the central narrative, the shooting itself. Called upon as the local representative of imperial power to put down a supposedly rampaging elephant, the narrator realizes on sighting the beast that in the interim it has calmed down. But the huge crowd of Burmese that has followed him forces him into crisis:

> I realized that I had to shoot the elephant after all. The people expected it of me and I had to do it . . . I was only an absurd puppet pushed to and fro by the will of those yellow faces behind. I perceived at that moment that when the white man turns tyrant it is his own freedom that he destroys. (*CO, X*, p. 504)

Recognizing the irresistible combination of duty and impotency, he shoots the animal. Analysing his actions later, he wonders 'whether any of the others grasped that I had done it solely to avoid looking the fool' (ibid., p. 506). The opposition of individual and group remains fundamental to the narrative and thematic direction of 'Shooting an Elephant'. In the moment the narrator attempts to overcome his sense of inadequacy, his fear of looking foolish, he becomes the crowd's plaything, an absurd puppet. Drained of any sense of self, his actions are determined not by personal or even by imperial dictates, but by the will of the crowd. The group triumphs over the individual, no matter that the narrator suspects (or hopes) that his true motivations remain hidden.

The dominance over the powerful mass over the puny individual signals an apparent transfer of power from imperial master to imperial subject. The narrator's existential crisis, it seems, turns the oppressor into the oppressed. But the crisis remains that of the individual, and this concentration on an unusually self-aware figure deflects attention away from the larger forces at work. While the narrator claims to recognize imperialism's evil, he fails to make a substantive critique of imperialism as a process that affects the local inhabitants. The essay's personal perspective necessarily focuses on the narrator's human frailties, and while these are presented with a compelling and sometimes confronting honesty, his more general assumptions go largely unexamined: the differences between British imperialism and comparable regimes; the normality of brutality and racism under imperialism; the disturbing 'otherness' of the Burmese. Emphasis, and a consequent empathy, on the colonial official's loss of freedom leaves that of the Burmese largely unconsidered.

Among the best of Orwell's early essays, 'Shooting an Elephant's qualities are manifest: a deftly handled scenario, the construction of a complex central figure psychologically and politically compromised by general circumstances and the specific dilemma he faces; a powerfully evoked dramatic build up to the shooting followed by a vivid depiction of the agonizing, pointless death of the elephant; the revelatory examination of internal motives and external forces. Lehmann immediately accepted it for the second number of *New Writing*. These literary qualities partly explain why 'Shooting an Elephant' remains unusual among Orwell's essays in having an 'afterlife' while he lived. Lehmann reprinted it in the first number of *Penguin New Writing* in November 1940 and it was included in the A. F. Scott-edited *Modern Essays* (1942). Extraordinarily, it was also broadcast on the BBC Home Service in October 1948 (Fenwick, p. 180). But for all its precision and concision, and its undoubted literary and rhetorical power, its detailed and illuminating examination of the mind of a colonial official ignores the important group of local figures: the Burmese. As with 'A Hanging', focusing on one group necessarily occludes others.

A rather more mundane reality forms the basis of 'Bookshop Memories', published in *Fortnightly* in November 1936. Confusingly, *Fortnightly* had been published monthly for all but its first year (1865). Anthony Trollope had helped in the setting up of the periodical, which had once boasted Frank Harris as its editor. By 1936 it concentrated on centre-left politics and the more genteel side of literature. As such, *Fortnightly* provides the right platform for some good-hearted criticism of a largely neglected and often idealized world. 'Bookshop Memories' evokes the period from October 1934 to January 1936 when Orwell worked in a second-hand bookshop, reflecting his early interest in the sociology of literature and his capacity to observe and depict the comic aspects of literary culture. He begins by immediately puncturing any romantic preconceptions, commenting that

> When I worked in a second-hand bookshop – so easily pictured, if you don't work in one, as a kind of paradise where charming old gentlemen browse eternally among calf-bound volumes – the chief thing that struck me was the rarity of really bookish people. (*CO*, X, p. 510)

Orwell sketches a dull, eccentric environment where somewhat 'moth-eaten and aimless' customers do not know good books from bad. He grabs an opportunity to satirize the stamp collectors who frequent the shop, and points out the tackiness of the Christmas card business, remembering an invoice for '2 doz. Infant Jesus with rabbits' (ibid., p. 511). Orwell comments that the bookshop's lending library allowed you to see people's real tastes, not their pretended ones, and 'the one thing that strikes you is how completely the "classical" English novelists have dropped out of favour. It is simply useless to put Dickens, Thackeray, Jane Austen, Trollope, etc. into the ordinary lending library: nobody takes them out' (ibid., p. 512). Ironically, the bookshop he fashions has Dickensian traces of eccentricity and dilapidation, mixed into a larger criticism of banality. Answering the rhetorical question of whether he would like to be a bookseller, he gives a slightly qualified 'no'. Despite the nostalgia suggested by its title, Orwell admits that his experiences in a bookshop have turned him away from books, at least as they are found in second-hand shops: 'The sweet smell of decaying paper appeals to me no longer. It is too closely associated in my mind with paranoiac customers and dead bluebottles' (ibid., p. 513). Rather than an investigation of the state of literature in a politically charged decade or a statement of purpose about what a writer might or should pursue in those circumstances, 'Bookshop Memories' more readily fits the model of the classical periodical essay that illustrates and comments upon aspects of everyday culture from a personal perspective. Mixing wry humour with highly selective accounts of odd or comically mundane incidents and people, the essay provides an early instance of Orwell's interest in social habits, customs and institutions that surround the literary industry.

The variety of active journals allowed the possibility of dealing with distinct areas of the literary world simultaneously. In the same month that 'Bookshop Memories' was published, the *New English Weekly* ran 'In Defence of the Novel'. Where Orwell's earlier essay for the journal gave a predominantly positive reading of Kipling's career, 'In Defence of the Novel' attacks reviewers. Novels and reviews are intimately linked, of course, Orwell blaming what he perceives as the low contemporary prestige of the novel on the abysmal standards of reviewing. The failure of reviewers to differentiate properly between good and bad writing, so that 'all novels are thrust upon you as works of genius', prompts a sceptical public to suspect that all novels must be mediocre. Orwell partly excuses reviewers, recognizing, as one himself, that to write frankly about all books received would be financial as well as literary suicide: bills have to be paid. In addition, the reviewer, possibly an admirer of highbrow novels and novelists, must of necessity assess works that fall criminally short of the ideal. Inevitably, hyperbole fills the abyss between the artist and the artisan. As he puts it:

> [T]o apply a decent standard to the ordinary run of novels is like weighing a flea on a spring-balance intended for elephants. On such a balance as that a flea would simply fail to register; you have to start by constructing another balance which revealed the fact that there are big fleas and little fleas. And this approximately is what [the reviewer] does. (*CO, X*, p. 519)

When such standards apply, intelligent readers dismiss the review. More seriously, those same readers might dismiss what is under review, so that 'it is possible for a novel of real merit to escape notice, merely because it has been praised in the same terms as tripe' (ibid., p. 520). Orwell proposes a solution to the dilemma:

> [J]ust *one* periodical (one would be enough for a start) which makes a speciality of novel reviewing but refuses to take any notice of tripe, and in which the reviewers *are* reviewers and not ventriloquists' dummies clapping their jaws when the publisher pulls the string. (ibid.)

Considering that Orwell himself was reviewing for the *New English Weekly* at the time, he seems at least to be nipping at the hand that feeds him. Acknowledging that certain periodicals do review novels with a certain degree of critical detachment, he asserts that

> these belong to the highbrow world, a world in which it is already assumed that novels, as such, are despicable. But the novel is a popular form of art, and it is no use to approach it with the *Criterion-Scrutiny* assumption that literature is a game of back-scratching (claws in or out according to circumstances) between tiny cliques of highbrows. (ibid.)

Orwell's targets here (hack reviewers, highbrow magazines) are puny, but the argument put forward in 'In Defence of the Novel' approximates that used against more powerful foes: the need for open debate. He even proposes a 'system . . . of grading novels into classes A,B,C and so forth, so that whether a reviewer praised or damned a book, you would at least know how seriously he meant it to be taken' (ibid., p. 521). No such system was set up, nor did Orwell apply it himself. The general purpose of improving the quality of the novel by improving the quality of reviews remains moot. He does, however, recognize the importance and effect of criticism done by a small group of periodicals.

Orwell's concern for the quality of novels and of their assessment are integrated in his review of Philip Henderson's *The Novel Today* in the *New English Weekly* on New Year's Eve, 1936. He describes Henderson's book as 'a survey of the contemporary novel from a Marxist standpoint', judging it 'a weaker version of Mirsky's *Intelligentsia of Great Britain*'. D. S. Mirsky, a Russian intellectual who had lived for a time in London, had written a venomous attack on British intellectuals on returning to the Soviet Union. In Orwell's view, Henderson's analysis is weaker because he is

> someone who has got to live in England and cannot afford to insult too many people . . .[and] is of some interest because it raises the question of art and propaganda which now rumbles like a sort of 'noises off' round every critical discussion. (*CO, X*, p. 532)

Henderson's propriety, from Orwell's perspective, results not from good manners, but from intellectual dishonesty: the position 'that a book is only a "good" book if it teaches the right sermon' (ibid., p. 533). The religious terminology is not arbitrary, for Orwell sees it as a tendency of 'extremists at the opposite poles of thought, the Communist and the Catholic'. While highly critical of these orthodoxies, he denies that these positions as universally accepted. The 'official attitude' is still one he illustrates by means of an old Punch cartoon depicting 'an intolerable youth telling his aunt . . . he intended to "write". "And what are you going to write about dear?" his aunt inquires. "My dear aunt," the youth replies crushingly, "one doesn't write *about* anything, one just *writes*." ' Officialdom preaches the code of aesthetic detachment, the drawing away from social reality; the writer is nothing more than a dilettante. Orwell ridicules this attitude, but more keenly attacks the tendentious criticism that gestures to aesthetic criteria while judging a book purely on the political or religious philosophy espoused. The linking of Communist orthodoxy with that of Catholicism (a connection he would also make in *The Road to Wigan Pier*) drives home the perverting effects of literary criticism that abdicates its aesthetic duty to political prejudices. The effects pervade beyond the boundaries of literary criticism or literature itself. Orthodoxy in one area necessarily infiltrates others. Orwell considers this very depressing for anyone who cares for the cause of Socialism. 'For what is it except the most ordinary chauvinism turned upside down? It simply gives you the feeling that the Communist is no better than his opposite number' (ibid., p. 534).

By the time the review was published, Orwell had sent Gollancz the manuscript of *The Road to Wigan Pier* and had arrived at the Lenin Barracks in Spain to fight in and write about the Spanish Civil War. His difficulties in getting his interpretation of events published are dealt with in the next chapter, as well as his increasingly radical political position. But it is worth considering here how far he had come as a writer after considerable struggle. At the end of 1936 he had published one semi-documentary and three novels, numerous reviews and several essays that in time would be reprinted repeatedly. His novels show him using his own experiences as the basis of several experiments in style that only partially succeed. *Down and Out* reveals a capacity to write vividly and compellingly about ignored sections of society. His essays also rework his own experiences, and in the best of them, 'A Hanging' and 'Shooting an Elephant' especially, he creates eloquent pieces that in their acuity and polish rival his longer work. Although he was still grappling with questions of form and style in his fiction, his essays already exhibit qualities that later would be recognized as central to his writing: clarity and precision; the ability to cast an illuminating light into neglected areas; an independent political and moral vision delivered with arresting force. At least in his essays, Orwell had found his literary voice.

Chapter 2

The Radicalized Orwell: From Spanish to Global Conflict (1937–9)

The years 1937–9 would witness a substantial radicalizing of Orwell's political position, much of it in response to the deteriorating political environment nationally and internationally. The impetus for this decline had been the onset of the Great Depression, the effects of which pulsated directly and indirectly through the decade. On the political Right, the rise of Adolf Hitler had led quickly to the suppression of political opposition in Germany, the persecution of minority groups – particularly Jews – rapid rearmament and attempts to overturn the conditions of the Treaty of Versailles. Appeasement policies instigated by the Baldwin government elected in 1935 encouraged Hitler's recklessness, leading to the reoccupation of the Rhineland in 1936. Germany, Italy and Japan signed the Anti-Comintern Pact in that year (Comintern being a contraction of the Communist International) and the proclamation of the German–Italian Axis displayed growing Fascist confidence. The threat of aggression materialized on a small scale in Italy's 1936 invasion of Abyssinia. Fascism also had a toehold in Britain, Oswald Mosley's British Union of Fascists enjoying limited but sometimes enthusiastic support among sections of society. On the Left, in the face of Fascism's menace, the 7th Congress of the Comintern in 1935 reversed its 'class against class' position that had mandated the violent denunciation of other left wing parties seen as reformist stooges; the Popular Front (sometimes People's Front) approach favoured working with those parties and bourgeois parties. This new policy was taken up enthusiastically in some sections of the Left as a sign that only the Soviet Union stood against Fascism, but was repudiated by other sections as a cynical Soviet exercise to maintain domination. Governments proclaiming themselves as supporters of the Popular Front were elected in Spain and France, but in the former case this precipitated a revolt by the Spanish military under General Francisco Franco and the ensuing Spanish Civil War, a conflict that Kingsley Martin wrote in *The Political Quarterly* exemplified the 'increasing clarity of the international choice between Fascism and Socialism' (Martin, 1936, p. 574).

The complexities and ambiguities of the Spanish Civil war were captured in Charles Fenby's assessment in the same journal that 'the Left Wing has inherited ideas of fair play which perhaps hinder its propaganda' (Fenby, p. 258). In the ensuing months Orwell would find himself dramatically at odds with the positions of Martin and Fenby, if not on the war itself, then on how events should be interpreted and communicated. His brief time fighting in Spain and the consequences of his efforts to publish his accounts of what he had seen would have a profound effect on Orwell's politics and writing, moving him further to the Left than when he had returned from Wigan the year before. The Spanish Civil War was not, obviously, the only political determinant of the late 1930s, for while the advance of Fascism was immensely troubling and potentially consequential. From Orwell's perspective, the Soviet Union's dominance as a model for socialism and communism was also worrying. The concentration of power around Stalin and the suppression of opponents, especially those linked to Leon Trotsky, indeed caused concern for many on the Left. The Great Depression still unsettled the world's major economies, and although unemployment in Britain was down from its worst peaks it would stay above one and a half million for the rest of the decade. Through most of the 1930s Europe was unnerved.

When it was published in March 1937 *Wigan Pier* itself exposed the grim circumstances for miners and others who had work, let alone the poor and unemployed whose miserable situation seemed entrenched. Beyond its contents, certain aspects of its publication and reception reflect the state of debate within the British Left at the time, aspects that would also have a radicalizing effect on Orwell. Researching and writing the book broadened his political awareness and hastened his political growth, putting him in touch with the actual conditions of key sectors of the working class. He maintained his *Adelphi* contacts, names supplied by Richard Rees helping him meet local workers and political organizers. He wrote semi-jokingly to Jack Common, now the *Adelphi*'s co-editor, about the 'barbarous regions' he had surveyed (*CO, X,* p. 458). The contract for *Wigan Pier* offered him the chance and the challenge of formulating a political position for public consumption, the eventual book arguing Orwell's peculiar and still maturing version of Socialism. It provided a detailed but selective report on conditions in the north, and more controversially, a highly personalized account of Orwell's own journey to Socialism. It also ridiculed respected Socialist writers who 'have all been dull, empty windbags: Shaw, Barbusse, Upton Sinclair, William Morris, Waldo Frank, etc, etc', on the grounds that in the face of the Fascism's attractions the only way to create 'an effective Socialist party' was to offer an objective which fairly ordinary people would recognize as desirable. Above all else, therefore, he wrote that 'we need intelligent propaganda' (*CO, V,* p. 214). Orwell attacked what he saw as the Soviet template for Socialism, revered uncritically as he saw it by Left intellectuals, one that did not take account of local conditions or traditions and was fixated on technological and materialist progress. And he crudely satirized middle class Socialists by provocatively caricaturing 'every fruit-juice drinker, nudist, sandal-wearer, sex-maniac' supposedly drawn to Socialism (ibid., p. 161).

Wigan Pier was published as a Left Book Club edition, by which time Orwell was already fighting on the Aragón Front with the P.O.U.M. militia. The book substantially cultivated his public profile within certain sections of the British Left, primarily because of the phenomenal success of The Left Book Club. Orwell's publisher Victor Gollancz established it in 1936 to extend and inform the British public sphere. He made this aim plain in the first number of the *Left News*, a monthly paper for LBC members, where he wrote that the club was attempting

> to provide the indispensable basis of *knowledge* without which a really effective United Front of all men and women of good will cannot be built. If we are to win, we must have, each one of us, not less but more knowledge than the best informed of our enemies. (Gollancz, 1936, p. 2)

The Club required members to pay for a special low-priced (2/6p) club edition of a selected book every month for six months. Books were selected by Gollancz, academic Harold Laski and Left intellectual John Strachey, and promoted left-wing ideas and analyses, often with more than a hint of Communist and Soviet sympathy. Strachey was decidedly pro-Communist, Ben Pimlott describing him as 'a fully committed Communist who found it convenient not to carry a card' (Pimlott, p. 158). Gollancz's biographer Ruth Dudley Edwards argues that while Gollancz never was a Communist, he could be described 'in his own words in private correspondence, as "no more than a 'fellow-traveller'" – though "an immensely admiring and sympathetic one", who was from time to time "carried away"' (Edwards, p. 213). She adds that in 1936 Gollancz believed that 'the only hope for future peace' lay in a Popular Front approach in Britain that 'would hold out hopes of a British/French alliance with the Soviet Union to resist Hitler and Mussolini, while at home it could do much to eradicate the social injustice that fuelled Mosley's fascist party' (ibid., pp. 228–9). But that hope blinded Gollancz to the darker aspects of Soviet and Communist policy, and as the decade wore on the Left Book Club became dominated by Communist personnel and opinion to the detriment of other leftist views.

The Left Book Club proved surprisingly successful; by May 1936 it had 9,000 members (Edwards, p. 231); a year later nearly 45,000 people were signed up, reaching 57,000 by April 1939 (ibid., p. 258). As a Monthly selection, *The Road to Wigan Pier* sold over 44,500 copies, far exceeding anything Orwell had produced and almost anything he would produce before *Animal Farm* nearly a decade later (the exception being a 1940 Penguin edition of *Down and Out*). Although the Club was a rising political and cultural force in the British polity in 1937 it commanded only a proportion of progressive thought in Britain. While 45,000 Left Book Club members easily surpassed the membership of the Communist Party of Great Britain – which languished below 10,000 – in 1934 the British Union of Fascists had peaked at between 40,000–50,000, before dropping to 5,000 in 1935, and then rising again to 15,000 in 1936 and

22,000 by 1939 (Pugh, p. 166). (The Fascists also understood the importance of the public sphere, publishing their own *Fascist Quarterly* along with papers such as the *The Blackshirt* and *Action*, both of which had circulations of over 20,000 (ibid., p. 223).) Still, the Left Book Club substantially contributed to the healthy diversity of views energizing public debate.

Despite selection as the Monthly choice *Wigan Pier* carried a Foreword by Gollancz that made a convoluted case that 'the People's Front is not the "policy" of the Left Book Club, but the very existence of the Left Book Club tends towards the People's Front' (*CO*, *V*, p. 217). Having added that 'it is a long time since I have read so *living* a book, or one so full of burning indignation against poverty and oppression', Gollancz declares that he 'had marked well over a hundred minor passages which I thought I should like to argue with' (ibid., p. 218). He goes on over eight pages to heavily criticize Orwell's '*emotional* Socialism' in the second half of *Wigan Pier*, where Orwell traces his development from a middle-class child to a polemically idiosyncratic Socialist. This Gollancz compares unfavourably to the ideal of 'scientific Socialism'. 'This book', he concludes, 'more perhaps than any other that the Left Book Club has issued, clarifies – for me at least – the whole meaning and purpose of the Club' (ibid., p. 225). He means the first half of the book – the second half he writes off, and in fact he attempted to persuade Orwell to publish the halves separately. Orwell refused, even if in a letter to his agent Leonard Moore, he had described the then-unfinished text as 'a sort of a book of essays' (*CO*, *X*, p. 510). Gollancz's clear desire to convert readers to Socialism by publishing *Wigan Pier* and his need to control their interpretation of an unorthodox but persuasive text largely gets repeated by Harold Laski's review of the book in *Left News*. Laski calls the first part of the book 'admirable propaganda for our ideas' (Meyers, 1975, p. 104) before criticizing Orwell for ignoring 'class antagonisms' and having 'no sense of the historical movement of the economic process' (ibid., p. 106). By the time the book appeared Orwell had been in Spain for several months, and while Crick calls Orwell's research for *Wigan Pier* 'The Crucial Journey', his time in Spain was to be equally transformative. The new lessons he learned about the control of language and the manipulation of history would later radiate through *Animal Farm* and *Nineteen Eighty-Four*. Ironically, people who had previously published his work would now find his independent views dangerous.

Orwell enlisted as 'Eric Blair' in the Partido Obrero de Unificación or P.O.U.M. militia, which had affiliations with the ILP in Britain. By the beginning of January 1937 he was living at the Lenin Barracks in Barcelona, before moving to the frontline at Alcubierre in February and then close to Huesca, where he saw action. Some of this activity was recorded in P.O.U.M.'s own newspaper *The Spanish Revolution*, where the activities of 'Eric Blair, the well-known British author' are mentioned, including that 'he is now fighting with the Spanish comrades of the P.O.U.M. on the Aragon front' (*CO*, *XI*, p. 10). Orwell would stay on the Aragon front until the end of April, after which he applied for leave with the intention of joining the International Brigade in Madrid. But while back in Barcelona he became entangled in skirmishes between the P.O.U.M. and its allies on one side and the Communists trying to suppress opposition on the Left. Instead of leaving for Madrid he returned to the front, where he was shot in the throat, recuperating in hospitals and a sanatorium before returning to the front in mid-June to get his discharge papers. Soon after, the Republican government declared the P.O.U.M. illegal and Orwell and his wife Eileen, who had visited him at the front as well as providing help to the ILP, went into hiding in Barcelona in fear of their lives. They later escaped Barcelona and Spain by train, returning back to England in July 1937.

Those are the bare facts of Orwell's time in Spain, which he set down with his impressions and analysis in *Homage to Catalonia*, published in May 1938. But those facts conceal more than they reveal, the most telling being that Secker and Warburg published the book after Gollancz refused the manuscript before a word had been written. Instead, it came out in a print run of only 1,500, its publisher Frederic Warburg later revealing that it sold only 683 copies in its first six months (Warburg, p. 238). This number was so small compared to the more than 40,000 for the Gollancz-sanctioned *Wigan Pier* that when Orwell's agent, Leonard Moore, sent a letter to Orwell, who was in Morocco convalescing from a tubercular lesion, Orwell wondered if the number of 'about 700' was 'a typist's error' (*CO, XI*, p. 221). As well as a financial disaster for Warburg, the poor sales negated Orwell's purpose in writing *Homage to Catalonia*, which was to counteract false reporting of events and the misrepresentations of ideological battles. He had recognized this in Spain, reading accounts by British newspapers and journals that were sent or brought over by Eileen. Writing to Gollancz on 9 May 1937, he wrote: 'I hope I shall get the chance to write the truth about what I have seen. The stuff appearing in the English papers is largely the most appalling lies – more I cannot say, owing to the censorship' (*CO, X*, pp. 22–3). Recovering from his bullet wounds a month later he wrote to Cyril Connolly on 8 June:

> I have just been reading one of your articles on Spain in a February New Statesman. It is a credit to the New Statesman that it is the only paper, apart from a few obscure ones such as the New Leader, where any but the Communist viewpoint has ever got through. (*CO, XI*, p. 27)

Gollancz and the *New Statesman* would refuse to print Orwell's views, underscoring the centrality of newspapers and periodicals to the flow and tenor of public information and debate. Orwell would need to use other platforms to prosecute his unconventional case on the war through articles, reviews and essays. Bizarrely, especially given *Homage to Catalonia*'s later status, far more people read those short works in Orwell's lifetime than read the book itself.

His realization of fallacious or biased reports in the British press on the war did not change the reality that most people in Britain cared little about it, *The Times* commenting that 'the conflict is regarded with the greatest detachment, except by a small group of enthusiasts on either side' (cited in Fenby, p. 248). But for those enthusiasts, the war – as all modern wars are to some degree – was one of perceptions as well as of relentless, violent battles, of ink as well as of blood. And it was fought in this larger – if far less hostile – sense within and beyond Spanish orders, between rival commanders in Madrid, Bilbao and Barcelona and between rival editors in London and elsewhere. A key problem for those in Britain attempting to understand conditions and prospects in Spain was the dearth of information. Kingsley Martin's 1936 survey of press coverage reported in *The Political Quarterly* indicated that 'from the beginning, the news from Spain was curiously contradictory' (Martin, 1936, p. 576). An August 1936 leader comment in *Time and Tide*, published months before Orwell went to Spain, stated baldly that it is 'quite impossible to form a general picture of what is happening in Spain. The news is fragmentary and unreliable' (Unsigned editorial, *Time and Tide*, 1936, p. 1090). Many periodicals such as *Time and Tide* could only give second-hand accounts, although Frank Pitcairn, from the *Daily Worker*, was reporting from Barcelona 'a few days after the Franco landings in the South', according to the official history of the paper (Rust, p. 39). *The New Statesman and Nation* carried eyewitness reports by Geoffrey Brereton, Liston Oak and Cyril Connolly. The ILP *New Leader* published accounts from activists John McNair, John McGovern, Jennie Lee, Bob Edwards, as well as a statement by Orwell – 'That Mysterious Cart'. *New Leader*'s 'Night Attack on the Aragon Front' contained extracts from letters sent to McNair by 'Bob Smillie, Eric Blair, Albert Gross and Paddy Donovan that were compiled and reworked by McNair (McNair, p. 3). Apart from the prospect of distortion, the obvious difficulty with eyewitness accounts remains that different individuals can provide conflicting reports of the same event, a situation complicated further when the various witnesses are political foes, even if ostensibly are fighting for the same cause. The paucity of information and the desire to secure victory creates the conditions where the depiction of events can be manipulated.

Returning to England, Orwell made plans for a book on his experiences that analysed the war and its implications. But after a conversation with Gollancz's Deputy Director Norman Collins, Gollancz wrote saying that he did not wish to publish it. Davison notes that while not a Communist Gollancz felt 'that he should never publish anything "which would harm the fight against fascism"'. As well as this odd claim about a book as yet unwritten, Davison comments that Gollancz 'saw the irony of rejecting an account by someone who had been on the spot whilst he sat quietly in his office, and he made plain that he thought Orwell as keenly anti-fascist as anyone' (*CO*, *XI*, pp. 37–8). At about the same time Orwell received a letter from Fredric Warburg observing that it would appear from a recent issue of the New Leader that you have had an exciting escape, and it has been suggested to us that an account of the full story would be of interest to the reading public. (Shelden, 1991, p. 307)

Corresponding with Leonard Moore, Orwell saw that while Seckers 'are rather obscure publishers, they cater for a public that would welcome a book of this kind' (*CO, XI*, p. 38). This belief seems confirmed by the minutes of a 1937 ILP National Administrative Council meeting, recording that the party 'has been at a great disadvantage owing to the absence of books stating our political philosophy and policy. The "Left Book Club" is a powerful instrument for the C.P. [Communist Party] in this respect.' The minutes suggest encouraging 'Messrs. Secker and Warburg to publish a number of books', one of which is listed as 'Barcelona Tragedy' by George Orwell – the future *Homage to Catalonia* (*CO, X*, pp. 39–40).

The urgency of the Spanish situation required that while he worked on the book Orwell communicate his knowledge and assessments with as little delay as possible to British audiences. Journals and weeklies provided the necessary sites, offering sufficient space for observations and comments. Orwell already had established connections with several important journals, allowing him to target specific readerships and to present analyses to different periodicals. The opportunity to write with known audiences in mind allowed him the chance to make slightly different arguments that fitted that journal's readership. Orwell submitted 'Eye-Witness In Barcelona' to *New Statesman and Nation*, but Kingsley Martin turned it down, later arguing that the British press 'was almost entirely in the hands of anti-Republican propaganda', and that 'I didn't see it as my function to play the other side's game' (Martin in Rolph, p. 228). This personalizing of the propaganda battle underlines how those in positions of power, including editorial power, could determine perceptions on the war. Martin also reveals an adversarial approach to the representation of the Spanish situation. He also refused Orwell's review of Franz Borkenau's *The Spanish Cockpit*, later justifying his decisions by describing Orwell's views as

violent anti-Negrin propaganda [Negrin led the Republican Government] – and of course anti-Communist too. I would no more have thought of publishing them than of publishing an article by Goebbels during the war against Germany. (Rolph, p. 228)

For the fervently committed, the stakes were that high, and those in the position to publish or not to publish unorthodox views had substantial power.

Orwell did get his work published outside *The New Statesman and Nation*, the significantly-titled 'Spilling the Spanish Beans' appearing in two parts only weeks after he had returned from Spain. The *New English Weekly* published what was Orwell's first attempt to divulge a concealed truth and consequently unsettle the misconceptions of *New English Weekly* readers. He charges into action:

> The Spanish Civil War has produced a richer crop of lies than any event since the great War of 1914-18, but I honestly doubt, in spite of the heca-tombs of nuns raped and crucified before the eyes of the *Daily Mail* report-ers, whether it is the pro-Fascists newspapers that have done the most harm. (*CO, XI*, p. 41)

This qualified criticism of the rabidly conservative *Daily Mail*, infamous for its 'Hurrah For the Blackshirts' article of 1934, signals a rhetorical feint, for the true targets of this opening barrage are the 'left-wing papers, the *News Chronicle* and the *Daily Worker*, [who] with their far subtler methods of distortion . . . have pre-vented the British public from grasping the true nature of the struggle' (ibid.). These assertions constitute a substantial challenge to the liberal readers of the *New English Weekly*, who, though they might not read the Communist Party's *Daily Worker*, might well take in the *News Chronicle*. (Indeed, had they done so the previous month they could have read a section of *The Road to Wigan Pier*, part of a *News Chronicle* series promoting the work 'of young writers already famous among critics, less well-known by the public' (Fenwick, p. 182).) Crucially, the charges against both papers go unsubstantiated. But that very lack of evidence, allowable in an essay, reinforces the suspicion of a tactic being subtly employed by the papers. Orwell insinuates that the crude exaggerations of the *Daily Mail* can be recognized easily, then defused and dismissed. The sophisticated meth-ods and strategies of the Left, by contrast, resist easy detection by trusting read-ers, making their damaging effect far more insidious and consequential.

These opening sentences raise any number of questions and counterclaims: What constitutes 'the true nature of the struggle'? What are the methods of distortion? Have left-wing papers done more harm than their ostensibly pro-Fascist rivals? How does Orwell know the truth? The apparently hyperbolic argument that damns left-wing papers while absolving their right-wing counter-parts requires substantial justification. Putting the opening paragraph under scrutiny reveals exaggerations, factual holes and plain inconsistencies. As a fully fleshed argument it fails, but as polemic it works, immediately engaging attention by planting uncertainty about the reader's own credulity while set-ting out basic – though contentious – premises about the correlation between the reality in Spain and its representation. Implicitly, the opening promises an antidote, the truth that has been obscured or falsified. That promise lies in the phrase that constitutes an implicit leitmotif in Orwell's non-fiction: 'I honestly doubt'.

Each word of that phrase warrants inspection. In general terms the openly sceptical position requires an inclination and a capacity to test out or ques-tion arguments, underpinned by obligations to an acceptable notion of truth. It relies on readers' willingness to trust the authority and integrity of the honest doubter. As *News Chronicle*'s *Wigan Pier* puff makes plain, Orwell was well-regarded by critics but relatively unknown to the public. Apart from occasional reviews, only 'In Defence of the Novel' had been published in *New English Weekly*. His argument rests in part on somehow conveying integrity, something he attempts by employing the first person pronoun. Here it underscores his right to make a case, for he reveals his presence in Spain only a month before: 'When I left Spain in late June the jails were bulging' (*CO, XI,* pp. 41–2). The currency of his account potentially supersedes earlier reports, the active term 'bulging' suggesting unresolved pressures. Simultaneously, the speed with which Orwell conveys his take on events and conditions in Spain implies a relative lack of manipulation, contrasting with what he contends are the distortions of the left-wing press. He asks readers to accept his independent eyewitness over politically partial newspapers, not because of the weight of counter-evidence presented, but by virtue of him claiming to be an honest doubter. We need not read this as a cynical manoeuvre, and for many readers and critics Orwell's approach distinguishes him positively from his peers. While there is no reason to doubt his sincerity, he uses the rhetorical purchase of the eyewitness perspective to prosecute his heterodox case.

The question raised in the opening paragraph about what constitutes the 'real nature of the struggle' gets immediately answered, Orwell contending that

> [t]he fact that these papers have so carefully obscured is that the Spanish Government . . . is far more afraid of the revolution than the Fascists . . . there is no doubt whatever about the thoroughness with which it is crushing its own revolutionaries. (ibid., p. 41)

As with the bold assertion of the harm done by certain left-wing newspapers, this statement openly challenges Left orthodoxies and reports about Spain. Orwell argues that these are distortions, beneath which a bedrock of facts exists. The struggle between those consciously distorting perceptions and others – like himself – attempting to uncover that foundation and transmit the truth generates the essay's rhetorical dynamic. Orwell claims that 'the real struggle is between revolution and counter-revolution' adding that it is

> unfortunate that so few people in England have yet caught up with the fact that Communism is now a counter-revolutionary force . . . using the whole of their powerful machinery to crush or discredit any party that shows signs of revolutionary tendencies. (ibid., p. 42)

The claims are damning and sweeping, and in recognizing the scope of the assertions comes the realization that Orwell has taken off the mantle of informed eyewitness to supply more general commentary. Admittedly, the specific instance of Communist suppression he cites (the jails of Barcelona bulging with non-Communist revolutionaries) derives from first-hand experience. Nevertheless, the broader claims (e.g. that 'Communists everywhere are in alliance with bourgeois reformism') logically cannot be the account of an individual eyewitness. In order to reinforce his claims, he resorts to history, contending that '[t]o see how the present situation arose, one has got to go back to the origins of the civil war' (ibid., p. 42). Several points of origin suggest themselves, but for Orwell's purposes it begins with Franco's military insurrection of July 1936, barely a year before 'Spilling the Spanish Beans' itself appeared. This telescoped perspective allows the setting up of a pivotal antagonism between the 'blatant reactionary' Franco on the one side, and an alliance of the working class, peasants and liberal bourgeoisie on the other.

Orwell the 'historian' argues for a crucial flaw in the alliance, for though the bourgeoisie might side against the reactionary, they are 'not in the least opposed to a modern version of Fascism, at least so long as it isn't called Fascism' (ibid., p. 42). Rather than seeing the anti-Franco alliance as cohesive and co-operative, Orwell argues that

> you get for a while a situation in which the worker and the bourgeois, in real-ity deadly enemies, are fighting side by side. This uneasy alliance is known as the Popular Front (or, in the Communist press, to give it a spurious demo-cratic appeal, People's Front). (ibid., p. 42)

Several points from the preceding extracts are worth considering; first, the question of nomenclature. Both political wings have problems with politi-cal labels, though for different reasons. The bourgeoisie would deny the Fascist label while supporting the practice of a modern form of Fascism. The Communists attempt to attach a 'spurious democratic' label onto something that in fact does not exist. Despite the superficial differences of approach and ideology, there is a common misuse or abuse of language, whether by com-mission or omission. Such abuse immediately signals duplicity for Orwell, the manipulation and distortion of language constituting a threat central to his understanding of totalitarianism.

A second, more oblique point integrated into the quotation above concerns the 'spurious democratic' label of the People's Front. In 'Spilling the Spanish Beans' Orwell explicitly forges links between the various national Communist parties under the control of the Soviet Union. He contends that Soviet self-interest requires that it influence the crushing of any genuine revolution in Spain – while he accepts that Spanish Communists would deny the charge. There follows the curious argument that such a denial 'even if true, is hardly relevant, for the Communist Parties of all countries can be taken as carrying out Russian policy' (ibid., p. 44). The circularity of the accusation scarcely gives Spanish Communists a possibility to rebut the claim. It does fit with Orwell's own take on Socialism, in which nations develop towards Socialism in accordance with their respective traditions and history, not from an imposed and alien theoretical template.

This concern illuminates a third point, Orwell's contention that there exists a monolithic 'Communist press' directed by – or subservient to – the Soviet Union. He does not balance this perception with the revelation of a monolithic Fascist press. In fact, he begins 'Spilling The Spanish Beans' by wondering whether, despite the blatant misreporting of Rothermere's right-wing *Daily Mail* the left-wing papers 'have done the most harm'. In a letter to Geoffrey Gorer written soon after his return from Spain, he praises Lord Beaverbrook's *Daily Express*, declaring that '[t]he only daily paper I have seen in which a glimmer of truth sometimes gets through is the *Express*'. Orwell advises Gorer that, '[w]hatever you do, don't believe a word you read in the *News Chronicle* or *Daily Worker*' (*CO, XI*, p. 69). In 'Spilling the Spanish Beans' the Communist press takes on massive and malevolent proportions, Orwell claiming at the end of the essay's first part that

> it is certain that the Spanish Communist Party, plus the right-wing Socialists whom they control, plus the Communist Press of the whole world, have used all their immense and ever-increasing influence upon the side of counter-revolution. (ibid., p. 44)

The generic conventions of the essay allow such grandiose statements without requiring the burden of proof. The material to substantiate these claims would require many pages, something Orwell hoped he could incorporate into what became *Homage to Catalonia*.

The salvo at Communist anti-revolutionary practice ending the first part of the essay prepares the ground for the second, which sets out to lay bare Communist propaganda. Orwell begins with a feigned withdrawal, admitting that '[a]ny Communist would reject . . . [my account] as mistaken or wilfully dishonest' (ibid.). While he naturally rejects the counterclaim, he nevertheless wants it published, because publication (within the confines of his own essay) provides him an opportunity for drawing attention to Communist propaganda, the easier to attack it. 'Broadly speaking,' he asserts, 'Communist propaganda depends upon terrifying people with the (quite real) horrors of Fascism'. This additionally involves 'pretending . . . that Fascism has nothing to do with capitalism', that it is 'an aberration', 'mass sadism' (ibid.). This argument attacks the Popular Front reversal that encouraged bourgeois participation in the broad alliance against Fascism, something requiring that Communists ignoring what they had only recently argued were undeniable links between Fascism and capitalism.

Acknowledging the partial success of the strategy, Orwell notes that not everybody is fooled. He depicts a certain sort of revolutionary, the 'troublesome

person who points out that Fascism and bourgeois "democracy" are Tweedledum
and Tweedledee' (ibid.). This irritant bears a strong familial resemblance to
the 'honest doubter' of the early part of the essay, and Orwell recognizes the
Communist need 'to get rid' of such people. He contends that the form such
action takes involves not force, but words. The irritated begin by calling the
irritant

> an impracticable visionary . . . confusing the issue . . . splitting the anti-Fascist
> forces . . . Later, if he still refuses to shut up, you change your tune and call
> him a traitor. More exactly, you call him a Trotskyist. (ibid., pp. 44–5)

This argument sets out Orwell's suspicion about the Communist need to
control language, which performs the useful political task of neutralizing
ideological opponents who might otherwise retain the potential to employ
language as a critical tool. In various forms, this idea underpins much of
his lifelong antagonism to Communism. He answers the question, 'what is
a Trotskyist?', revealing that, although commonly used in Spain to describe
or decry a disguised Fascist posing as a revolutionary, 'it derives its peculiar power from the fact that it means three separate things': a supporter
of world revolution; a member of Trotsky's organization, or a disguised
Fascist. These three meanings can be 'telescoped one into the other at
will', so that in

> Spain, to some extent even in England, *anyone* professing revolutionary
> Socialism (i.e. professing the things the Communist Party professed until a
> few years ago) is under suspicion of being a Trotskyist in the pay of Franco
> or Hitler. (ibid., p. 45)

The linking of Trotsky and Fascism had been spurred on by the Moscow trials of supposed Trotskyist collaborators including Zinoviev and Kamenev.
Their confessions led to allegations in the Communist press that Trotsky's
activities were funded by Fascists. British Left journals carried varied assessments, the ILP's *Controversy* staging a torrid debate. Some, like Jon Evans,
admitted that '[n]o trial in all history is as bewildering and as baffling . . .
[and] no complete and feasible explanation has yet been given' (Evans,
p. 25) while for Pat Sloan 'They *Were* Guilty' (Sloan, p. 6). The Left Book
Club backed the trials' veracity, Ivor Montagu in the October 1936 *Left News*
declaring that Trotsky

> is called counter-revolutionary, Fascist. That is right . . . Trotsky today speaks
> of the Soviet Union *in precisely the same terms . . . as those used by Hitler at
> Nuremberg* . . . Is it any accident that Trotsky and Fascism should speak the
> same language? No. (Montagu, p. 127)

Orwell would fall victim to this branding, the *Daily Worker* labelling him a Trotskyist and a Fascist, to the point where he asked Gollancz to intervene with the Communist Party, which Gollancz did.

Orwell ends 'Spilling the Spanish Beans' with a stinging attack on the failure of the British left-wing press to depict properly the events in Spain. The rationale behind this deception, he argues, is 'that if you tell the truth about Spain it will be used as Fascist propaganda' (*CO*, X, p. 46). Orwell derides this attitude as one of 'cowardice'. Yet the long-term dangers are more serious, for failing to tell the truth about Spain stops the British public understanding Fascism and how it can be combated. Consequently, he judges, the *News Chronicle* version of Fascism as a kind of

> homicidal mania peculiar to Colonel Blimps bombinating in the economic void has been established more firmly than ever. And thus we are one step nearer to the great war 'against Fascism' . . . which will allow Fascism, British variety, to be slipped over our necks during the first week. (ibid.)

This grim warning expresses Orwell's belief in the importance of print media to informed public debate. Admittedly, he argues for a rather crude causality between the printed word and public perceptions: the public, after all, can question what it reads. He also overstates the importance of the Spanish Civil War in the general understanding of Fascism. Spanish Fascism provided only one variety of the creed; suspicion of – and antagonism to – Germany and to a lesser extent Italy remained a feature of much of the press. Nevertheless, his broad argument, that public debate depends on available information, seems worth making. Certainly, this requirement is built into Habermas's conception of an active, productive public sphere. As the decade progressed, Orwell came to consider that Britain's limited press freedoms were in danger of being lost. It was a prospect he feared, tried to highlight, and wrote against.

He achieved one small victory over Kingsley Martin by getting his review of Borkenau's *The Spanish Cockpit* published by *Time and Tide*. *Controversy*'s printing of another rejected piece, 'Eye-Witness in Barcelona', in one sense constituted an even greater win. But *Controversy* was a far more marginal journal than *The New Statesman*, having begun in 1932 as the ILP's internal bulletin (*CO*, XI, p. 61, n.1) before being reconfigured in 1936. Styling itself 'The Monthly Forum for Socialist Discussion', *Controversy* argued that 'the Left is cursed by a variety of fake forums which are merely disguised propaganda organs of one Party' (Smith, C. A., p. 1). A signed statement to mark the second anniversary of the revamped journal acknowledges that while no one

> is in agreement with all that appears in its columns . . . each of [the contributors'] views has found repeated expression – by members of the Labour

Party and Communist, by Anarchists, Trotskyists and Pacifists. (Orwell et al.,
'S.O.S.', October 1938)

Political figures James Maxton, Aneurin Bevan and Fenner Brockway signed,
along with writers Naomi Mitchison and Orwell. For all this support, *Controversy*
struggled on as a threepenny monthly (the cost kept low to attract workers),
its survival dependent on circulation drives and direct appeals for cash dona-
tions. Compared to *The New Statesman and Nation*, which in 1937 had a readership of nearly 25,000 and a prominent national profile, *Controversy* was lively
but far less significant. It did publish unorthodox views, though, including
'Eye-Witness in Barcelona'.

The perspective made explicit in that title reinvokes the potential opposition between appearance and reality that informed 'Spilling the Spanish
Beans'. Yet, whereas in that essay different constructions of 'reality' competed
for dominance, in 'Eye-witness in Barcelona' Orwell changes tack, arguing
that a sound basis of fact has already been established: 'the major events have
been carefully tabulated in [ILP member] Fenner Brockway's pamphlet "The
Truth About Barcelona", which so far as my knowledge goes is entirely accurate'. Brockway's report allows Orwell to concentrate on his own task 'in my capacity as eye-witness . . . to add a few footnotes on several of the most-disputed
points' (*CO, XI*, p. 55). This rhetorical tactic works by a neat circularity: as an
eye-witness, Orwell verifies Brockway's 'entirely accurate' account, while simultaneously using that account as the foundation for his own assessments.

In accepting Brockway's account, however, Orwell takes up a problematic
political stance. Brockway and others in the ILP had long been embroiled in a
furious verbal row with the Communist Party, carried out through their respective party newspapers, the *New Leader* and the *Daily Worker*. Mutual antagonism
had preceded the war in Spain: an article in the April 1934 *New Leader* claims,
for example, that 'Communists Take Wrong Turning' (Unsigned, 13 April 1934,
New Leader, p. 2). By December 1935 the war of words had escalated, the *New
Leader* publishing an 'Open Letter' to Communist Party leader Harry Pollitt
asking 'Where Does the Communist Party Stand?' (Unsigned, 13 December
1935, *New Leader*, p. 2). A reply to another 'open letter' drew the haughty
response from Brockway that '[n]o letter could reveal more clearly the mental
confusion and blind faith of the typical loyal member of the Communist Party'
(Brockway, p. 2). John McGovern kept up the tide of abuse in 'Socialism without
Compromise'. Counterpunching against Communist attacks, McGovern argues
that 'in the "Daily Worker," J.R. Campbell is asking, "Where Does the I.L.P.
Stand?" I will tell him; but first it is worth asking where the Communist Party
stands?' (McGovern, p. 2). Although hardly a debating *coup de grâce*, McGovern's
question does register the degree of animosity between the parties.

The existing debate over ideological purity provided the kindling for disputes over the war in Spain, as the respective parties lined up with their Spanish

counterparts. The degree of ILP identification was high, a June 1936 article declaring that 'the Workers Party of Marxist Unity [P.O.U.M.] is the I.L.P. of Spain' (Unsigned editorial, 28 August 1936, *New Leader*, p. 3). This association continued through the war, Brockway contending a year later that

> Sincere revolutionary Socialists will increasingly turn to the Parties in each country which carry on the revolutionary tradition. In Spain that Party is the P.O.U.M. In this country that Party is the I.L.P. (Brockway, 1937, p. 3)

These were the groups Orwell fought for inside Spain; he was to argue their cause in Britain. While the commitment of the ILP to P.O.U.M. remained steadfast, it generated opprobrium from some Leftist sections in Britain, requiring repeated refutation in the *New Leader*. An 'Eye-witness Story by an I.L.P.er in Madrid' in January 1937, for example, howls 'How's This "Daily Mail?"', in rejecting anti-P.O.U.M. claims (Unsigned, January 1937, 'How's This "Daily Mail"', p. 2). In February 1937, an article considers 'Why Communists Attack P.O.U.M.' and two weeks later the paper announces defiantly: 'We Are Proud of P.O.U.M' (12 March 1937, p. 3). Yet a column in *Time and Tide* registers the dark colours in which the Anarchists and P.O.U.M. were being portrayed, charging that they have 'let the winning of the war fall a very secondary place . . . [their] ranks have become the happy hunting ground for the agents of General Franco' (Unsigned, May 1937, 'Spain's New Government', *Time and Tide*, p. 680). With a fine irony, Orwell had been shot through the throat two days before the article appeared.

'Eye-Witness in Barcelona' attempts to repair the political damage caused both to P.O.U.M. and the ILP by reports in the British press. The essay covers similar territory to 'Spilling the Spanish Beans' and in several instances almost the same words are employed. Yet 'Eye-witness in Barcelona' has a sharper focus, primarily considering events surrounding the May 1937 uprising in Barcelona, and the subsequent Communist suppression of dissent. This concentration allows (even necessitates) a first-hand account. Despite its title, 'Eye-witness in Barcelona' is not exclusively an eye-witness report. It comprises two parts: the first, an account of events surrounding the May uprising in Barcelona that Orwell himself had witnessed; the second, a more general analysis of the suppression of the P.O.U.M. Orwell challenges perceptions of three aspects of the uprising written up in the *Daily Worker* and the *New Statesman and Nation*: the purpose of the uprising; the people involved; arms supposedly hidden by the P.O.U.M. In the first instance – the Communist press's insistence that the uprising was designed to overthrow the Government and perhaps hand over Catalonia to the Fascists – Orwell counters

> I cannot . . . say with certainty that a definite revolutionary intention was not in the minds of a few extremists . . . [but the] ordinary rank and file behind

the barricades never for an instant thought of themselves as taking part in a revolution. We thought . . . that we were simply defending ourselves. (*CO, XI*, p. 55)

This rhetorical manoeuvre takes account of the fact that, as in a piece of narrative fiction told in the first person, the eyewitness perspective has inherent limitations; the intentions of all the participants cannot be known. Yet these uncertainties are dismissed in favour of the limited certainties of the eyewitness. Proof of the fact that the P.O.U.M. and its supporters were ordered not to shoot again comes from the narrator, this time from his actions: 'I personally was fired at a number of times, but never fired back' (ibid., p. 56). Yet the authority of the eyewitness comes from the ability not simply to describe but to analyse. In answer to the self-generated question of

Whether the revolutionary opportunity ought to have been taken advantage of . . . [s]peaking solely for myself. I should answer 'No.' . . . . I still think it was a little better, though only a very little, to lose the revolution than to lose the war. (ibid., p. 55)

Orwell leaps from merely recording the facts to interpreting them. The false modesty at the beginning of the essay, the professed wish only to 'add a few footnotes' to Brockway's 'entirely accurate' account, provides a springboard for an alternative to the Communist press's explanation. The perspective employed in 'Eye-witness in Barcelona' is anything but neutral, carrying an inherent political dimension.

The same argument applies in Orwell's rebuttal of the other two claims – about the people involved and the supposed hidden caches of arms. A few examples should suffice. Contesting the Communist accusation that the uprising was solely the work of P.O.U.M., Orwell replies that '[a]nyone who was in Barcelona at the time knows that this is an absurdity' (ibid., p. 56). Denying a charge that the P.O.U.M. secretly stockpiled arms, he argues that '[a]s a matter of fact the P.O.U.M. possessed pitifully few weapons . . . During the street-fighting I was at all three of the principal strongholds of the P.O.U.M' (ibid., pp. 56–7). He then catalogues the party's meagre arms. The eyewitness perspective justifies the replacement of misinformation by observed 'facts'. The full effect of the rhetorical momentum built up in the first half of the essay can be best seen in the second, which defends the P.O.U.M. against charges that its leaders are in the pay of the Fascists, and uncovers how the suppression of the P.O.U.M. was concealed from the troops at the Front.

The fact that Orwell did not see these events means that the second half of the essay stitches together hints and suppositions in patchwork fashion. For example, while certain that many connected with the P.O.U.M. were arbitrarily jailed, Orwell admits that 'probably it would be impossible to get hold of accurate figures, but there is reason to think that during the first week there were 400 arrests in Barcelona alone' (ibid., p. 58). While in the first part of the essay, the uncertainty of the motives of all involved in the uprising could be overruled by the narrator's certainty of his own motives, in the second, the 'certainty' over the numbers arrested depends on guessing totals from fragments of information gathered first-hand.

On the question of the concealment news on the P.O.U.M. Orwell stands on firmer ground, for in leaving the front to see a medical board '[t]ogether with a number of others I had the disagreeable experience of getting back to Barcelona to find that the P.O.U.M. had been suppressed in my absence' (ibid., p. 59). Eye-witness accounts rely on such luck, and in fact as the result of a timely warning Orwell was able to escape imprisonment, although 'others were not so fortunate' (ibid.). The essay ends with Orwell once again using his first-hand knowledge to interpret the complexities of the situation in Spain, much of which he himself had not seen. Arguing that the loyalty of the militia would not have been affected had they known of the suppression of the P.O.U.M., he draws two final conclusions, which bring the essay to a close:

> the present Government has more points of resemblance to Fascism than points of difference . . . Secondly, the elimination of the P.O.U.M. gives warning of the impending attack upon the Anarchists. (ibid., p. 59)

Orwell was correct on the second prediction, but his view of the correlations between the Government and the Fascists was merely a contentious interpretation. Founding his position on the bedrock of first-hand knowledge, he rebuts what he judges are the distorted accounts of others. He cuts out the middlemen, plying his description direct to the British readers. Yet a bedrock of facts does not eliminate bias. In a December 1938 letter to the American journalist Frank Jellinek, whose *The Civil War in Spain* Orwell had reviewed, he writes that in *Homage to Catalonia*

> I've given a more sympathetic account of the P.O.U.M. 'line' than I actually felt . . . I had to put it as sympathetically as possible, because it had no hearing in the capitalist press and nothing but libels in the left-wing press. (*CO*, *XI*, p. 256)

Orwell was not averse to a little distortion in a good cause, nor was he ignorant of the potential impact of his views on different audiences and editors.

New English Weekly's Philip Mairet considered 'Spilling the Spanish Beans' an 'illuminating article' (Mairet, p. 129). While the circulation of the *New English Weekly* did not approach that of the *New Statesman and Nation*, it still allowed the opportunity of quickly placing 'a more sympathetic account of the P.O.U.M. "line"' before a politically interested section of the public. Such accounts were in short supply in the middle of the Spanish Civil War. Given the *New Statesman and Nation* rejection, the *New English Weekly* provided Orwell's best means of publicizing an unpopular view. The smaller, more radical audience of *Controversy*, by contrast, could be given a more considered argument. Orwell's tactical use of specific arguments for particular periodical audiences can be seen in the fact that neither essay seems entirely appropriate for the journal in which it appears. The general argument in 'Eye-witness in Barcelona' fits more easily with the politically moderate leanings of the *New English Weekly* than the more radical *Controversy*. Similarly, the relatively measured assessment in 'Spilling the Spanish Beans' would have found a more sympathetic audience in *Controversy*. As they stand, however, Orwell gets the opportunity of challenging rather than merely reinforcing the preconceptions of both sets of readers.

These essays put Orwell's take on the events in Spain quickly into the forum of leftist ideas while he worked on *Homage to Catalonia*, not published until April 1938. In the same month that 'Eye-Witness in Barcelona' appeared, though, he responded to one of the main attempts to categorize the political position of writers on the war: the pamphlet, *Authors Take Sides on the Spanish Civil War*, published by the *Left Review* in 1937. A questionnaire sent to writers by the journal attempted to gauge, and no doubt to generate, commitment; the replies eventually were issued in pamphlet form. Writers were asked: 'Are you for, or against, the legal Government and the people of Republican Spain? Are you for, or against, Franco and Fascism?' The questionnaire left no room for misunderstanding the severity of the situation: 'The equivocal attitude, the Ivory Tower, the paradoxical, the ironic detachment, will no longer do' (Cunningham, p. 438).

Faced with the passionate call, 149 writers were said to have replied, among them such literary luminaries as T. S. Eliot, Ezra Pound, Sean O'Casey, Stephen Spender, Evelyn Waugh and W. H. Auden. Yet Valentine Cunningham plausibly casts doubt over the handling of replies, and their inclusion in one camp or the other (Cunningham, pp. 28–9). One name not recorded was Orwell's, who did reply, after a fashion. Part of his response reads:

> Will you please stop sending me this bloody rubbish . . . I am not one of your fashionable pansies like Auden and Spender, I was six months in Spain, most of the time fighting, I have a bullet-hole in me at present and I am not going to write blah about defending democracy or gallant little anybody. (*CO, XI*, p. 67)

He continues in this vein for many more lines (including another homophobic attack on Spender) asserting that those behind *Authors Take Sides* wouldn't print his response: 'You wouldn't have the guts.' Later, having met Spender, Orwell apologized for various attacks upon him, but that troubling aspect of the reply aside, his response registers genuine anger about how the war was being interpreted and an unwillingness to be press-ganged into service.

A *Daily Worker* statement by Frank Frankford produced another vigorous response. Frankford had been with the ILP contingent and had fought with Orwell in Spain, as well as having been imprisoned, but in the *Daily Worker* he made several allegations suggesting that the P.O.U.M. and the Fascists were collaborating, that the P.O.U.M. was hiding weapons, and that a cart was moving at night between the P.O.U.M. and Fascist positions, suggesting illicit communication between the groups. Orwell wrote a counter-statement, published as 'That Mysterious Cart', refuting the claims and suggesting that Frankford's 'wild statements' had been put into his 'mouth by Barcelona journalists, and that he had chosen to save his skin by assenting to them' (*CO, XI*, p. 85). Orwell's statement was signed by fourteen other members of the contingent and published in the ILP's *New Leader*, a further sign of Orwell's increasing closeness to the party. He attended its summer school that same month and offered to write regularly for the paper, an offer Fenner Brockway turned down. Brockway later regretted his decision, calling it 'one of the two great mistakes of my life. I turned him down because *New Leader* was a propaganda sheet for the factory floor, and it did not seem to me that it was his type of writing' (Crick, p. 348).

Orwell also communicated his views on Spain through other journals in the form of reviews of books on the war, again allowing him to speak to a broader array of audiences. The impact of these pieces should not be exaggerated (they are only reviews, after all) but they prove the general point about how Orwell transmitted his views. His July 1937 review of Borkenau's *The Spanish Cockpit* in *Time and Tide* actually considers two books, but Orwell writes off *Volunteer in Spain*, by International Brigade Member John Sommerfield, as 'sentimental tripe' (*CO, XI*, p. 52). *The Spanish Cockpit* receives high praise, Orwell wondering whether he is rash 'in saying that it is the best book yet written on the subject, but I believe that anyone who has recently come from Spain will agree with me' (ibid., p. 51). Once again, Orwell uses his Spanish experience to check the accuracy of Borkenau's account, allowing it to past muster. In a letter to Geoffrey Gorer, Orwell wrote that Borkenau had contacted him to say that Orwell was the only reviewer who had picked up on this point (*CO, XI*, p. 81). Still, Orwell must have known that their reading of events would be controversial. Perhaps this explains his later admission to Raymond Mortimer, the literary editor of *The New Statesman and Nation*, that 'the [rejected] review I wrote was tendentious and perhaps unfair' (*CO, XI*, p. 117). He also reviewed Arthur Koestler's *Spanish Testament* in *Time and Tide*, judging the part of the book that tells of Koestler's time in prison as 'probably one of the most honest and unusual documents that have been produced by the Spanish war', but commenting that other parts look as though they have 'been "edited" for the benefit of the Left Book Club' (*CO, XI*, p. 113). He begins with the statement, 'It goes without saying that everyone who writes about the Spanish war writes as a partisan' (ibid., p. 112) and ends it with the alarming thought that because of the vast stakes involved and the ghastliness of the Fascists the conclusion to be reached is:

> if someone drops a bomb on your mother, go and drop two on their mother. The only apparent alternatives are to smash dwelling houses to powder, blow out human entrails and burn holes in children with lumps of thermite, or to be enslaved by people who are more than ready to do these things than you are yourself; as yet no one has suggested a practicable way out. (ibid., p. 113)

The excessiveness of the final images is meant to provoke readers but it runs the risk of freezing them in fear. Generally, reviews such as these presented Orwell's unorthodox reading of events, one that challenged entrenched views and tried to influence broad left-wing opinion. They were unsuccessful.

Homage to Catalonia was published in April 1938 to highly polarized reviews. Crick observes that the

> *Daily Worker* savaged it in a few words, giving a lead followed by the smaller Left-wing journals. Again and again it was pictured as a defence of 'Troskyites and anarchists' who betrayed the Republican cause. (Crick, p. 363)

Orwell complained to the editor of *The Listener* about their anonymous reviewer using 'about four-fifths of his space in resurrecting from the Communist Press the charge that . . . the P.O.U.M. is a "fifth column" organi-sation in the pay of general Franco' (*CO, XI*, p. 160), adding caustically that he has the right to ask that 'when a book of mine is discussed at the length of a column there shall at least be some mention of what I have actually said' (ibid., p. 161). With rare evenhandedness *The Listener* published the reviewer's response with the editor's comment 'that we consider it hardly meets the points raised by Mr Orwell, to whom we express our regrets' (ibid.). Others lavishly praised the book, Geoffrey Gorer in *Time and Tide* calling it 'a work of first-class literature and a political document of the great-est importance' (Meyers, 1975, p. 121), adding (correctly) that 'it will prob-ably be abused both by Conservative and Communists' (ibid., p. 123). Philip Mairet, in the *New English Weekly*, observes that 'knowing already something of this writer's vigour of mind and honesty of purpose, as remembering the illuminating column ['Spilling the Spanish Beans']' he had contributed, the journal's readers would expect 'something new and revealing'. They will not be disappointed:

> The book is likely to stand as one of the best contemporary documents of the struggle. Its frank individuality of outlook, combined with a certain political näiveté, gives internal evidence of its freedom from political obscurantism, for what bias it has is naked and wholly unashamed. (Mairet, p. 127)

Despite Mairet's perceptive comments, and the positive reviews of others, the work now considered a classic (if still contested) account of the Spanish Civil War sold less than 700 copies. The contrast to the 40,000 plus copies of the Left Book Club-sanctioned *Wigan Pier* could hardly be a starker indication of the publishing dynamics of the time and of the different perceptions being promoted. The war gave Orwell a revelatory awareness of the great and sometimes insidious power publishers and editors potentially commanded to block contentious opinions and facts and simultaneously to promote views closer to their own.

1938 proved a difficult year. Diagnosed with bronchiectasis, Orwell spent half of 1938 in a Kent sanatorium, largely unable to write, and the following six months recuperating in the dry heat of French Morocco, a treatment recommended to him on medical grounds. Looking back on the year in November he wrote in a letter to John Sceats that 'with all this illness I've decided to count 1938 as a blank year and sort of cross it off the calendar' (*CO, XI*, p. 237). Yet it was also a significant year, for he joined the ILP. He announced the decision publically in the *New Leader* piece 'Why I Join the I.L.P.', registering an important radicalization of Orwell's political stance. One might see the piece itself as an exercise in preaching to the converted, but that its primary purpose being to record affiliation rather than to persuade. Publically making such a declaration also meant a form of allegiance to a party vilified by Communists as a Trotskyite (and, therefore, in their demonology, a crypto-Fascist) group. To claim membership, then, meant making enemies. That said, in practical terms the ILP had little real political influence. Having disaffiliated from the Labour Party, its membership plummeted from over 16,000 to less than 5,000 by 1934 and in the 1935 election the ILP won four seats of the over 600 available and only 0.7 per cent of the vote. Even so, key assumptions of ILP thought – that Fascism was a variant of capitalism; that the Popular Front was a cover for Communist and Soviet power, and that any future war would likely be between competing imperialist powers and therefore should be resisted – were positions Orwell would promote until the eve of that war.

The ILP's brand of anti-Fascism distinguished it from those on the Left (including the Communists and the Left Book Club) supporting a Popular Front. For the ILP, the struggle against Fascism was merely an aspect of the broader struggle against capitalism. 'Why I Join the I.L.P.' begins with Orwell acknowledging himself as a writer, before making the initially surprising admission that 'the impulse of every writer is to "keep out of politics"'. This impulse, he acknowledges, is no longer practicable, for

> To begin with, the era of free speech is closing down . . . We have seen what
> has happened in Italy and Germany, and it will happen here sooner or later.
> The time is coming – not next year, perhaps not for ten or twenty years,
> but it is coming – when every writer will have the choice of being silenced

altogether or of producing the dope that a privileged minority demands. (*CO, XI,* pp. 167–8)

Despite the dark prediction of the end of free speech, the very vagueness of the timetable for what is deemed inevitable undercuts any sense of immediate crisis. Tensions between certainty and uncertainty, between what is destined and what merely is a potentiality, run through the piece. Orwell considers, for example, that 'if Fascism triumphs, I am finished as a writer' (ibid., p. 168); much depends, clearly, on that 'if'. Orwell develops this point in the following paragraph, linking the intellectual threat of having to produce copy on demand to a physical threat: 'I have got to struggle against [the end of free speech], just as I have got to struggle against castor oil, rubber truncheons and concentration camps' (ibid.). He commits himself to physical struggle, something plausibly backed up by his recent fighting in Spain. The potential role for the writer has changed, and Orwell maps it in personal terms:

> In so far as I have struggled against the system, it has been mainly by writing books which I hoped would influence the reading public. I shall continue to do that, of course, but at a moment like the present writing books is not enough . . . One has got to be actively a Socialist, not merely sympathetic to Socialism. (ibid.)

He deems the ILP the only party 'likely to take the right line either against imperialist war or against Fascism when it appears in its British form' (ibid.). While appearing to expect Fascism, 'Why I Join the I.L.P.' is invigorated by the sense of purpose that strives to combat the ideology.

Given Orwell's argument in *Wigan Pier* about the need for Socialism to take account of specific national characteristics, his belief that Fascism would take a British form is understandable. In part, it reprises the position set out in 'Spilling the Spanish Beans'. The link between British Fascism and imperialist war, however, distinguishes 'Why I Join the LL.P.' from the earlier essay. Orwell acknowledges the ILP line that the impending war would result from the (inevitable) clash of imperial interests, rather than as an ideological battle between democracy and Fascism. The war would involve equally rapacious capitalist nations fighting for imperial dominance. This contentious premise allows Orwell to criticize those (such as supporters of the People's Front) who urge Britain and its allies to rearm against the Fascist threat. He comments that experiences in Spain

> brought home to me the fatal danger of mere negative 'anti-Fascism'. Once I grasped the essentials of the situation in Spain I realized that the I.L.P. was the only British party . . . I could join with at least the certainty that I

would never be led up the garden path in the name of Capitalist democracy. (*CO, XI*, p. 169)

In joining the ILP Orwell adopts its analysis of Fascism's threat and the need for revolutionary Socialism, and 'Why I Join the I.L.P.' publicizes that acceptance. It might be read against Orwell's perversely comic depiction of two of the Socialist 'cranks' he lampooned in *The Road to Wigan Pier* among the sandal-wearers and sex-maniacs drawn to Socialism. There he recalls riding through Letchworth on a bus and seeing two old men, 'both very short, pink and chubby, and both hatless', 'dressed in pistachio-coloured shirts and khaki shorts into which their huge bottoms were crammed.' The men produce a 'mild stir of horror on top of the bus,' causing the man next to Orwell to murmur '"Socialist", as one would say, "Red Indians". He was probably right – the I.L.P. were holding their summer school in Letchworth' (*CO, XI*, p. 162). Less than a year after writing this Orwell himself attended the 1937 ILP Summer School at Letchworth, and a further year on had joined the party, an illuminating measure of his political development.

Having left the sanatorium on 1 September 1938 Orwell and Eileen sailed for Morocco the following day, arriving in Marrakech twelve days later. Within another fortnight the Munich crisis had erupted, destabilizing Europe, confirming the efficacy of Germany's expansionary tactics, and giving Neville Chamberlain one of modern history's most pyrrhic victories. With actual war now ominously possible Orwell, working from Marrakech, put his name to a *New Leader* manifesto 'If War Comes, We Shall Resist'. This blames the imperialist treaties signed at the conclusion of the First World War, and calls for 'world supplies' to be made equally available to all people 'on a basis of co-operation and social justice'. It charges that the British government's 'policy of economic imperialism' has 'aggravated the evils of world distribution, and therefore has a heavy responsibility for the present crisis'. The signatories repudiate

> all appeals to the people to support a war which would, in effect, maintain and extend imperialist possessions and interests . . .
>
> If war comes, it will be our duty to resist, and to organize such opposition as will hasten the end of that war . . . [and then build] a new world order based on justice and fellowship. (*CO, XI*, p. 213)

The manifesto was signed by 149 people including Orwell, Vera Brittain, Havelock Ellis, C.E.M. Joad, Ethel Mannin, James Maxton, Fenner Brockway. the Chairman of the League of Coloured Peoples (H. A. Moody) an' Chairman of the International African Service Bureau (Georg^ (*CO, XI*, p. 212, n.1). Orwell would maintain the views pre^ turbulent year before the feared war began.

His other immediate response to Munich was the essay 'Political Reflections on the Crisis', published in the December issue of *The Adelphi*, which makes the case against war and attacks those on the Left whose acceptance of the Popular Front position means promoting the case for war against Fascism. Orwell scornfully lumps together

> the *News Chronicle*, the *Daily Worker, Reynolds's*, the *New Statesman*, and the sponsors of the Left Book Club [who for two years have been] deluding themselves and part of their public that the entire British nation, barring a few old gentleman in West End Clubs, wanted nothing more than a ten-million-dead war in defence of democracy. (*CO, XI*, pp. 242–3)

The essay's general line against war mapped on to *The Adelphi*'s pacifist stance (one that Middleton Murry heavily supported but which had caused Richard Rees to leave the journal). It attacked the Popular Front call for war and the belief that were an election held the public would vote in a Popular Front government. From Orwell's ILP position, the populace in fact was anti-war, if not for quite the same anti-imperialist reasons as his own. The Munich crisis, he argues, revealed that 'the British public will go to war if they are told to' but that 'they don't want war and will vote against any party which stamps itself as a war party' (ibid., p. 242). Part of the argument in 'Political Reflections on the Crisis' acts to warn the Labour Party against becoming a war party to save its skin. War preparation, in Orwell's reading of the circumstances in 1938 and for most of 1939, is part of a 'fascising process' that 'can be used as an excuse for anything' (ibid., p. 245). By refusing the attractions of joining the government in its preparations for war, the Labour Party will return to 'an anti-militarist and anti-imperialist line' (ibid.). Sent from Marrakech, the essay's argument holds to the accepted ILP position.

'Political Reflections on the Crisis' has another target: the English intelligentsia. Orwell had attacked this group regularly at least as far back as *Wigan Pier*. But whereas there they were pilloried for their slavish devotion to the Soviet model of Socialism, in this essay they are blasted for their support of the Popular Front's call for war. He lashes them for declaring that 'we' must fight without any knowledge of what war entails and without any real likelihood (given their privileged positions) of experiencing combat should it occur. For the intellectual, he declares, 'war is something that happens on paper, and consequently they are able to decide that this or that war is "necessary" with no more sense of personal danger than in deciding on a move at chess' (ibid., p. 244). This observation rates as a crude if effective simplification, the foregrounding of the word 'necessary' a deliberate link to W. H. Auden's poem 'Spain' which Orwell gets to by passing through one of his grimmer exaggerations, that British civilisation produces in increasing numbers two types, the gangster and the pansy. They never meet, but each is necessary to the other. Somebody in eastern Europe 'liquidates' a Trotskyist; somebody in Bloomsbury writes a justification of it. And it is, of course, precisely because of the utter softness and security of life in England that the yearning for bloodshed – bloodshed in the far distance – is so common in our intelligentsia. (ibid.)

Stripped of its alarming prejudices and blatant excesses, Orwell's underlying point, that intellectuals can fail to understand the sometimes horrific implications and consequences of their ideas, is valid enough. But he does his argument no justice by using such vulgar and simplistic stereotypes, which he then goes on to personalize by commenting that 'Auden can write [in 'Spain'] about "the acceptance of guilt in the necessary murder" because he has never committed a murder, perhaps never had one of his friends murdered, possibly never even seen a murdered man's corpse' (ibid.). Here Orwell is on firmer ground at the individual level (in fact Auden would later edit that line and then repudiate the poem entirely, although Edward Mendelson argues that Orwell was not the cause of the editing). But he immediately moves from the specific to the general, taking Auden as an exemplar of the 'utterly irresponsible intelligentsia' who, he argues, ' "took up" Catholicism ten years ago, "take up" Communism to-day and will "take up" the English variant of Fascism a few years hence' (ibid.). Orwell considers this progression as 'a special feature of the English situation', although, as with most exaggerations used for rhetorical effect, it was falsified by reality (Auden, who was never a Communist, became a Christian rather than a Fascist).

Orwell's anti-war position in 1938 and for most of 1939 fed into larger concerns about the prospects for free speech and the expression of unorthodox political ideas if, as he feared, a variant of totalitarianism was imposed or tamely accepted in Britain. Replying from Marrakech to a letter from the poet, critic and art expert Herbert Read he declares that

it is vitally necessary for those of us who intend to oppose the coming war to start organising for illegal anti-war activities . . . At present there is considerable freedom of the press and no restriction on the purchase of printing presses, stocks of paper etc., but I don't believe for an instant that this state of affairs is going to continue. If we don't make preparations we may find ourselves silenced and absolutely helpless when either war or the pre-war fascising processes begin. (*CO, XI*, p. 313)

And in March he replied to another letter from Read asking for contributions to *Revolt*, a journal that 'ran for six issues, from 11 February to 3 June 1939' and that 'aimed at presenting the Spanish civil war from an anti-Stalinist point of view' (ibid., p. 341, n.1). While making his usual cautionary statement that 'till

I've seen what kind of paper it is to be I don't know whether I could be of any use' Orwell adds that

> [i]f we could keep a leftwing but non-Stalinist review in existence (it's a question of money, really) I believe a lot of people would be pleased. People aren't all fools, they must soon begin to see through this anti-fascist racket. (ibid., p. 340)

His own contribution to understanding the Spanish War from an anti-Stalinist position was 'Caesarean Section in Spain', published in *The Highway* in March 1939. This essay concentrates not on the specifics of the war but on the role of Spanish workers in defending democracy, wholly appropriate given that *The Highway* was the journal of the Workers' Educational Association (WEA). Priced 2p, *The Highway* was a monthly paper with a circulation in excess of 20,000, larger than most independent journals of the Left. Despite this, a message of thanks from the General Secretary of the WEA in April 1939 underlines the economic difficulties faced by such organs: 'if we can increase the circulation to 30,000 we can produce without financial loss' (Unsigned, April 1939, *The Highway*, p. 198). Several aspects distinguish this piece from Orwell's other essays on Spain. Although he does utilize perceptions drawn from his experiences, the bulk of the essay surveys more general issues, most notably the effect the war might have on the development of Spanish democracy. This attention to broader questions rests on the smoothing over of the divisions within the Spanish Left. These are mentioned briefly, but the central conflict portrayed in 'Caesarean Section in Spain' lies between Franco and the Republican Government, the latter being portrayed as the defender of liberal, democratic aspirations. In painting this picture of an essentially harmonious Left, Orwell tactfully leaves out the attacks on the distortions of Communists and the British press that had informed his earlier essays. Instead, 'Caesarean Section in Spain' incorporates a vote of confidence in the Spanish people's ability to resist Franco, Orwell considering that

> [t]he people have seen and learned too much . . . The desire for liberty, for knowledge, and for a decent standard of living has spread too far too widely to be killed by obscurantism or persecution. (*CO, XI*, p. 355)

Throughout 'Caesarean Section in Spain' he mixes the plucky, the sombre, the hopeful and the realistic, in clear distinction from the stridency of 'Spilling the Spanish Beans' and 'Eyewitness in Barcelona'. One reason for this change lies in the periodical's readership. The WEA set itself a didactic brief and in his essay Orwell blends an account of the situation in Spain with a lesson on the importance of workers in the struggle for democracy. The Spanish Civil

War operates as a 'hopeful portent', for 'in Government Spain bot
and the spirit of democracy have survived to an extent that no one
foreseen' (ibid., p. 333). By the time the essay had been published 'ʟ
Spain' had ceased to exist in any meaningful form, but Orwell's tactic remains
plain enough: to publish a defence of the Spanish workers while using their
struggle as a 'hopeful portent' for the future of democracy. The WEA audience
again partly explains this strategy. In employing the democratic aspirations
and successes of the Spanish workers (at least at the time the essay was written) he suggests to the British readers of *The Highway* their potential strength.
'Caesarean Section in Spain' works, then, as a general examination of the resil-
ience of democracy. It functions partly as an analysis of the Spanish Civil War,
but potently as an assertion of the democratic potential of British workers.

At the end of March 1939 Orwell and Eileen sailed back to a Britain. Two
days later Franco took control of Madrid. Other omens were equally bleak,
Germany having occupied all of Czechoslovakia (in defiance of the Munich
agreement) earlier in the month. Orwell by then had completed the manuscript of *Coming Up for Air*, which was published in June.

At the end of May 1939 Orwell had begun to write the essays for the
collection *Inside the Whale*, which would be finished in December, several
months into the war, and published in March 1940. It offers a nostalgic
reflection on a simpler pre-First World War England seen through the eyes
of George Bowling, a chubby everyman. Bowling temporarily escapes the
tatty reality of a suburban life with ghastly wife and children – threatened
by bombers and bombs – for the half-remembered world of his childhood.
He finds this equally soiled. *Coming Up for Air* was reasonably well-received
and sold well enough in Britain to be reprinted. Interestingly it was published by Gollancz, who had first call on Orwell's fiction, even though Ruth
Dudley Edwards observes that Gollancz disapproved of the novel's politics
'which included a parody of an LBC meeting' (Edwards, p. 289). She also
notes that since November 1938 at least Gollancz had himself become worried about the direction of the Left Book Club and that by early 1939 had
told Communist Party leader Harry Pollitt that 'no longer would he allow
the Club to peddle the party line' and that 'discussion and consultation
would have to be in an atmosphere of real freedom on both sides' (ibid., p.
289). Under the threat of war and in the light of reappraisals, the dynamics
of publishing would change again.

He had two other essays published on the eve of war, the first being the
highly polemical 'Not Counting Niggers', published in the July 1939 issue
of *The Adelphi*. Davison suggests that this piece possibly uses material from
Orwell's pamphlet 'Socialism and War' which may have been rejected by the
Publications Committee of the ILP, and which was never published (*CO, XI*,
p. 169, n.1). Technically, 'Not Counting Niggers' is more a review article as it
assesses Clarence K. Streit's *Union Now*, which argues for an anti-Fascist bloc of

western democracies. Orwell uses the opportunity to aim a rhetorical scatter-gun at the British Left, contending early on that

> In a prosperous country, above all in an imperialist country, left-wing politics are always partly humbug. There can be no real reconstruction that would not lead to at least a temporary drop in the English standard of life, which is another way of saying that the majority of left-wing politicians and publicists are people who earn a living by demanding something they don't really want. (ibid., p. 358)

To ignore the economic reality that British power wealth had been built on the backs of the subjected imperial races, he argues, makes a mockery of the overthrow of the economic system, a plan beloved of the Left. Implementing the plan necessitates the breakup of the Empire, and with it the inevitable loss of the economic power that underpinned hopes of a prosperous Socialist Britain. The essay forcefully exposes this putative contradiction. Before considering *Union Now*, Orwell launches an attack upon the supposed anti-militarists of the Left who in arguing for Peace Blocs, Peace Fronts and Democratic Fronts against the Fascists ignore the iniquities at the heart of the democracies. The Labour Party draws flak for its 'pettifogging grizzle against conscription' but Orwell also targets 'the warriors of the *New Statesman . . .* pretending that the world is an assemblage of [democratic] sheep and [fascist] goats, neatly partitioned off by national frontiers' (ibid., p. 359). Streit suggests a union of the Western democracies and British colonies against the Fascists, a proposal Orwell rates as 'the sheep and goats theory at its best'. He fires a broadside at another Left bastion, suggesting that if the reader cannot accept Streit's version 'you will certainly never accept it in the form handed out by the Left Book Club' (ibid.). But the chief target of 'Not Counting Niggers' is something greater than the individual failings of *The New Statesman and Nation* or the Left Book Club, for the essay attacks all those who, under the guise of defending Britain against fascism, merely want the retention of the imperialist status quo. Crucially, for Orwell, the unspoken clause is always

> 'not counting niggers'. For how can we make a 'firm stand' against Hitler if [by dismantling the Empire] we are simultaneously weakening ourselves at home? In other words, how can we 'fight Fascism' except by bolstering up a far vaster injustice?
>
> For of course it *is* vaster. What we forget is that the overwhelming bulk of the British proletariat does not live in Britain, but in Africa and Asia. It is not in Hitler's power, for instance, to make a penny an hour a normal industrial wage; it is perfectly normal in India, and we are at real pains to keep it so. (ibid., p. 360)

Orwell fudges any precise definition of 'proletariat' in making his point, but the point itself is clear and controversial. Controversial, at least, for readers of *The Adelphi* – but orthodox for the ILP. Indeed, almost a year before 'Not Counting Niggers', James Maxton, in a *New Leader* article titled 'So This Is Empire!', puts the same point plainly: 'I say deliberately that the poverty conditions and denial of freedom in the Empire are worse than in the Fascist States of Germany and Italy' (Maxton, pp. 4–5). Fenner Brockway argues similarly in the polemic, 'Has Hitler Anything to Teach Our Ruling Class?', a contribution to the *New Leader*'s eight-page 'Empire Special' of April 1938. In this, Brockway writes that we 'may be free in Britain from the worst tyrannies of Fascism, but they exist in the British Empire. Hitler cannot teach the British Ruling Class anything in technique of suppression' (Brockway, 1938a, p. v). In a published talk with Jawaharlal Nehru, Brockway proposes that the ILP would 'give support to the Indian people in their struggle against British Imperialism, whether in circumstances of peace or of war' (Brockway, 1938b, p. 3). The argument set down in 'Not Counting Niggers', then, jibes neatly with party proclamations. Indeed, in ILP terms it might even be seen as restrained.

'Not Counting Niggers' again illustrates Orwell's use of reviews as covers for what effectively are polemical essays. The fact that it was published in the pacifist *Adelphi* adds to its argumentative bite, operating as might a heckler at a sedate political meeting, unsettling the certainties of those attending. Access to the centre-left pages of *The Adelphi* audience also broadens the impact of the short, sharp attacks upon both *The New Statesman and Nation* and the Left Book Club. Beyond this, the haymaking swipes at 'the majority of left-Wing politicians and publicists', and all those who employ 'such phrases as "Peace Bloc", "Peace Front" [and] "Democratic Front"' are more likely to connect with the chins of an *Adelphi* readership. Orwell wants to tear away what he sees as the masks disguising hypocrisy, ignorance and self-interest being worn by many on the Left. The essay incorporates an explicit image of disguise to explain the last few years, a 'sort of monstrous harlequinade in which everyone is constantly bounding across the stage in a false nose – Quakers shouting for a bigger army, Communists waving Union Jacks, Winston Churchill posing as a democrat' (*CO, XI*, p. 358). The absurd alliances generated by the British Empire provide a stick with which to beat the blinkered, ignorant or dissembling supporters of the status quo. Where 'Shooting an Elephant' had considered imperialism in moral terms, in 'Not Counting Niggers' economics exposes the reality of the process, making it absurd for Orwell that Streit 'has coolly lumped the huge British and French Empires – in essence nothing but mechanisms of exploiting cheap labour – under the heading of democracies!' (ibid., p. 360). He adds that 'One gets some idea of the real relationship of England and India when one reflects that the per capita annual income in England is something over £80, and in India about £7.98' (ibid.). He then utilizes the image of 'an Indian coolie's leg . . . thinner than the average Englishman's arm' to reinforce his argument. Illuminating as the image is, it would carry less rhetorical force without the statistic. The bleak economic picture reinforces the attack on those who preach the defence of British power without acknowledging the economic corruption at its base. 'Not Counting Niggers' marks a highpoint in Orwell's radical criticism of British imperialism. The onset of war only months after its publication would prompt a substantial rethinking of his ideas on a number of subjects, but as with all periodical pieces 'Not Counting Niggers' provides a vivid record of his thinking at a given moment, a moment soon to be folded into a horrendous and massively transformative war.

'Democracy in the British Army' was published in *Left Forum* (the new name for *Controversy*, for which he had written 'Eye-Witness in Barcelona') the very month that the Second World War began. One measure of the rapid political developments taking place was that the key issue engaging *Left Forum* readers at the time (the Nazi–Soviet non-aggression pact) receives no mention in 'Democracy in the British Army'. Indeed much of it looks to the distant past, Orwell giving a short history of class stratification in the British army from the time of the Duke of Wellington. The history lesson establishes that 'the British army remains essentially the same machine as it was fifty years ago': reactionary and class-ridden. This is the crux of the essay, for Orwell charges that

> [a] little while back any Socialist would have admitted this . . . But we happen to be at a moment when the rise of Hitler has scared the official leaders of the Left into an attitude not far removed from jingoism. Large numbers of left-wing publicists are almost openly agitating for war. (*CO, XI*, p. 406)

The slight qualifications in this accusation ('not far removed from jingoism'; 'almost openly agitating for war') do little to temper its provocativeness; indeed, they provide the camouflage behind which Orwell can launch his assault. *Left Forum* was contributed to – and read – by supporters of the Labour Party and the Communist Party; their leaders certainly fall under the label 'official leaders of the Left'. By not naming specific individuals, though, Orwell achieves the effect of a blanket condemnation with little rhetorical effort. The additional snipe at 'left-wing publicists' reinforces the repeated attacks upon the distortions of the Left press and constitutes a thinly veiled jibe at the Left Book Club and his own publisher, Victor Gollancz.

In 'Not Counting Niggers' Orwell had attacked sections of the Left for turning a blind eye to the iniquities of British imperialism. By contrast, in 'Democracy in the British Army' he attacks the belief that in the expected war, the reactionary, class-ridden army will be transformed: ' "this time" things are going to be "different". Militarization is not going to mean militarization. Colonel Blimp will no longer be Colonel Blimp'. Instead, Orwell notes, the 'more soft-boiled left-wing papers' urge and expect the 'democratizing of the army' (ibid.). Attacking the Left press, Orwell once again highlights its ability to manipulate and direct Left opinion. Not all the arguments for Socialism in Britain come under the heading of 'intelligent propaganda' he had argued for in *Wigan Pier*. Some, in fact, hamper the proper understanding of the consequences of left-wing tactics and arguments. Orwell's only practical means of countering such manipulation remained periodicals.

Given the lessons of military history delivered in the first part of 'Democracy in the British Army', Orwell is vigorously sceptical of the potential for a democratized army. In the later part of the essay he considers what democratizing the army might mean, judging that

> if it means anything, [it] means doing away with the predominance of a single class and introducing a less mechanical form of discipline. In the British army this would mean an entire reconstruction which would rob the army of efficiency for five to ten years. Such a process is only doubtfully possible while the British Empire exists, and quite unthinkable while the simultaneous aim is to 'stop Hitler'. (ibid.)

The purpose of Orwell's lesson in military history is clear; the inherited class divisions that give the British army its cohesion cannot and will not be transformed radically within the time available. Further, in undermining the possibility of 'democratizing' the army, Orwell cuts the ground from under those on the Left whose justification for war against Germany in defence of the Soviet Union rests on the argument that militarization is not going to mean militarization. Without the transformation of the army, the Left case for supporting war against Germany collapses.

In line with ILP fears, Orwell predicts an expansion of the army on existing lines. He disparages the idea that new democratic militias, of the type he had fought in during the Spanish Civil War, will signal real change in the makeup of the army hierarchy. Few Socialists, he warns, grasp the fact that 'in England the whole of the bourgeoisie is to some extent militarized' (ibid., p. 407). Whatever the pretensions towards democracy in the army, the training received by the middle classes in public school give them an advantage over the untrained worker. This advantage makes promotion more likely, thus entrenching bourgeois control. Orwell writes bluntly that '[o]nce the novelty [of conscription] has worn off some method will be devised of keeping proletarians out of positions of command' (ibid.). Not only does the Left belief in democratizing the army increase the possibility of war, but the outcome of conflict will be the imposition of class divisions on the conscripts. In any case, and as Orwell had argued in 'Not Counting Niggers', such a war would in reality merely defend one imperial power against another.

He develops the idea of increasing militarization to encompass the potential for military domination within Britain. Adopting the position that 'what is true within the armed forces is true of the nation as a whole', he contends that 'every increase in the strength of the military machine means more power to the forces of reaction' (ibid.). Again, this argument accords with the ideas of the ILP. Yet it also repeats a theme running through Orwell's essays on Socialism, that the activities of sections of the British Left have consequences at odds with their alleged aims. Sometimes, the discrepancy between aims and consequences is the result of naivety, while at other times it results from hypocrisy, but in all cases the Left periodical or daily press is involved in the justification of flawed policies and actions. Orwell ends 'Democracy in the British Army' with a broadside against the shortcomings of one section of the Left press, charging that possibly

> some of our left-wing jingoes are acting with their eyes open. If they are, they must be aware that the *News Chronicle* version of 'defence of democracy' leads directly *away* from democracy, even in the narrow nineteenth-century sense of political liberty, independence of the trade unions and freedom of speech and the press. (ibid.)

Not only is 'freedom of speech and the press' vital to democracy – the self-same press can threaten the democracy it supposedly protects.

Despite the beguiling opening stroll through British military history, 'Democracy in the British Army' constitutes a vigorous attack on large sections of the British Left in general, and support for war against Germany in particular. Along with 'Not Counting Niggers', 'Democracy in the British Army' indicates how Orwell's political thinking in the lead-up to the Second World War reflects ILP radicalism. This radicalism tends to be ignored in studies of Orwell, largely as a consequence of Orwell's abrupt realignment of his views on the need for war, the iniquities of British imperialism and the necessity of patriotism once the war began. The war-time position is taken as a kind of destination point, a place where Orwell's views solidify into a prickly but patriotic Socialism. The attention to a supposed destination, however, ignores the 'journey', the development of ideas in relation to changing situations, or changing perspectives. At the turbulent end of a tumultuous decade such changes were to be expected, and indeed required. Through his essays, Orwell could publicly reassess his views, a process that would only accelerate when war began.

His writing during this period, with its engaged arguments and hard political edges, its tenacious insistence on some form of observable and describable reality, tests the boundaries of the essay form. In *The Complete Works of George Orwell* several of the pieces this chapter examines are labelled 'articles', a term that could be applied without serious dispute. Yet the capacious arena of the essay allows for work that is factual and avowedly fragmentary, as well as challenging to entrenched ideology – the essay can be the critical form *par excellence*. There is also the matter that Orwell's work gets published in journals and periodicals that allow for something more extended and personal than might appear in newspapers. Significantly, the malevolent control of debate in newspapers and journals, and the need for them to publish ignored or uncomfortable views and facts, becomes central to arguments Orwell presents in some of his writing, reflecting his fear that totalitarianism actively threatens to extinguish free thought and speech. He was not alone in thinking this, of course, and his engaged work in the late 1930s contributes to a far larger discussion about the transmission and regulation of ideas. They are interventions into what he takes as the dangerously patrolled sphere of public debate. His pieces regularly foreground the personal perspective (often employing an eyewitness view) as part of their rhetorical and polemical strategies, registering the peculiar insights available to those who honestly report what they witness, while recognizing the potential for limitations and bias. In 'A Hanging' and 'Shooting an Elephant' Orwell had compellingly employed that position, fusing it with elements regularly seen in creative fiction to fashion essays that blur towards the short story end of the essay spectrum. With his late-1930s essays on Spain, written while that war still eviscerated the country and while ideologies and parties contested for dominance in Spain and elsewhere, the eyewitness perspective was necessary and potentially illuminating. It supplied an antidote to the poisonous changing of facts and the suppression of reports in newspapers and politically inclined periodicals that constituted an adulteration of history at its draft stage. These pieces try not to evade or erase their own incompleteness or partiality, often drawing attention to this aspect. But as the work connected to Orwell's membership of the ILP declares, self-awareness need not require the pulling of punches.

For all their vigour, we need to remember that these works mostly were published in relatively obscure journals and reviews. A danger exists that the sincere and intense commitment of individuals or relatively small groups becomes falsely magnified as a popular concern. The periodicals where Orwell's views were published comprised only a small, highly politicized subset of broad opinion. Small fires can still blaze bright, though, and cumulatively the audiences who read his essays were sometimes larger and more diverse than those who read his longer works. This was particularly the case with *Homage to Catalonia*, a work designed for immediate and maximum impact that failed to find a large audience, partly at least because of negative reviews in some journals and papers whose political position it offended. When war broke out Orwell still was merely a reasonably well-considered novelist and for many on the British Left an intriguing if somewhat eccentric documentary writer; in no sense was he a major figure in the British literary or political worlds. Nor did he have much of an international presence. All that accepted, he was an energetic participant in many of the decade's debates, and was considered significant enough to be attacked by his political enemies. He had no equivalent literary enemies, despite his scathing remarks about writers such as Spender and Auden. Or, more correctly, he had no literary enemies who published (Auden was certainly capable enough of wounding, but he and Spender were substantially better considered at the time than Orwell and perhaps did not see the need). Keeping Orwell in his place and in his context (as much as is possible) helps chart his development and his position in the cultural and political sphere. And it cautions against retrospective distortions, as when Kingsley Martin, recalling later his rejection of 'Eye-witness in Barcelona', declared that 'we didn't have *Homage to Catalonia* to publish – nothing balanced like that' (Rolph, p. 228). Martin appears not to have recognized the manifest hypocrisy in that statement.

Chapter 3

Orwell in Wartime: Socialism, Patriotism and Cultural Threat (1940–5)

Robert Hewison calls the end of the 1930s in Britain 'the grand slaughter of magazines', presenting a sobering list of defunct journals from 1939 and 1940: '*The Cornhill Magazine, Criterion, Fact, London Mercury, New Stories, New Verse, Purpose, Seven, Twentieth-Century Verse, Wales, Welsh Review*, and the *Voice of Scotland* all fell silent' (Hewison, p. 12). Others survived, but only just, as John Lehmann acknowledged in the first number of *Folios of New Writing*:

> In the Christmas Number I announced the death of *New Writing*. In the early days of the war, it seemed that *New Writing* could scarcely hope to survive: against the bombs, the calling up of writers, the scarcity of paper, the difficulties of transport, and, as much as anything else, the transformation of thought and feeling that total warfare would bring with it. (Lehmann, 1940, p. 5)

The inside cover signalled the precarious state of things, announcing that '*Folios of New Writing* will appear at irregular intervals'. Other journals such as *Scrutiny* would appear only seasonally during the war. The transformation of thought and feeling can be measured by Cyril Connolly's opening statement in *Horizon*, begun on the cusp of the 1940s:

> The moment we live in is archaisitic, conservative and irresponsible, for the war is separating culture from life and driving it back on itself, the impetus given by Left Wing politics is for the time exhausted, and . . . there is a certain suspension of judgement and creative activity. (Connolly, 1940, p. 5)

The shape, scope and purpose of cultural debate were reconfigured by the start of war. By 1942, as Orwell commented in a BBC talk 'Paper is Precious', essentially 'no new periodicals have appeared during the past year. Most of the highbrow magazines, "Scrutiny", "Horizon", the "New Statesman" . . . are greatly reduced in size' (*CO, XIII*, p. 119). Lehmann's list of hurdles speaks from the editor's position, to which could be added those felt by writers – what

to write about? How to write it? Readers too had to decide whether periodicals were unjustifiable indulgences or crucial symbols of the culture being
defended. All three groups had to adjust to new conditions to ensure intelligent cultural discourse survived.

Orwell's own position was complicated. Before the war he had argued forcefully the ILP line against the war, but when fighting began the ILP continued
to argue against an imperialist venture. Was political consistency plausible
when circumstances had changed so markedly? He explained in an April 1940
letter that he left the party

> at the beginning of the present war because I considered that they were
> talking nonsense and proposing a line of policy that could only make things
> easier for Hitler. In sentiment I am definitely 'left', but I believe that a writer
> can only be honest if he keeps free of party labels. (*CO, XII*, p. 148)

Orwell sought to adapt his Socialist beliefs to the unique circumstances war
produced. We can see him as a resolute but not inflexible writer and thinker,
engaged, but without a systematic blueprint or theory.

His war was not purely political. He developed his interests in the sociological examination of literature and popular culture generally, his essays on
these areas substantially cultivating his range and speaking to a broader audience. His job as a Talks Producer for the BBC's Eastern Service (from August
1941 until November 1943) allowed him to fashion literary programmes alongside the more news-related features. (His contract, interestingly, named him
'E.A. Blair'.) Paying £640 per year, the job gave him a financial stability that
he had not enjoyed before, which he supplemented with journalism, regularly reviewing or writing articles for *Time and Tide* (where he became drama
critic in May 1940), *The Observer* and *Manchester Evening News*. He contributed
to the magazines *Listener* and *Picture Post*, and less frequently to *New English
Weekly* and *The Adelphi* – even to the *New Statesman and Nation*. And there were
occasional pieces (mostly reviews) for an eclectic assortment of journals: *Life
and Letters, Folios of New Writing, English Digest, New Republic, Daily Express, Now
and Then, Poetry (London), World Digest, The Nation, Persuasion, Synopsis, War
Commentary – For Anarchism, Politics, New Saxon Pamphlets, Contemporary Jewish
Record*, and *Forward*. He wrote essays for the LBC's *Left News*, improving his profile as a literary and social commentator with a weekly 'As I Please' column in
the Labour-aligned paper, *Tribune*. Substantial pieces on literature and popular culture appeared in *Horizon*. His regular 'London Letter' to the left-wing
American journal *Partisan Review* established his name among the intellectual
Left in the United States. Fenwick records over 400 wartime 'Contributions
to periodicals' (Fenwick, pp. 186–218). Much of these were lightweight, but
there remained a crop of significant essays. Although *Animal Farm* was finished by 1944, Gollancz, Faber, and Jonathan Cape all rejected it, meaning

that Orwell published no fiction between *Coming Up for Air* in 1939 and Secker and Warburg's publication of *Animal Farm* in 1945. During that prolonged (and unwanted) gap, periodicals, weeklies and newspapers published most of his writing. He regularly employed the essay's vigour and pliability, establishing himself as a provocative and engaging essayist able to entertain, instruct and cajole on subjects as diverse as Charles Dickens, patriotic socialism, comic postcards, crime novels and anti-Semitism.

His first essay published during the war was a holdover from the pre-war period. John Lehmann had written to him in Morocco requesting new material. By 1939, *New Writing* had gone through several administrative changes, partnerships with The Bodley Head and the Communist-leaning Lawrence and Wishart having ended. Lehmann had hoped to 'publish a "*New Writing* Library" of novels, autobiographies and books of poems', but Lawrence and Wishart's political affiliations made that unviable, Lehmann lamented: 'A publishing house with the political ties that bound Lawrence and Wishart could never have carried the project through, or have given me a freehand indefinitely' (Lehmann, 1957, p. 309). Bort observes that the constant element for Lehmann was his 'faith in his own independence as spokesman for his generation and decision maker on the magazine's destiny and identity' (Bort, p. 677). Finding their positions incompatible, Lehmann arranged a deal with Leonard Woolf for Hogarth Press to publish the magazine. Lehmann convinced Christopher Isherwood and Stephen Spender 'to accept formal roles as advisory editors'. Both writers soon left, Isherwood departing with W. H. Auden for New York in January 1939 and Spender eventually transferring his energies to the new *Horizon*. Spender's move angered Lehmann (Shelden, 1989, p. 36) but he was energetic and well-connected enough to carry on cultivating and shaping the journal on his own. Changes in personnel were a regular part of journal publication, underscoring the interactive, mutable culture periodicals created.

New Writing was only published twice a year, the longer time between issues suiting Lehmann's aim to promote quality over topicality. Its length gave scope for more reflective and discursive work than many other journals. Still, it would be undergoing its near-death experience when Orwell's essay was published in the Christmas 1939 number. 'Marrakech' reads the city as a site for multivalent colonial relationships. A more personal essay than 'Not Counting Niggers', it comprises a series of vignettes around the seemingly reactionary central point that to individuals like Orwell the local people are 'invisible'. In 'A Hanging' and 'Shooting an Elephant' imperial masters reduced the Burmese to a state of near-invisibility, but 'Marrakech' addresses the very act of making invisible, of not fully recognizing the locals as human beings. Orwell gives an eyewitness account, but also examines his alien status and consequent inability to comprehend the 'people with brown skin'. The first vignette presents a Moroccan funeral without the trappings of European cemeteries: '[n]o gravestone, no name, no identifying mark of any kind. The burial ground is merely a huge waste of hummocky earth, like a derelict building site' (*CO, XI*, p. 417). This 'anti-catalogue' figuratively buries the Moroccans, preceding the subsequent search for some form of commonality.

Orwell wanders among beings he finds difficult to construe as human:

> Are they really the same flesh as yourself? . . . Or are they merely a type of undifferentiated brown stuff, about as individual as bees or coral instincts? They rise out of the earth, they sweat and starve for a few years, and then sink back into the nameless mounds of the graveyard and nobody notices that they are gone. (ibid.)

The massive presumption (how can it be known that nobody notices?) registers how his limited perspective determines interpretations within the essay, a point reinforced later when he gives a coin worth slightly more than a farthing to an old woman. Her reaction elicits a telling interpretation:

> She answered with a shrill wail . . . which was partly gratitude but mainly surprise. I suppose that from her point of view, by taking notice of her, I seemed to be violating some law of nature. (ibid.)

This attempt to comprehend the woman's reaction reads not so much as correct supposition as the imposition of Orwell's view. But where in the correlation of Moroccans to bees the locals are denigrated by the superior outsider, here he tries to think through why the woman reacted as she did. Although the resulting comments remain patronizing, they take account of an alternative point of view based on different cultural assumptions.

In the final vignette Senegalese soldiers march past Orwell, one of them turning with what Orwell reads as 'a look of profound respect'. Thinking further, he suggests the soldier 'has feelings of reverence before a white skin. He has been taught that the white race are his masters, and he still believes it' (ibid., p. 420). The odd interweaving of the religious ('reverence') and the colonial ('race' and 'masters') indicates a complex and unresolved relationship. In *Wigan Pier* Orwell admits that the middle classes had been taught to believe that the working class smells; here, conditioning imposes African submission. But where the middle class had been taught its superiority, the soldiers have been fooled into believing their inferiority. Or so Orwell appears to think. The sight of the large, potentially powerful group of Africans prompts more troubling notions, for

> There is one thought that every white man . . . thinks when he sees a black army marching past. 'How much longer can we go on kidding these people? How long before they turn their guns in the other direction?' (ibid.)

The overturning of the putative power relationship requiring nothing more than a realization on the part of the soldiers, quickly supplants comforting thoughts of reverence. Only a vague criticism of imperialism underpins these observations, but they acknowledge mutual perceptions and misperceptions. The alienated condescension of the essay's opening images gives way to awareness of potentially transformative political energies. Even so, Orwell remains unable to move beyond a revelation that white mastery hinges on the compliance of the locals, comforting himself that:

> It was a kind of secret which we all knew and were too clever to tell; only the Negroes didn't know it. And really it was like watching a flock of cattle to see the long column, a mile or two miles of armed men, flowing peacefully up the road, while the great white birds drifted over them in the opposite direction, glittering like scraps of paper. (ibid.)

This strangely evocative ending again reduces the colonized to something less than fully human, even with the troubled and troubling idea of a mile or two of armed men flowing peacefully. The ending exposes how 'Marrakech' offers an impressionistic account of a place from the perspective of an eyewitness more interested in depicting and conveying mood and texture than in undertaking a thorough political analysis, but whose reflections nevertheless expose submerged anxieties. In this it fits within the concerns and tenor of *New Writing*, which favoured the literary over the purely political, and contrasts with 'Not Counting Niggers', a far more politically engaged reading of motives for a very different readership. 'Marrakech' has more obvious kinship with 'A Hanging' and 'Shooting an Elephant', but where they convey 'messages' – hanging is immoral; colonialism destroys colonizers and colonized – 'Marrakech' is more inquisitively open-ended, more tentative. The earlier essays constructed tight narratives with discernable characters and moral payoffs, but 'Marrakech' strings together snapshots and impressions that readers can explore, investigating their biases and deficiencies.

Orwell made his most significant step as an essayist with the publication of the collection *Inside the Whale* in March 1940. Much of it was written before the war. As mentioned in the previous chapter, after returning to England from Morocco in March 1939, he began the essays that comprise the book, completing them by December 1939. He explained to Leonard Moore that

> I don't know whether Gollancz will want them. They may be a bit off his track, and as they are sort of literary-sociological essays they touch at places on politics, on which I am certain to say things he wouldn't approve of. The subjects are Charles Dickens, boys' weekly papers (the Gem, Magnet, etc) and Henry Miller, the American novelist. (*CO, XI*, p. 365)

Inside the Whale in several ways is detached from the political turmoil of the time, and distinct from the more polemical work Orwell had been writing for periodicals. All three essays deal with literature in the broad sense: 'Charles Dickens' considers the writer and his works; 'Boys' Weeklies' examines pulp magazines for adolescent boys; 'Inside the Whale' provides a comparative reading of the motivations influencing writers of the 1920s and 1930s through an assessment of the American writer Henry Miller. A book of essays was a departure for a writer who was seen and seemed to present himself primarily as a novelist and writer of documentary work – not that writing essays precluded other work. Adding 'essayist' to his credentials registered a desire to publicize new interests and take new approaches. As essayists back to Montaigne had understood, no area was off-limits, and no stance or style was required or imposed. Essayists had metaphorical passports to travel wherever their interests and imagination took them. An essay collection of this type also suggests Orwell's wish to address different audiences, or established audiences in new ways. Such a book represented a publishing risk, though, given his relative obscurity. Gollancz only printed 1,000 copies, and some of those were 'destroyed by bombing' (*CO, XII*, p. 19). Orwell later wrote to Geoffrey Gorer: 'I find this kind of semi-sociological literary criticism very interesting . . . but unfortunately there's no money in it. All Gollancz would give me in advance of the book was £20!' (*CO, XII*, p. 137). Orwell could not have known that in time essays like these would be considered among his best and most distinctive work.

Almost perversely for a collection published in March 1940, with a world war going very badly, the first essay faces towards the nineteenth century. 'Charles Dickens' is more than an extended piece of literary criticism, or a character study, though it is both of these things. It begins with the arresting assertion that 'Dickens is one of those writers who is well worth stealing' (*CO, XII*, p. 20). Why? And by whom? The implied grave robbers are classic Orwell villains: Catholics and Marxists. In reviewing *The Novel Today* he had abused both groups as discarding aesthetic criteria for political orthodoxy in their literary assessments. Here he argues that each desires to 'claim' Dickens: 'G.K. Chesterton credit(s) Dickens with his own highly individual brand of medievalism . . . (while the Marxist T.A. Jackson) has made the spirited attempt to turn Dickens into a bloodthirsty revolutionary' (ibid.). Orwell aims to understand why Dickens should elicit advances from such diverse suitors, while eluding the clutches of both. He is less interested in the literature as purely an aesthetic product than as a social portrait and indicator of Dickens' relation to that society.

Orwell addresses Dickens' continuing importance in the essay's first and last sections, while in the central sections he deals in detail with aspects of Dickens' personality and novels: his fear of the proletariat; the melodramatic plots of his novels; the cartoonish simplifications of his characters; his lack of 'vulgar nationalism'. He portrays a complex, acute, though limited writer, a sharp observer of appearance rather than a methodical or sophisticated thinker. What binds these elements together is Dickens' sense of human decency. Decency might be mistaken for decorum or gentility, but for Orwell the attribute has a critical cutting edge. He treats Dickens as 'a subversive writer, a radical, one might truthfully say a rebel' (ibid., p. 21) rather than a revolutionary writer, one who hopes for the overthrow of a system, noting that 'Dickens' criticism of society is almost exclusively moral' (ibid., p. 22). The revolutionary agitates for transformative change in the political system, Dickens for change in the human heart.

This distinction has complex implications, for Dickens directs his moral critique at institutional authority. Where the revolutionary writer aims to topple authority, Orwell asserts that Dickens' 'whole "message" is . . . If men would behave decently the world would be decent' (ibid., p. 23). Accepting that this message 'at first glance looks like an enormous platitude', he declares that it calls into question the revolutionary's argument: 'Useless to change institutions without a "change of heart" – that, essentially, is what [Dickens] is always saying' (ibid., p. 30). For Orwell, Dickens' message functions as a 'tenable' alternative to the revolutionary desire for systemic change. He considers these positions in a broader context:

> The moralist and the revolutionary are constantly undermining one another. Marx exploded a hundred tons of dynamite beneath the moralist position, and we are still living in the echo of that tremendous crash. But already . . . sappers are at work . . . to blow Marx at the moon. Then Marx, or somebody like him, will come back with yet more dynamite, and so the process continues, to an end we cannot yet foresee. (ibid., p. 31)

The essay's first part ends with this struggle unresolved. Elevating Dickens to Marx's level as a social critic underlines the importance of Dickens' moral standpoint. Grave-robbing Catholics and Marxists had been accused of enlisting Dickens. Orwell does this as well, but goes further, positioning Dickens in the forefront of the larger fight against orthodoxies.

The first part dominates the essay's argument, the following sections analysing Dickens' literary output, noting his shortcomings and strengths. In Part II Orwell suggests that (like H. G. Wells) Dickens' urban bourgeois upbringing turns him against the aristocracy, but only vaguely for the urban proletariat. Dickens' narrow social vision has two aspects, being 'a great advantage to him, because it is fatal for a caricaturist to see too much' (ibid., p. 33) while restricting him to the level of a caricaturist, even if a great one. Comparing Dickens to what Orwell takes as xenophobic writers such as Thackeray, Orwell notes his striking 'lack of vulgar nationalism', something akin to his own flaying of the British Empire in 'Not Counting Niggers' and 'left-wing jingoes' in 'Democracy in the British Army'. Keeping up the attack on some of his leftist

contemporaries, he makes the wildly speculative and juicily provocative claim
that 'if Dickens were alive today he would make a trip to Soviet Russia and
come back with a book like Gide's *Retour de l'U.R.S.S.*' – a modern-day *Martin
Chuzzlewit*. As he knew, though, for some on the Left Gide's renunciation of
the Soviet Union deserved metaphorical deportation to the intellectual gulag.
The manoeuvre remains merely a rhetorical gesture, a way of anachronistically
mobilizing Dickens for Orwell's benefit.

Part III challenges the accepted notion that Dickens was 'a champion of the
"oppressed masses"' (ibid., p. 36). Orwell argues that Dickens' support had
crucial limits: as a 'south of England man' Dickens cannot relate 'to the bulk
of the real oppressed masses, the industrial and agricultural labourers' and
his childhood 'experiences have given him a horror of proletarian roughness'.
Orwell utilizes the observation to mount another contemporary attack, suggesting that 'In rather the same way the modern doctrinaire Socialist con-
temptuously writes off a large block of the population as "lumpenproletariat"'
(ibid.). He connects the term 'lumpenproletariat' emotively to a supposed
doctrinaire horror, rather than in the primarily descriptive way it operates in
Marxist analysis. Misrepresentation though this is, the tactic fits with Orwell's
pervasive antagonism to what he sees as theoretically determined and politically duplicitous Communism. Dickens does not write about work, Orwell
contends, and his plots become convoluted so that the desired character development can occur, again in opposition to doctrinaire dogma. He also observes
that Dickens is not mechanically minded:

> When he speaks of human progress it is usually in terms of *moral* progress –
> men growing better; probably he would never admit that men are only as
> good as their technological development allows them to be. (ibid., p. 44)

Orwell admits in Part V that his discussion has concentrated on Dickens' 'message' at the expense of his literary qualities, but counters that every writer has
a message: 'All art is propaganda. Neither Dickens himself nor the majority of
Victorian novelists would have thought of denying this. On the other hand, not
all propaganda is art' (ibid., p. 47). This argument has a contemporary resonance, echoing Orwell's call for intelligent socialist propaganda to replace the
platitudes and alienating Soviet idealization of socialist orthodoxy.

Why does anyone still care about Dickens? The first answers are rather banal:
Dickens' ubiquity ('ladled' down the throats of children, buried in the subcon-
scious of adults); the vivid eccentricities of his characters; his ability 'to reach
simple people'. (This point rather contradicts Orwell's comment in 'Bookshop
Memories' that nobody takes out Dickens in second-hand bookshops.) What
motivated Dickens, Orwell thinks, what makes him memorable, was that he was
a moralist conscious of having 'something to say'. 'He is always preaching a sermon, and that is the final secret of his inventiveness. For you can only create if

you can *care*' (ibid., p. 53). Orwell revives the relationship between moral critique and radicalism, this time leavened by an understanding of Dickens' humour:

> A joke worth laughing at always has an idea behind it, and usually a subversive idea. Dickens is able to go on being funny because he is in revolt against authority, and authority is always there to be laughed at. (ibid., p. 54)

Again, Orwell distinguishes moral radicalism from revolutionary desire for systemic change, adding contentiously that '[m]ost revolutionaries are potential Tories, because they imagine that everything can be put right by altering the *shape* of society' (ibid.). Instead, Dickens calls for a change in human nature. Stressing these differences, Orwell emphasizes Dickens' broad audience:

> The common man is still living in the mental world of Dickens, but nearly every modern intellectual has gone over to some or other form of totalitarianism . . . But in his own age and ours he has been popular chiefly because he was able to express in a comic, simplified and therefore memorable form the native decency of the common man. (ibid., p. 55)

Dickens functions almost as a means of political and social classification: on the one side, totalitarianism, Tories, Fascists, Marxists, and the belief in the benefits of systemic change; on the other, Dickens, decency, moral radicalism, common humanity. These qualities contribute to the final imagined portrait of Dickens, the

> face of a man who is always fighting against something, but who fights in the open and is not frightened, the face of a man who is generously angry – in other words, of a nineteenth-century liberal, a free intelligence, a type hated with equal hatred by all the smelly little orthodoxies which are now contending for our souls. (ibid., p. 56)

Taking Dickens as an exemplary free intelligence naturally calls into question those willing to subscribe to the smelly little orthodoxies. Dickens measures the shortcomings of modern writers, their failure to fight openly and fearlessly.

For the most part *Inside the Whale*'s second essay, 'Boys' Weeklies', analyses what could be called unintelligent propaganda, the cheap weeklies. Unintelligent need not signify unsuccessful; weeklies such as *Magnet* and *Gem* might re-create a world of stereotypes perpetually frozen in 1910, but they remained an immensely popular form of mass entertainment. While Orwell admits to finding this a 'rather startling phenomenon' (*CO, XII*, p. 59) in the 1930s, he understands the potential for inculcating conservative values. By contrast, 'in England popular imaginative literature is a field that left-wing thought has never begun to enter' (ibid., p. 76). Orwell desires that this situation should change. Although he documents specific weeklies he repeatedly pulls back from sharp focus to a wide shot, assessing the social impact of supposedly marginal literature. So, after detailing the contents of the average small newsagent, he makes the larger claim that '[p]robably the contents of these shops is the best available indication of what the mass of the English people really feels and thinks' (ibid., p. 58), and the fact that 'the combined public of the ten papers [analysed] is a very large one', suggests the paper as an influential medium for transmitting values. Orwell distinguishes two general types of weekly for boys: the long-established purveyor of public school shenanigans, and the racier post-1914 adventure model. The peculiar attractions of the older type include the creation of an unchanging though 'extraordinary little world . . . not easily forgotten'; a world he recognizes as 'the debasement of the Dickens technique' (ibid., p. 60). Public school-based weeklies are 'peculiar to England' he informs readers, and they emphasize the 'unbridgeable gulf between the "public" school and the "private" school', portraying 'life at a "posh" public school as wildly thrilling and romantic' (ibid., p. 62). Their surprisingly broad readership, which Orwell claims includes members of the lower-middle and working classes, ensures that this portrait gets viewed widely. Accepting the conservative political standpoint of *Gem* and *Magnet*, Orwell judges it of 'a completely pre-1914 style, with no Fascist tinge. In reality, their basic political assumptions are two: nothing ever changes, and foreigners are funny' (ibid., pp. 65–6). He adds that both papers are patriotic, but 'their patriotism has nothing whatever to do with power politics or "ideological" warfare. It is more akin to family loyalty'. Their patriotism provides a 'valuable clue to the attitude of ordinary people', who are

> patriotic to the middle of their bones . . . When England is in danger they rally to its defence as a matter of course, but in between times they are not interested. England is always in the right and England always wins, so why worry? . . . Failure to understand it is one of the reasons why left-wing political parties are seldom able to produce an acceptable foreign policy. (ibid., p. 67)

The passage exemplifies how Orwell uses the specific focus of 'Boys' Weeklies' to address larger topics, in this instance dubiously judging the success of Left foreign policy relative to *Magnet*'s patriotism.

The soporific Conservatism of the established weeklies contrasts with their post-1914 counterparts. By ranging widely beyond the school story, the latter 'have far greater opportunity for sensationalism', especially in terms of the newly included scientific theme. Orwell writes that '[w]hereas the *Gem* and *Magnet* derive from Dickens and Kipling, the *Wizard, Champion, Modern Boy*, etc . . . owe a great deal to H.G. Wells' (ibid., p. 69). Given his own championing of Dickens, Orwell's sympathies are plain, although he notes the emergence 'in the post-war boys papers' of 'bully-worship and the cult of violence' (ibid.). The post-war weeklies glorify the strong leader, a character 'intended as a superman' (ibid., p. 70). Tempering this rampant sadism, Orwell notes, is that 'the scenes of violence in all these stories are remarkably harmless and unconvincing.' The same cannot be said, however, for their American counterparts, and in this lies a danger, for

> the process of Amercanisation is going on . . . The American ideal, the 'he-man', the 'tough guy', the gorilla who puts everything right by socking everybody else on the jaw, now figures in a majority of boys' papers. In one serial now running in the *Skipper* he is always portrayed, ominously enough, swinging a rubber truncheon. (ibid., p. 71)

In Orwell's iconography, the rubber truncheon always symbolizes totalitarianism.

For the most part contemporary politics are excluded from the weeklies: 'The clock has stopped at 1910. Britannia still rules the waves, and no one has heard of slumps, booms, unemployment, dictatorship, purges or concentration camps' (ibid., p. 72). Does it matter? Orwell responds by moving from the specifics of boys' weeklies to a more general social critique:

> [M]ost people are influenced far more than they would care to admit by novels, serial stories, films and so forth . . . the worst books are often the most important, because they are usually the ones that are read earliest in life . . . [Boys' magazine readers ingest] a set of beliefs which are considered hopelessly out of date in the Central Office of the Conservative Party. (ibid., p. 74)

The vacuous anachronisms of *Magnet* have a political aspect: 'Considering who owns these papers,' Orwell asserts, 'it is difficult to believe that this is unintentional' (ibid., p. 74). We are back in the world of *Ami du Peuple*. The propaganda of the Conservatives might not be particularly intelligent, but, being ubiquitous, it works. Inevitably, Orwell asks 'why is there no such thing as a left-wing boys' paper', and though this allows him to lampoon the lame didacticism of the Left, the question has a serious purpose, for he claims to have seen Left-leaning popular literature in Spain. He also cites the Soviet film *Chapayev* as having 'all the usual paraphernalia . . . heroic fight against odds, escape at the last moment, love interest, comic relief . . . except that its tendency is "left"' (ibid., p. 75). These international examples have no British equivalent, where 'popular imaginative literature is a field that left-wing thought has never begun to enter'. Orwell ends 'Boys' Weeklies' by reiterating how Conservative publishers have grasped the propaganda opportunity, criticizing the Left with the sarcastic statement that this

is only unimportant if one believes that what is read in childhood leaves
no impression behind. [Conservative publisher] Lord Camrose and his colleagues evidently believe nothing of the kind, and, after all, Lord Camrose
and his colleagues should know. (ibid., p. 76)

As with 'Charles Dickens', Orwell combines a detailed study of an ostensibly
literary topic with a critique of contemporary political attitudes. Neither essay
stays within the boundaries marked out by their respective titles, but 'Boys'
Weeklies' charts a fresh course, its nuanced examination of popular culture
revealing a curiosity about the supposedly ephemeral. This essay might seem
worryingly irrelevant to a war-time environment, but the invitation to consider
the hidden influence of marginal culture has a larger political implication, for
it addresses how views are promoted and stifled, and with it the nature of public discourse. The Left's failure to engage in this area, Orwell suggests, ensures
that conservative norms dominate.

   The title essay uses Henry Miller to assess the relationship between literature and political commitment. Orwell had reviewed Miller's banned
Tropic of Cancer in a 1935 *New English Weekly* issue, praising it for 'passages of
rather Whitmanesque enthusiasm' (*CO*, X, p. 405), for its attempts to get at
real facts and for bridging the frightful gulf that exists, in fiction, between
the intellectual and the man-in-the-street. Miller's avowedly apolitical views
seem to make him a strange choice given the essay's wider focus, but he acts
as a instructive point of difference from young 1930s writers and a point of
contact with writers of the 1920s. The first of three sections analyses *Tropic of
Cancer*, while the second surveys recent British literature, launching a searing attack upon the left-wing orthodoxy of young thirties writers. The third
section returns to Miller, comparing his quietist acceptance of the collapse
of civilization to impassioned Marxist-leaning writers; Edward Upward and
Louis MacNeice are singled out for special attention. Ultimately, Orwell
sides with Miller for recognizing before others that 'literature, in the form
in which we know it, must suffer at least a temporary death' (*CO*, XII, p.
110). Miller symbolizes that temporary death, and his significance lies in
demonstrating 'the *impossibility* of any major literature until the world has
shaken itself into its new shape' (ibid., p. 112). That statement bears a striking similarity to one written for the first number of *Horizon* by Connolly.
His much-quoted phrase – 'Our standards are aesthetic and our politics are
in abeyance' – seems to prove the periodical's artistic detachment, but the
statement continues:

This will not always be the case, because as events take shape the policy
of artists and intellectuals will become clearer . . . At the moment civilization is on the operating table and we sit in the waiting room. (Connolly,
1940, p. 5)

War undeniably crushes individual action initially, but Connolly can contemplate a time after the operation when life will continue. For Orwell, too, the 'death' major literature suffers will only be short-term. That assumes that totalitarianism does not prevail, something unknowable in early 1940.

Orwell champions Miller not because of Miller's ghoulish nihilism, but because he faces reality without fear. 'Good novels,' Orwell writes, 'are written by people who are *not frightened*' (*CO, XII*, p. 106). He makes the same point in 'Charles Dickens', the essential difference being that Miller will not fight, withdrawing contented inside the metaphorical whale, into 'a womb big enough for an adult' (ibid., p. 107). Orwell begins his critique of *Tropic of Cancer* by dodging the issue of its sexual explicitness and instead noting that the book was praised by writers (Eliot, Pound, Huxley and others) who are not '"in fashion"' (ibid., p. 86). This sparks the important point that 'the subject-matter of the book, and to a certain extent its mental atmosphere, belong to the twenties rather than the thirties'. One of the defining principles of the now-unfashionable writers of the 1920s was the truthful depiction of life, and Miller sets down the facts of human existence vividly and faithfully. Orwell compares *Tropic of Cancer* to James Joyce's *Ulysses*, which he also praised. Accepting the necessary differences, he sees them both writers as capable of writing 'a novel which opens up a new world not by revealing what is strange, but by revealing what is familiar', and values their ability to depict the 'recognisable experience of human beings' (ibid., p. 87).

Miller's individuality links him to Eliot, Joyce, Wyndham Lewis, D. H. Lawrence and others who comprise 'the movement' of the mid- and late 1920s. Orwell points out 'the first thing to notice about the group . . . is that they do not look like a group. Moreover several would strongly object to being coupled with several of the others' (ibid., p. 96). He contrasts this individuality with the group mentality of 'the movement' of the 1930s, 'the Auden-Spender group'. With the 1920s writers, 'what "purpose" they have is very much up in the air' (ibid., p. 97). The 1930s is different:

> Suddenly we have got out of the twilight of the gods into a sort of Boy Scout atmosphere of bare knees and community singing. The typical literary man ceases to be a cultured expatriate with a leaning towards the Church, and becomes an eager-minded schoolboy with a leaning towards Communism. (ibid., p. 99)

This caricature of the 'typical literary man' of the 1930s is intentionally tendentious, but the ramifications are important. Orwell sees in the rise of 'orthodoxy sniffers' the passing of liberalism and the potential triumph of the mental slavery of totalitarianism. 'Inside the Whale' berates orthodoxy sniffers and forewarns of totalitarian malevolence.

Why did young 1930s writers turn to an ideology dominated by foreign ideas? And '[w]hy should *writers* be attracted by a form of Socialism that makes mental honesty impossible?' (ibid., p. 102). His answer, 'middle class unemployment', seems odd, but he means unemployment of talent and a consequent lack of belief. Communism, Orwell declares

> was simply something to believe in. Here was a church, an army, an orthodoxy, a discipline. Here was a Fatherland and – at any rate since 1935 or thereabouts – a Fuehrer . . . Patriotism, religion, empire, military glory – all in one word, Russia. Father, king, leader, hero, saviour – all in one word – Stalin. The devil – Hitler. Heaven – Moscow. Hell – Berlin . . . It is the patriotism of the deracinated. (ibid., p. 103)

Such rootless 'patriotism' for a foreign country determined that 'by 1937 the whole of the intelligentsia was mentally at war' (ibid., p. 104). Anti-Fascism provided a mask for ideological control, the retailing of lies, the suppression of opposition. Ultimately, these efforts failed 'because the actual course of events has made nonsense of the left-wing orthodoxy of the last few years' (ibid., p. 105). Orwell warns that the next orthodoxy might not be any improvement. Envisaging the possibility that it might be totalitarian, he suggests that literature produced under such a regime 'will be quite different from anything we can now imagine. Literature as we know it is an individual thing, demanding mental honesty and a minimum of censorship' (ibid., p. 105). This perception underpins his central argument, that 'good novels are not written by orthodoxy-sniffers, nor by people who are conscience stricken about their own unorthodoxy' (ibid., pp. 105–6). What distinguishes him is that Miller faces the end of civilization squarely: he fiddles while Rome burns, but 'unlike the majority of people who do this, fiddling with his face towards the flames'.

Orwell notes Miller's desire to accept the destruction and withdraw inside the whale. He appreciates that desire, for 'being inside a whale is a very comfortable, cosy, homelike thought' (ibid., p. 107). Comfort and homeliness contrast to the potentially bleak future:

> Almost certainly we are moving into an age of totalitarian dictatorships – an age in which freedom of thought will be at first a deadly sin and later on a meaningless abstraction. The autonomous individual is going to be stamped out of existence. (ibid., p. 110)

Orwell's prediction proved false, but at the beginning of a transformative and highly destructive conflict in which some of the most powerful aggressors were totalitarian, it was not wildly implausible. Quietist comfort held out a tempting prospect.

But the age of dictatorships is only 'almost' certain; the future remains provisional, the gloomy timetable blurry. Orwell had predicted something similar in 'Why I Join the I.L.P.', though it might happen 'not next year, perhaps not for ten or twenty years'. Now he suggests:

> Seemingly there is nothing left but quietism – robbing reality of its terror by simply submitting to it. Get inside the whale – or rather, admit that you are inside the whale (for you *are*, of course). Give yourself over to the world-process, stop fighting against it or pretending that you control it: simply accept it, endure it, record it. (ibid., p. 111)

But if the quietism favoured by Miller is rational, it does not preclude other stances. Jonah's time inside the whale was temporary – eventually the whale vomited him up. And the qualifier – this time 'seemingly there is nothing left' – suggests that there might be something left. Orwell's praise for Miller itself is qualified: he does not consider Miller 'a new hope for English prose', describing him as 'essentially a man of one book' (ibid., p. 111). Although that book was important, its significance was 'merely symptomatic' or writers like Joyce who describe 'the recognisable experience of human beings'. Joyce reconstructs at many levels the experience of Dublin's denizens. Miller's passivity allows him

> to get nearer to the ordinary man than is possible for more purposive writers. For the ordinary man is also passive . . . So far from endeavouring to influence the future, he simply lies down and lets things happen to him. (ibid., p. 91)

In this sense, many ordinary people have already taken up residence in the whale's belly. Miller's book records that passivity, and he personifies the creed. Orwell's fear of mass passivity also proved misguided. Indeed, he questioned his own supposition before *Inside the Whale* was published. Writing to Gollancz he admits that Gollancz might be right in considering his predictions 'over-pessimistic', continuing that 'it is quite possible that freedom of thought etc. may survive in an economically totalitarian society' (ibid., p. 5). This is radically at odds with the gloomy forecasts made in the book itself. Yet the discrepancy can be explained by Orwell's additional comment:

> What worries me at present is the uncertainty as to whether the ordinary people of countries like England grasp the difference between democracy and despotism well enough to want to defend their liberties . . . The intellectuals who are at present pointing out that democracy and fascism are the same thing etc, depress me horribly. However, perhaps when the pinch comes the common people will turn out to be more intelligent than the clever ones. I certainly hope so. (*CO, XII*, p. 115)

people proved equal to the task. As Orwell's letter suggests, the
the Whale were written for readers on the brink of war, or experi-
rly days of the 'phoney war'. The nightmare prophesy, as with
edictions Orwell made, was not fulfilled, the essay recording a
prospect that never eventuated.

'Inside the Whale' was meant to provoke. But the small print run limited
the collection's impact. Even so, it received appreciative reviews in the *New
English Weekly*, *The Adelphi* and *Time and Tide*. In the last of these Arthur Calder-
Marshall begins with emphatic and truncated advice: 'Must read . . . Brilliant
writer. Superb' (Meyers, 1975, p. 175). He then spends most of the review on
'Inside the Whale' 'because it is going to prove a centre of political controversy', taking Orwell to task for accepting Miller's quietist position (ibid.).
Ironically, the small sales initially undermined Calder's expectation of contro-
versy, and 'Inside the Whale' would prove far more contentious after Orwell's
death. Orwell and the book were given insightful assessment by Q. D. Leavis in
Scrutiny. Wrongly assuming he belongs to the 'Bloomsbury racket' along with
Connolly and Spender, she distinguishes him from them and others by the fact
that he has 'grown up' (ibid., p. 187). Leavis gives each essay a thoughtfully critical and positive appraisal, but her opinion of Orwell himself deserves attention.
Comparing her very positive judgement of the quality of his 'promisingly' different essays, she declares that the only impression his 'dreary [novels] had on
me is that nature didn't intend him to be a novelist. Yet his equivalent works in
non-fiction are stimulating' (ibid., p. 188). She adds later that

> if he were to give up trying to be a novelist Mr Orwell might well find his
> métier in literary criticism . . . He is evidently a live mind working through
> literature, life and ideas. He knows what he is interested in and has some-
> thing original to say about it. (ibid., p. 189)

Her incisive assessment reveals that for all the faults of his fiction she rates his
non-fiction and essays inventive and persuasive. Orwell's approach connected
to some degree with *Scrutiny*'s own with its call for the play of free intelligence
upon the underlying issues. Clearly, Leavis felt 'Inside the Whale' manifested
those qualities, for she ended the review claiming: 'If the revolution were to
happen that he wants and prophesies . . . he would be the only man of letters
we have whom we can imagine surviving the flood undisturbed' (ibid., p.
190). This is an extraordinarily generous claim about a writer only in his late
thirties who had published just four 'dreary' novels, three documentary or
pseudo-documentary works and now a book of essays. As it happens Orwell
never again wrote the dreary novels Leavis complained about. Had Orwell
lived longer, of course, he might well have returned to novels like *Keep the
Aspidistra Flying* and *Coming Up for Air*; several ideas were projected but none
was produced. In the second half of his truncated literary career, though,

he developed, as Leavis might have hoped, into an astute, engaging and independent-minded essayist.

More people probably read 'Boys' Weeklies' and 'Inside the Whale' initially when they appeared in periodicals. ('Charles Dickens' would not be reprinted until the *Critical Essays* collection of 1946). A shortened version of 'Boy's Weeklies' was printed in *Horizon*, which had quickly established itself as one of Britain's leading literary and cultural journals. Admittedly *Horizon* had less competition than equivalent journals of the 1930s, but conditions were difficult and the requirement repeatedly to gather quality material during a war created substantial and ongoing impediments. Despite anxiety about whether it would succeed, by the time 'Boys' Weeklies' appeared in the third issue *Horizon* was already selling 7,000 copies (Shelden, 1989, p. 42). Orwell's friendship with Connolly – begun at prep-school but non-existent after Eton until Connolly reviewed *Burmese Days* and found that George Orwell was also his old school friend Eric Blair – proved mutually beneficial. Connolly admired Orwell's essays and was pleased to publish, while *Horizon* gave Orwell a sizeable and sophisticated audience along with the space to develop sustained reflections on cultural topics without the need that they be topical.

There was no American edition of the collection, but the title essay was published in the 1940 American anthology, *New Directions in Prose and Poetry*. First printed in 1936, the anthology presented itself as 'an annual volume of "advance-guard" literature – an exhibition gallery where young writers offer their "new directions" to the public'. Over that time it had included in its yearly collections the works of Jean Cocteau, William Carlos Williams, Gertrude Stein, Lawrence Durrell, Dylan Thomas and Henry Miller, so selection in the 1940 edition was no small matter. There was the more prosaic aspect that the critical analysis of Henry Miller underpinning 'Inside the Whale', as well as comparisons between British and American authors which occur in the essay, slotted into the general concerns of *New Directions*. This was the first time one of Orwell's essays had been published outside Britain, and apart from translations it was the only time 'Inside the Whale' was printed in Orwell's life. But selection itself spoke to the essay's quality, and that it had attracted attention from outside the British public sphere.

Not all Orwell's essays were substantial, but the brief 'Charles Reade' deserves a moment's consideration. Published in *New Statesman and Nation*, it represents Orwell's partial rapprochement with the weekly after the breakdown during the Spanish Civil War. It also exemplifies his occasional efforts to publicize the work of neglected literary figures. Reade had been a respected novelist in the mid-1800s, but as Orwell notes at the start of his short analysis, although the publication of cheap editions of Reade's work indicates 'that he still has his following, . . . it is unusual to meet anyone who has voluntarily read him' (*CO, XII*, p. 232). Orwell spruiks Reade's qualities, balancing praise for the 'charm' of conveying 'useless knowledge' and an interest with social reform against the fact that Reade 'has no sense whatever of character and probability' (ibid., p. 234). Part of the fascination of a short essay like 'Charles Reade' is its almost inappropriate taking up of space on a largely forgotten Victorian writer (although Orwell suggests that he is one of the 'best "escape" novelists we have' and so would be good to send to soldiers). The piece reflects Orwell's nostalgic bent, his own love of useless knowledge, the essay's capacity to address any subject matter from a personal perspective, and the periodical function of promoting cultural discussion. Its ephemeral aspects contrast with the significance of 'My Country Right or Left'.

As with 'Shooting an Elephant' and 'Marrakech', 'My Country Right or Left' resulted from John Lehmann's prompting. Eager to keep the salvaged *Folios of New Writing* afloat, he sent letters to Orwell, V. S. Pritchett, William Plomer and others he hoped would contribute (Lehmann, 1960, pp. 45–6). Lehmann's pressure worked, 'My Country Right or Left' appearing in the second issue. The essay advertises Orwell's brand of patriotic Socialism and begins with a regular tactic, swiftly undercutting an established idea: 'Contrary to popular belief, the past was not more eventful than the present' (*CO, XII,* p. 269). He considers the ambiguities involved in memories, observing that images of the First World War for those living through the Second World War are an amalgam of 'books, films and reminiscences' (ibid.). He examines the interconnection between personal history, the changing perceptions of historical events, and the imprint of history upon individuals and groups. Much of the essay's first part recounts Orwell's memories of the First World War. He reveals how the war's lack of genuine impact on his generation engendered a cynical 'pacifist reaction' that outlived the war itself: 'For years after the war, to have any knowledge of or interest in military matters . . . was suspect in "enlightened" circles' (ibid., p. 270).

Despite his generation's cynicism he admits that as 'the war fell back into the past those who had been "just too young" became conscious of the vastness of the experience they had missed'. To compound the problem, '[y]ou felt yourself a little less of a man, because you had missed it' (ibid.). He argues, though, that feelings of inadequacy can breed expectation in those who missed out: a future war might allow those too young for the Great War to achieve manhood. Orwell develops this argument for psychological motivation in revealing himself 'convinced that part of the reason for the fascination that the Spanish civil war had for people of about my age was that it was so like the Great War' (ibid., p. 271). Still, he admits that the Spanish Civil War was slightly disappointing, a 'bad copy of 1914-18' (ibid.).

For all that disappointment, something more fundamental gets hinted at, for he suggests the emotional or psychological processes at work in his attitude to the Spanish Civil War. Acknowledging that 'only part of the reason' for fighting in Spain was a supposed similarity between it and the First World War, he advances very few arguments in the essay. Emotional or psychological explanations dominate, underpinning the general proposition that motivating factors exist outside political ideology or rational argument. Justifying fighting in the Second World War, he incorporates a political element but introduces it through the unusual medium of a reported dream:

> The night before the Russo-German pact was announced I dreamed that the war had started . . . It taught me two things, first, that I should be simply relieved when the long-dreaded war started, secondly, that I was patriotic at heart, would not sabotage or act against my own side, would support the war, would fight in it if possible. (ibid.)

Two points strike home immediately: the enormous lesson Orwell takes from the dream, and the lack of information about its content. Its potent import is only enhanced by the fact that it occurs the night before the announcement of the Russo-German pact. Its timing and 'message' appear implausibly symbolic, but are presented unquestioningly.

The dream marks a moment of transformation, the dividing line between his anti-war speeches and pamphlets of the 1930s and accepting the need to fight. In effect the dream negates his ILP-inspired anti-war activities of the late 1930s. Orwell almost apologetically admits that 'at times I even made speeches and wrote pamphlets against [war]' (ibid.). Given the vehemence of 'Not Counting Niggers' and 'Democracy and the British Army' – never mind his membership of the ILP – this comment reconfigures his efforts and arguments. The dream's neutralizing effect gets accentuated by juxtaposing it to the nightmare of impending war. It brings relief, and the certainty of an appropriate stance to take. That this stance founds itself upon patriotism reveals the gap Orwell has leapt since writing 'Not Counting Niggers' and 'Democracy in the British Army' the previous year. Having established his patriotic credentials by way of a revelatory dream, Orwell then provides reasons for supporting war against Fascism:

> There is no real alternative between resisting Hitler and surrendering to him, and from a Socialist point of view I should say that it is better to resist; in any case I can see no argument for surrender that does not make nonsense of the Republican resistance in Spain, the Chinese resistance to Japan, etc., etc. (ibid.)

This makes up all of the rational argument Orwell employs for supporting the war. Yet even this political position does not stand for long, Orwell immediately knocking it down by revealing the 'emotional basis' of his actions: 'What I knew in my dream that night was that the long drilling in patriotism the middle classes go through had done its work' (ibid.). He confesses not to able to sabotage an England 'in a serious jam'. A year before he had publically claimed that the British Empire was a 'far vaster injustice' than Fascist Germany.

Although the dream in 'My Country Right or Left' reveals the success of the 'long drilling in patriotism', the concept itself requires rationalizing in the conscious world. Orwell takes on the most damning political argument against his position, stating that patriotism 'has nothing to do with conservatism' (ibid.). Instead, he considers it 'devotion to something that is changing but is felt to be mystically the same', exemplifying this by using the supposed devotion 'of the ex-White Bolshevik to Russia' (ibid.). This example hardly defuses the charge that in England patriotism equates with conservatism. The mythical ex-White Bolshevik clearly is meant to fuse in an image the Socialist and the patriot, though its vagueness does not of itself convince. Orwell overcomes these shortcomings by employing a technique he used in 'Why I Join the I.L.P.' and 'Inside the Whale' – projecting into the future. He develops the quasi-philosophical notion of something changing but being the same in to a forecast and a warning that '[o]nly revolution can save England'. Orwell forecasts the possibility that a year or two on from 1940

> I dare say the London gutters will have to run with blood. All right, let them, if it is necessary. But when the red militias are billeted in the Ritz I shall still feel that the England I was taught to love so long ago and for such different reasons is somehow persisting. (ibid., p. 272)

London's gutters never ran with the blood of revolutionaries, and the *Ritz* stayed free of red militias. Yet the faulty predictions are less important than the idea of England changing but staying 'mystically' the same. Making this argument, Orwell reveals that as a result of childhood training he feels a 'faint feeling of sacrilege' at not standing during 'God Save the King' (ibid.). Acknowledging his feelings as 'childish', he contends that this is preferable to those 'left-wing intellectuals who are so "enlightened" that they cannot understand the most ordinary emotions' (ibid.). This constitutes a sweeping claim, the basis for a far more substantial accusation: 'It is exactly the people whose hearts have *never* leapt at the sight of the Union Jack who will flinch from revolution when the moment comes' (ibid.). This assertion about the inspirational qualities of the Union Jack interweaves patriotism with revolutionary success. The Orwell of 'My Country Right or Left' knows the value of 'drums, flags and loyalty parades'.

The essay ends with a literary flourish, Orwell drawing parallels between the poetry of two widely divergent writers: Sir Henry Newbolt, patriotic balladeer, and John Cornford, the model of politically committed young Left writers of the 1930s. Newbolt had lived on to ripe, conservative old age, while Cornford, a *Cambridge Left* contributor, had been killed at 21 while fighting in Spain. The comparison itself would be enough to inflame the passion of those still cherishing Cornford's memory, but Orwell also compared Cornford's Civil War poem 'Before the Storming of Huesca' with Newbolt's 'There's a breathless hush in the Close tonight', coming to the startling conclusion for supporters of both poets that 'the emotional content of the two poems is almost exactly the same'. From this piece of off-the-cuff comparative literature, he declares that '[t]he young Communist who died heroically in the International Brigade was public school to the core' (ibid.). As a judgement on Cornford, a writer who had warned of the 'very dangerous attempt to deck out the old class in new revolutionary utopian trappings', Orwell's statement requires something more substantial than a quick comparison of poems. Yet Cornford's alleged 'core' prompts a rhetorical question before the final assertion of this assertion-laden essay:

> What does this prove? Merely the possibility of building a Socialist on the bones of a Blimp, the power of one kind of loyalty to transmute into another, the spiritual need for patriotism and the military virtues, for which, however little the boiled rabbits of the Left may like them, no substitute has yet been found. (ibid.)

The reading of Cornford's poem that provides the foundation for these assertions is worryingly insubstantial, hardly constituting proof of the need for patriotism and 'military virtues', or the blanket vilification of the unnamed 'boiled rabbits of the Left'. The sheer tendentiousness of the composite parts gives the essay the impetus for that final impassioned attack. Examined separately, the individual statements are highly challengeable: can the 'possibility of building a Blimp on the bones of a Socialist' be taken seriously? Does Cornford's poem illustrate the transmutation of loyalty? Is there a spiritual need for patriotism and the military virtues? Can no substitute for these be found? All the questions can be asked, but Orwell withholds answers. Instead, like some rhetorical snowball, the assertions in 'My Country Right or Left' increasingly gather speed as they hurtle at the reader.

The essay publically registers a clean break from the politics of 'Not Counting Niggers' and 'Democracy in the British Army'. Orwell contradicts some of his earlier arguments, even adopting the same positions he reproached in those earlier pieces. 'My Country Right or Left' signals a significant and public change of political position, one that Orwell continued to test and develop in the essays he wrote during the war.

These changes should not be written off as mere revisionism: rapidly developing circumstances often necessitate dramatic realignments. Nor was Orwell alone on the Left in changing his position in the face of global conflict. Victor Gollancz had supported much that Orwell had derided through the 1930s: the various incarnations of the 'Popular Front'; the Soviet Union; the Communist Party of Great Britain. His publishing house and the Left Book Club had disseminated views he supported to tens of thousands of people. In the late 1930s, however, his suspicion of Communist subversion of the Left Book Club, coupled with a political reassessment after the Munich crisis, led him to a change of heart, a signal being 'Thoughts after Munich', his editorial in the November 1938 *Left News*. Gollancz claims that the original purpose of the Club had been to educate readers, with the laudable goals of 'the preservation of peace, and the creation of a juster social order' (Gollancz, 1938, p. 1032), but admits that

> Passionately believing in certain ideas, I have allowed myself . . . to become too much of a propagandist and too little of an educator . . . only by the *clash* of ideas does a mind truly become free. (ibid., p. 1035)

Gollancz's admissions also represent a sharp break with the past, provoked by the extraordinary political movements and events at the turn of the decade. Arguing for the illuminating clash of ideas, he can be seen promoting some form of an active public sphere. His increasing anxiety over the Communist activity in Britain, made plain in the *Left News* essay, 'The CP, Revolutionary Defeatism, and the "People's Convention"', was reinforced by the searing attack on the party in *The Betrayal of the Left: An Examination and Refutation of Communist Policy* (1941). He edited this book, to which Orwell, Harold Laski and John Strachey contributed. Orwell's political realignment, then, was not unique. Nor did his disavowal of the ILP entail a rejection of Socialism. In his mind, breaking from the party liberated him from the prospect of having to produce work needing official sanction.

'Our Opportunity' supplies the first major explication of his new position. It was published in *Left News* in January 1941 and would be reprinted as 'Patriots and Revolutionaries' in *The Betrayal of the Left*. While Left Book Club membership had dropped since the peak of 1939, it still commanded many thousands of readers, so publication in its official organ *Left News* gave Orwell access to a large, engaged audience. The title refers to two opportunities, one missed, the other still a potentiality. Orwell considers that, in the immediate aftermath of the retreat from Dunkirk, 'Had any real leadership existed on the Left . . . [it] could have been the beginning of the end of British capitalism' (*CO, XII*, p. 344). Even so, an opportunity still lies in the potential for another crisis:

> At that moment it may be decided once and for all whether the issues of this war are to made clear and who is to control the great middling mass of people, working class and middle class who are capable of being pushed in either one direction or the other. (ibid., p. 348)

Patriotism provides the binding agent for this middling mass and the key motivating force for a successful war and a successful revolution.

The title 'Patriots and Revolutionaries' that the essay carries in *The Betrayal of the Left* better reflects its argumentative thrust. The combination of patriotism and revolution somewhat echoes the call for the fusing of Socialist and Blimp in 'My Country Right or Left'. 'Our Opportunity' develops this argument in a more political direction. In part, the differences of approach can be explained by the nature of the respective periodicals in which the essays appear. *Folios of New Writing*'s literary-cultural bent suited Orwell's use of two writers (Cornford and Newbolt) to substantiate his case, but in the more openly political *Left News* the tactic would have been less effective. Where the earlier essay founds its argument for patriotic Socialism on the lessons from Orwell's dream, in 'Our Opportunity' he discerns an almost universal patriotism in the 'middling masses'. Criticising the Left leadership for its indecision at the time of Dunkirk, he judges that at that moment the willingness for sacrifice and drastic changes extended not only to the working class but to nearly the whole of the middle class, whose patriotism is stronger than its self-interest.

As well as teaching hard military lessons, Dunkirk revealed the crucial fact he feels that 'the common people were patriotic' (ibid., p. 345). He uses this assertion to call for the Left to understand the power of patriotism, harnessing it for revolution. Recognizing that in the early days of the war '[t]he notion that *England can only win the war by passing through revolution* had barely been mooted' (ibid., p. 344), Orwell argues that the disasters of mid-1940 changed the situation. The patriotism then shown by the working class, especially, resulted in 'a huge effort to increase armaments production and prevent invasion'. Simultaneously, recruiting huge numbers of soldiers in the Home Guard revealed a mass desire to defend England. This did not mean the defence of the country as it stood, but rather as it might be. Orwell detects a general perception that people have a 'duty both to defend England and to turn it into a genuine democracy' (ibid., p. 345).

This argument approximates Orwell's view of England changing, but 'mystically the same'. Here, he employs overtly political language:

> [T]he feeling of all true patriots and all true Socialists is at bottom reducible to the 'Trotskyist' slogan: 'The war and the revolution are inseparable'. We cannot beat Hitler without passing through revolution, nor consolidate our revolution without beating Hitler. (ibid., p. 346)

Orwell sees no third option: England either gets transformed into a 'Socialist democracy' or is subsumed within the 'Nazi empire'. Neither alternative is vouchsafed: the middling masses might or might not grab the opportunity the next crisis offers, and will only take the opportunity if their patriotism is channelled properly.

Orwell realizes that his argument for revolutionary patriotism rests on several debatable notions, most notably that middle class patriotism will override

self-interest 'when it comes to the pinch'. He had argued for the importance of
the middle class for Socialism in *Wigan Pier*, but there the call went out to that
group to lose their aitches. 'Our Opportunity' acknowledges that what Orwell
calls 'British extremist parties' have declared the winning over of the middle
classes 'unnecessary and impossible' (ibid.). He takes the pragmatic view that
the middle class contains 'practically the whole of the technocracy . . . without
which a modem industrial country could not last for a week' (ibid.). Without
the co-operation of this group, any Socialist revolution must fail. He asks rhetorically whether it would be possible to convert the airman or the naval officer
into a 'convinced Socialist', answering that it matters not so much whether the
middle class might support a Socialist revolution, as whether they would sabotage it. Orwell trusts in patriotism to stay the saboteur's hand:

> [A]t this moment of time a revolutionary has to be a patriot, and a patriot
> has to be a revolutionary, 'Do you want to defeat Hitler? Then you must be
> ready to sacrifice your social prestige. Do you want to establish Socialism?
> Then you must be ready to defend your country' . . . [A]long these lines our
> propaganda must move. (ibid., p. 347)

Revolution had to be argued for, and required informed and active citizenry,
something the essay aims in its small way to encourage.

'Our Opportunity' does not simply call for the integration of the middle
class in Socialist plans. Orwell understands the efforts, aspirations and revolutionary potential of the working class, seeing it driven by an instinctive
patriotism. He illustrates this point late in the essay by recalling such slogans
as 'Poor, but loyal' chalked on the walls of London slums at the Silver Jubilee
of George V; the slogan 'Landlords keep away' adorns the same walls (ibid.;
p. 349). Acknowledging that the writers of such slogans have a misguided
sense of political power, he sees the slogans proving his central point that the
slum dwellers 'were patriotic, but they were not Conservative. And did they not
show a sounder instinct than those who tell us that patriotism is something
disgraceful and national liberty a matter of indifference?' (p. 350). The question indicates a number of oppositions: between the nobly poor slum dwellers, and those who pillory patriotism; between soundness and indifference,
personal instinct and hectoring doctrine, patriotism and disgrace. In Orwell's
view there exists a fundamental dichotomy between an instinctual, patriotic
working class, and a shadowy, haranguing group falsely attributing negative
attributes to patriotism.

The fusing of national liberty and patriotism provides him with the rhetorical momentum for the question with which 'Our Opportunity' ends:

> [W]as [patriotism] not the same impulse that moved the Paris workers in
> 1793, the Communards in 1871, the Madrid trade unionists in 1936 – the

impulse to defend one's country, and to make it a place worth living in? (ibid., p. 350)

The historical episodes Orwell cites are examples of internal conflict rather than the defence of a nation from external threat. Even so, they buttress his general point: that progressive forces do defend their nation, as well as over-throwing reactionary powers. The heroes of Paris and Spain carried with them a sense of defending something that was changing while staying 'mystically the same'. 'Our Opportunity' develops the argument for patriotic Socialism spelt out in 'My Country Right or Left'. The later essay has a harder political edge than the earlier: instead of nostalgia, 'Our Opportunity' faces the future. What that future might be remains undetermined, and 'Our Opportunity' functions as a rallying cry rather than a plan of action. That would come later in 1941 with Orwell's major war-time essay on Socialism, 'The Lion and The Unicorn'.

Before that piece he sent off the first of his 'London Letters' to *Partisan Review*. A journal established in 1934 by the John Reed Club of New York, and initially affiliated to the Communist Party of the USA, *Partisan Review* had proclaimed its revolutionary purpose and support for the Soviet Union, seeing itself as a cultural counterpart to *New Masses*, the established journal of the C.P.U.S.A. An interesting transatlantic parallel can be drawn to the British radical journal *Left Review*, also set up in 1934. While not formerly tied to the Communist Party of Great Britain, *Left Review* nevertheless was sympathetic to the party, regularly expressing support for the Soviet Union and providing a culturally inflected platform for Marxist thought. One of *Partisan Review*'s two initial editors, William Phillips, later recalled that in order to get the journal off the ground *Partisan Review* arranged a fund-raising lecture by the 'suave British Marxist' John Strachey on the topic 'Literature and Dialectical Materialism'. Strachey's reputation in New York was such that his lecture 'raised the unbelievable sum of eight hundred dollars', recalled Phillips, 'enough to run a magazine for a year in a collapsed economy' (Phillips, 1976, cited in Cooney, p. 39). Although the details of Phillips' memory have been challenged (Cooney, p. 283, n.3) he conveys New York's committed political and intellec-tual environment in the 1930s. Engagement, though, often entails vituperative arguments, and by 1937 theoretical and tactical disputes caused Phillips and his major collaborator Philip Rahv to suspend the journal. When they started it up again, *Partisan Review* declared a new orientation:

Formerly associated with the Communist Party, *Partisan Review* strove from the first against the drive to equate the interests of literature with those of factional politics. Our reappearance on an independent basis signifies our conviction that the totalitarian trend is inherent in that movement and that it can no longer be combated from within. (Kurzweil, p. 1)

During the rest of the 1930s the journal became increasingly anti-Stalinist, while still arguing for democratic socialism.

Desmond Hawkins had provided a 'London Letter' for *Partisan Review*, but when he was forced by wartime commitments to give up the task, he suggested Orwell to replace him (Hawkins, p. 159, cited in *CO, XII*, p. 351). They had worked together at the BBC, another instance where personal contacts in a smallish network of the like-minded assisted Orwell; he was an insider's outsider. The art critic and *Partisan Review* contributor Clement Greenberg, who had written for *Horizon* in September 1940 (Latham, p. 865), contacted Orwell in December:

> The editors of *Partisan Review* would like very much to have you do an English letter for them. There are things that news reports do not tell us. For instance, what's happening under the surface in the way of politics? Among the labor groups? What is the general mood, if there is such a thing, among writers, artists and intellectuals? . . . You can be as gossipy as you please and refer to as many personalities as you like . . . You can use your own judgment as to length. (*CO, XII*, p. 351)

The flexible guidelines and encouragement to draw on his own opinions was a particularly liberating way to connect with a guaranteed American audience of sceptical leftists. By the early 1940s *Partisan Review* had already established itself as an influential new journal of literary, cultural and political criticism and comment in the United States, functioning as a nursery for what eventually would be seen as a distinctive type, the New York intellectual. When Orwell's first 'London Letter' appeared in the March-April issue of 1941, *Partisan Review* was nothing like as powerful as it would later become, but publication in a journal whose contributors included Greenburg, Edmund Wilson, Mary McCarthy and Lionel Trilling was no small thing. *Partisan Review*'s high intellectual and literary standards and its avowed anti-Stalinism made it a politically engaged version of *Horizon* and it provided an important entry point for Orwell's writing and reputation into the United States. It also added a small extra income, the journal paying $11.00 per 'Letter' (ibid.).

Orwell included part of Greenberg's invitation in his first contribution, indicating perhaps that he was not quite certain what *Partisan Review* expected. He dealt in a matter-of-fact way with the political and social conditions of Britain, and, as with his *Inside the Whale* essays, when turning to more literary matters he kept his account focused on the sociological. He notes pertinently that 'the economic foundations of literature are shifting, for the highbrow literary magazine, depending ultimately on leisured people who have been brought up in a minority culture, is becoming less and less possible' (ibid., p. 355). He exemplifies this point by commenting that '*Horizon* is a sort of modern democratized version of this (compare its general tone with that of the *Criterion* of ten years ago), and even *Horizon* keeps going only with difficulty' (ibid.). Beyond the economic difficulties was the wartime transformation in thought and feeling noted by Lehmann, which also influenced what got printed and read:

> There is such doubt about the continuity of civilization as can hardly have existed for hundreds of years, and meanwhile there are the air-raids, which make continuous 'intellectual life' very difficult. (ibid.)

As well as the shrinking of the public sphere, the quality of debate and of creative work inevitably was suffering. As a group, the London Letters primarily were informative pieces rather than essays, addressed to an American audience eager to find out about political and occasionally cultural developments from an unofficial but reliable source, one whose political attitudes roughly equated with those of *Partisan Review*. The 'London Letters' were far less polemical, and less personal than his work for British periodicals. He clearly saw his task as keeping readers abreast of political and social developments so that they remained more reports from the frontline rather than the type of essays Orwell continued to produce for British journals.

His first 'London Letter' for 1942, published in the March-April number, was something of an exception. Ironically, he begins by commenting that 'At this moment nothing is happening politically in England' (*CO, XIII*, p. 107) before going to address a series of topics: Whom Are We Fighting Against? Our Allies; Defeatism and German Propaganda. The last of these would upset some *Partisan Review* readers, for he remarks that

> the really interesting development is the increasing overlap between Fascism and pacifism, both of which to some extent overlap with Left 'extremism'. The attitude of the very young is more significant than that of the *New Statesman* pinks who war-mongered between 1935 and 1939 and then sulked when the war started. (ibid., p. 110)

He also lashes the ILP for 'never clearly stating whether or not it "supports" the war' (ibid.) and 'the pacifist monthly the *Adelphi* (sic)' for accepting 'at its face value the German claim to be a "socialist" state fighting against "plurocratic" Britain' (ibid., pp. 110–11). Personalizing his attack, he names from 'the little anti-war newspaper *Now*' a list of pacifists who by their antagonism to all war aid the Germans. Presumably this was meant to prompt a response, and it did, under the title 'Pacifism and the War: A Controversy' in the September-October number (*CO, XIII*, pp. 392–400). D. S. Savage, George Woodcock and Alex Comfort vehemently denied the charges of aiding Fascism, mounting several ethical arguments for the neutrality of pacifism; Woodcock in particular strongly criticized Orwell's attack upon journals and political parties to which he had once belonged. Orwell's active defence of his own arguments and of his changing views was also printed. The 'Controversy' was not resolved, but it registers the type of vigorous and sometimes-vituperative debates promoted at times by periodicals. More obliquely, it shows how the 'Letters' introduced Orwell to an argumentative subsection of the American left intelligentsia.

Orwell's owns interactions with the reviews and periodicals that were functioning were deepening and widening. 'Fascism and Democracy' was the second essay to appear in the *Left News* (February 1941). Orwell spends most of the space examining the case for democracy, and the attacks upon it by Communists and Fascists. Where he had swiped wildly at the pervasive Communist press in his essays on the Spanish Civil War, in 'Fascism and Democracy' he also acknowledges the 'bolder methods of propaganda' of the Fascists. Whatever the differences between the two, however, Orwell considers that 'the basic contention of all apologists of totalitarianism is that Democracy is a fraud' (*CO, XII*, p. 376). He reviews the anti-democratic case, willing, he writes, 'to admit the large measure of truth it contains'. The primary arguments are simple enough: the opportunity to vote is 'negatived' he argues 'by economic inequality'; the monied class keeps all effective political and economic power (ibid.). He exposes another force in democratic nations, which he describes as the '[m]ost important of all':

> nearly the whole cultural and intellectual life of the community – newspapers, books, education, films, radio – is controlled by monied men who have the strongest motive to prevent the spread of ideas. The citizen of a democratic country is 'conditioned' from birth onwards, less rigidly but not much less effectively than he would be in a totalitarian state. (ibid., p. 377)

This judgement broadens Orwell's attack about the restriction of ideas. Previously, he largely directed his venom at the left-wing print media; in recognizing the conditioning carried out in democracies as well as in totalitarian states, he appears on the verge of a radical cultural critique. The key phrase in the preceding argument, however, is 'not much less effectively'. Orwell is willing to grant that democratic nations exhibit many of the negative aspects of their totalitarian counterparts: 'all government, democratic or totalitarian, rests ultimately upon force' (ibid.). Yet his central attack upon critics of democracy insists that their 'implied argument . . . that a difference of degree is not a difference' (ibid., p. 378). Differences of degree between the oppressiveness in totalitarian and democratic states are fundamental. While democracies condition their inhabitants, in Orwell's view they do so 'less effectively' than totalitarian regimes. In democracies a newspaper like the Communist *Daily Worker* might be suppressed, but it had been allowed to survive ten years, and its editors had not been liquidated as would have happened under a totalitarian regime. Refugees have not fled the British Empire; heterodox opinions can be expressed in pubs; nothing in recent

American or British history approximates the purges and pogroms the Soviet Union or Germany. 'Fascism and Democracy' itself could not be printed in a totalitarian nation. This exposes crucial differences of degree between the two forms of rule, leading him to the question that employs his yardstick for totalitarian oppression: 'How many people personally known to you have been beaten with rubber truncheons or forced to swallow pints of castor oil?' (ibid.).

The answer to the loaded question being obvious, Orwell can come down in favour of democracy over totalitarianism. He comprehends the threat posed by totalitarian regimes, arguing that Britain as it stands at the beginning of 1941 cannot hold out against German power. He advocates Socialist revolution as the only hope, one that takes account of the historical and cultural heritage of England. This he contrasts to the Soviet-dominated assertions of local Communists who act as 'mere publicity agents' for the Soviet Union:

> Instead of pointing out that Russia was a backward country from which we might learn but could not be expected to imitate, the Communists were obliged to pretend that the purges, 'liquidations', etc. were healthy symptoms which any right-minded person would like to see transferred to England. (ibid., pp. 380–1)

In the absence of a viable alternative party with an avowed revolutionary intent, the Communists dominated, Orwell judging that their actions may have spread defeatism, consequently helping Hitler. He proposes 'a real English socialist movement', one that

> will be both revolutionary and democratic. It will aim at the most fundamental changes and be perfectly willing to use violence if necessary. But it will also recognize that not all cultures are the same, that national sentiments and traditions have to be respected if revolutions are not to fail. (ibid., p. 381)

'Fascism and Democracy' prefigures part of the argument of 'The Lion and the Unicorn', published that month. It and 'Our Opportunity' were printed in Gollancz's *The Betrayal of the Left* in March 1941. Only 1,593 copies were printed of which '293 were assigned to the Left Book Club and 1,300 were for the public. A second impression appeared on 2 May; of its 1,050 copies, 450 were allocated to the Left Book Club' (*CO, XII*, p. 442). It seems likely, then, that a far larger audience read the essays in *Left News* than the chapters of *The Betrayal of the Left*, a book that signals a degree of accord between Orwell and Gollancz. It did not last, Gollancz later refusing *Animal Farm*. Orwell then requested to be let free of his contract with Gollancz, which the publisher accepted. Although neither knew it at the time, *The Betrayal of the Left* would be the last book Gollancz would publish with Orwell's work in it.

Essays in the *Left News* reconnected Orwell to Gollancz and to the Left Book Club, still a major element of political and cultural debate. 'The Lion and the Unicorn' opened a new venture, Searchlight Books, one of several attempts by publishers to stimulate the public sphere. As far back as 1937 'Penguin Specials' had published cheap topical books quickly and cheaply. Partly perhaps because they cost only sixpence, by 1939 'almost every political Special sold 100,000 [copies] in a matter of weeks and the most successful achieved a phenomenal quarter of a million sales in less than four weeks' (Morpurgo, p. 135). The Specials continued through the war, and drew writers from across the political spectrum: the Soviet sympathizer and Labour MP, D. N. Pritt, for example, produced *Light on Moscow*, while the Liberal MP Richard Acland's *Unser Kampf* argued for common ownership in Britain and a new international order. Gollancz published the fantastically successful *Guilty Men* (a withering attack on the duplicity of British rulers) that sold nearly 220,000 copies, prompting him to begin the 'Victory Books' series. One of them, *The Trial of Mussolini*, sold nearly 150,000 copies (Edwards, p. 393). The impressive sales of these works suggest a public keen to participate in ongoing debates over the current state of affairs and the post-war future.

Orwell's contribution with Tosco Fyvel was to edit Searchlight Books. Initially suggested by Fyvel in 1940, the series was published through 1941 and 1942 by Martin Secker and Warburg at a price of two shillings a copy. An advertisement stressed that

> the aim of Searchlight Books [is] to do all in our power to criticise and kill what is rotten in Western civilization and supply constructive ideas for the difficult period ahead. The books will be written in simple language without the rubber-stamp political jargon of the past. (cited in Crick, p. 273)

Fyvel remembers he suggested Orwell set the tone 'with an optimistic book about the future of a democratic socialist Britain' (Fyvel, p. 107), a suggestion which became 'The Lion and the Unicorn'. Seventeen books were planned, although only ten were published (Fenwick, pp. 163–5). Looking back, Fyvel gave a synoptic view of the rise and eventual demise of the series:

> For a moment in the increasingly harsh course of the war, the Searchlight books were much discussed and Warburg could regard them as a success. However, they were mostly published in the early part of 1941 and by the end of the same year of 1941, the optimistic era of the Searchlight books was in a sense already over. (Fyvel, pp. 115–16)

His comment illustrates the constant movements, realignments, successes and failures fashioning war-time literary and political production and discussion.

'The Lion and the Unicorn' consists of three sections – 'England Your England'; 'Shopkeepers at War'; 'The English Revolution' – broken into sub-sections. This format enables Orwell to roam freely while constructing a coherent argument. The essay begins and ends by acknowledging the importance of patriotism. In the first instance, though, the patriots are German enemies, 'highly civilized human beings, flying overhead, trying to kill me' (*CO, XII*, p. 392). Orwell accepts that the individual German pilot is doing his duty, by 'serving the country that has the ability to absolve him from evil'. This seeming magnanimity has a hidden dimension:

> One cannot see the modern world as it is unless one recognizes the over-whelming strength of patriotism . . . [A]s a *positive* force there is nothing to set beside it. Christianity and international Socialism are as weak as straw in comparison with it. Hitler and Mussolini rose to power in their own countries very largely because they could grasp this fact and their opponents could not. (ibid.)

This opening sets the strategy for 'The Lion and the Unicorn', for in 'England Your England' Orwell focuses on what differentiates England from other countries, what makes it worth defending. He rather casually uses England as a synonym for Britain, contending that the differences between the Scots, say, and the English, 'fade away' the moment 'they are confronted by a European' (ibid., p. 398). He is more justified in suggesting that the traveler returning to England from Europe registers that, for all the formlessness, '[t]here is something distinctive in English civilisation.' Despite the supposed inclusiveness, however, Scotland, Wales and Northern Ireland are shortchanged.

Orwell begins to tease out some of these 'national' characteristics, reintroducing ideas sketched out in 'My Country Right or Left'. The first aspects are decidedly banal: a lack of artistic talent and a love of flowers. Others, such as the belief in individual liberty, the lack of power worship in the working class and the belief in the rule of law, are more substantial, as is his assertion that 'the totalitarian idea that there is no such thing as law, there is only power, has never taken root' (ibid., p. 397). In the third section he concedes a less engaging characteristic of English society, its class system. Even this is not all-powerful, he judges, for '[p]atriotism is usually stronger than class hatred', and while middle-class patriotism might seem unsurprising, he sees it as also important for the working class, whose

> patriotism is profound, but . . . unconscious. The working man's heart does not leap when he sees a Union Jack . . . but the working class are outstanding in their abhorrence of foreign habits. (ibid., p. 399)

This statement contradicts the position put forward in 'My Country Right or Left', that 'it is exactly the people whose hearts have *never* leapt at the sign of the Union Jack who will flinch from revolution when the moment comes', but the qualification that working-class patriotism is unconscious fudges the issue.

Subsection iii ends with what would become a famous analogy of England as a stuffy Victorian family, one where 'most of the power is in the hands of irresponsible uncles and bedridden aunts . . . A family with the wrong members in control' (ibid., p. 401). The image allows him to tell some home truths about the more disreputable members of the family. He notes the general decline of the ruling class, uncles and aunts helpless against the new forms of totalitarian power. In Subsection iv he targets an unlikely set of twins, the imperialist middle class and the left-wing intelligentsia. These siblings exhibit signs of enervation: the imperialists, unable to retain power in a disintegrating empire; the intellectuals, reduced to adopting European theories and spouting negative critiques.

These 'relatives' are indicative of outmoded facets of English life. He also notes a new development, 'the upward and downward extension of the English middle class' (ibid., p. 407). The 'England Your England' segment ends with the highly contestable case that the past 20 years had witnessed the breakdown of class distinctions between the working and middle classes in terms of tastes and habits. Further, Orwell predicts erroneously, the war 'will wipe out most of the existing class privileges' (ibid., p. 408). These developments, he predicts, will not adulterate essential English features:

> England will still be England, an everlasting animal stretching into the future and into the past, and, like all living things, having the power to change out of recognition and yet remain the same. (ibid., p. 409)

'Shopkeepers at War' connects the broad social analysis of 'England Your England' and the call for an English Socialist revolution in the essay's final part. Having argued rather vaguely for the unity of England in 'Shopkeepers at War' Orwell takes a more politicized stance, exposing the deficiencies of England's economic organization, enabling him to fuse coherent patriotism and economic re-organization to produce an 'English Revolution'.

'Shopkeepers at War' is relatively brief, partly because Orwell has a relatively simple case to put: capitalism has failed; unless England institutes a planned economy along Socialist lines, inevitably it must face defeat by a planned economy based on Fascist ideology. The war has provided the necessary proof (remembering that Orwell is writing in 1940, when Germany seemed almost invincible), demonstrating that

> private capitalism – that is, an economic system in which land factories, mines and transport are owned privately and operated solely for profit – *does not work*. It cannot deliver the goods. (ibid.)

Orwell's specific point, though, is that German victories in Europe have 'proved that a planned economy is stronger than a planless one' (ibid., pp. 409–10). Accept this argument, and a dark future awaits unless a planned economy is instituted. Faced with an enemy organized on superior economic logic, England must adopt that logic or be conquered. But the national characteristics discerned in 'England Your England' decrease the likelihood that Germany's Fascist path would be taken. For Orwell, Socialism offers clear and far-reaching benefits, for 'only by revolution . . . [can] the native genius of the English people be set free' (ibid., p. 415). He emphasizes that such transformative freedom lies within reach, asserting that

> England has got to assume its real shape. The England that is only just beneath the surface, in the factories and the newspaper offices, in the aeroplanes and the submarines, has got to take charge of its own destiny. (ibid.)

The call to destiny invigorates the essay's final part, 'The English Revolution', a title meant to connect with other 'national' revolutions – the American, French and Russian versions most obviously. As the call to factories and offices signals, Orwell envisages a populist revolution that eradicates class barriers. The

> suffocating stupidity of left-wing propaganda [has] frightened away whole classes of necessary people, factory managers, airmen, naval officers, farmers, white-collar workers, shopkeepers, policemen. (ibid., p. 420)

War, however, 'has turned Socialism from a text-book word into a realizable policy' (ibid., p. 421) and without the transformation of England into a Socialist state, the war cannot be won. Orwell proposes a loose, six-point plan involving nationalization, income limitation and Dominion status for India. The specifics are less important than the general aim, which is to turn this war into a revolutionary war and England into a Socialist democracy. Emphasizing the populist tenor of his revolutionary message, Orwell claims to

> have deliberately included in it nothing that the simplest person could not understand and see the reason for. In the form in which I have put it, it could have been printed on the front page of the *Daily Mirror*. (ibid., p. 422)

This represents another clear case of Orwell tailoring his argument to his expected audience. Having said this, as Crick has pointed out, Orwell's proposal 'of a ten to one differential of *tax-free* income' would have created 'a far more stratified society than the one he lived in', showing that 'his amateur economics did not match his amateur sociology' (Crick, p. 407).

The essay ends by appealing to the reader's patriotism. Orwell claims that 'patriotism has nothing to do with Conservatism', that instead 'it is a devotion to something that is always changing and yet is felt to be mystically the same', almost exactly the words from 'My Country Right or Left'. The war strengthened his conviction in patriotism and the need for revolution, so that where the earlier essay ends defensively, 'The Lion and The Unicorn' concludes positively, Orwell declaring that

> by revolution we become more ourselves, not less . . . We must add to our heritage or lose it, we must grow greater or grow less, we must go forward or backward. I believe in England, and I believe that we shall go forward. (*CO, XII*, p. 432)

A decent number of readers agreed, so that more than 12,000 copies of the essay were published (Warburg, p. 15): sizeable in itself, though small by comparison with the figures for *Guilty Men*. At 64 pages it was the longest expression of Orwell's Socialist ideas, but it remains very much an essay, an attempt at a complex multidimensional argument, rather than a fully resolved plan.

Publication in book format by Secker and Warburg led to the unusual consequence that 'The Lion and the Unicorn' was reviewed soon after publication. Contemporary critical reception was mixed, several commentators acknowledging the provocativeness of the argument while disagreeing with the substance. Others were not so positive. Margaret Cole, considering six war-time pamphlets in *Tribune,* dismisses 'The Lion and the Unicorn' as 'too slight and hasty a sketch to be worth much, and [that] it contains some very half-baked remarks' (Cole, p. 14). Orwell's old friend Max Plowman did not let fraternal feelings cloud his judgement, writing in *The Adelphi* that 'Orwell's faith is based on a credulity so naive it seems almost cruelty to examine it' and calling the essay an exemplar of the 'ardent superficiality' of contemporary political thinking (Plowman, 1941, p. 249). Winifred Horrabin, writing in the radical Left periodical *The Plebs,* admits to finding the essay 'stimulating', but argues that while 'Orwell's chief merit is that he is very challenging . . . [h]is chief fault is that he over-simplifies' (Horrabin, p. 149). It received one of its most detailed and perhaps perceptive critique in *Partisan Review.* Written by editor Dwight Macdonald, the review appeared a year after the essay's publication in Britain, Macdonald arguing that

> In its virtues and in its defects, *The Lion and the Unicorn* is typical of English leftwing political writing. Its approach to politics is impressionistic rather than analytic, literary rather technical, that of the amateur, not the professional. (Meyers, 1975, p. 191)

Macdonald sees two main advantages of the essay's impressionistic approach: the inclusion of cultural observations most analytic theorists would exclude; and a '*human* quality [to the writing] . . . you feel it engages him as a moral and cultural whole' (ibid., p. 191). Yet, he notes counterbalancing defects, for

> if Orwell's scope is broad, it is none too deep; he describes where he should analyse, and poses questions so impressionistically that his answers get nowhere; he uses terms in a shockingly vague way; he makes sweeping generalizations. (ibid.)

As a sustained treatise it fails for Macdonald. But the very qualities he notes – its impressionistic approach, literariness, amateurishness, the discernable human voice – are central to the essay form. What are defects in one form are virtues in another. Read as an essay 'The Lion and the Unicorn' succeeds, working consciously to provoke and engage readers, its fragmentary, partial and impressionistic argument demanding a response. Horrabin suggests that it 'calls for another book in reply' and in this regard the essay had accomplished one task. Macdonald ends his review by applauding the Searchlight Book series for providing 'the ideal medium for political pamphleteering, more topical and pointed than a full-length book and yet offering enough space to go deeper than a magazines article' (Macdonald, p. 194). Although he finds fault with much of Orwell's argument he values the medium in which it appeared, suggesting that 'The time would seem ripe for a "Searchlight Series" of our own' (ibid.).

A series of short essays published in mid-1941 in the BBC magazine *The Listener* (which sold over 70,000 copies) provided another point of entry in cultural debate. Collectively they provide one sense of Orwell's take on the place and function of literature and criticism in wartime. In 'The Frontiers of Art and Propaganda', he surveys literary criticism in Britain over the preceding ten years, recycling arguments from 'Inside the Whale' and opinions expressed as far back as his 1936 review of Philip Henderson's *The Novel Today*. Indeed, he uses similar phraseology as that earlier piece, damning left wing writers such as Henderson, Christopher Caudwell and Edward Upward for looking on 'every book virtually as a political pamphlet' and Upward for asserting 'that books can be "good" only when they are Marxist in tendency' (*CO, XII*, p. 484). He also reprises the distinction made in 'Inside the Whale' between the aesthetic writers of the 1920s (Pound, Eliot, Joyce, et al.) and the 'didactic, political writers' of the 1930s (Auden, Spender, MacNeice, et al.). He softens his attack on the latter group, acknowledging that 'in a world in which Fascism and Socialism were fighting one another, any thinking person had to take sides . . . Literature had to become political' (ibid., pp. 485–6). While this appears to go against Orwell's stated case in 'Inside the Whale', a change of stance should by now come as little surprise. Orwell tempers his forgiveness by arguing that the imposition of political orthodoxy 'led for the time being into a blind alley' (ibid., p. 486). Nevertheless, he does see a benefit in the politicization of literature in the 1930s, in that the 'art for art's sake' orthodoxy of the 1920s has been undermined. The collapse of that position in turn reveals that

> propaganda, in some form or other lurks in every book, that every work of art has a meaning and a purpose – a political literary and religious purpose – that our aesthetic judgements are always coloured by our prejudices and beliefs. (ibid.)

No correct political or aesthetic path, no 'discoverable literary trend' is made manifest. Importantly, however, the understanding of the purpose behind art has the salutary effect of helping 'to define, better than was possible before, the frontiers of art and propaganda' (ibid.). This ability to define marks a necessary advance.

In the second published talk, 'Tolstoy and Shakespeare', Orwell modifies his argument somewhat by examining an essay in which Tolstoy attacks Shakespeare. While every work of art has an underlying purpose, reducing criticism to the analysis of these underpinnings creates fresh biases; Orwell denies that 'there is no such thing as an aesthetic judgement' (*CO, XII*, p. 491). Tolstoy's essay exemplifies the dangers. Orwell accepts Tolstoy's charge that Shakespeare was not a great thinker, that his plots often stretch plausibility, that his characters can be inconsistent. He counters, however, that while Tolstoy succeeds in demolishing Shakespeare as a thinker and teacher, and while Tolstoy undercuts whatever 'political, social and religious purpose' Shakespeare may have, Shakespeare survives. The reason, according to Orwell, is that Tolstoy ignores Shakespeare's gifts as a poet; and, as a poet Shakespeare remains inviolable:

> Evidently a poet is more than a thinker and a teacher, though he has to be that as well. Every piece of writing has its propaganda aspect, and yet . . . there has to be a residuum of something that simply is not affected by its moral or meaning – a residuum of something we can only call art. (ibid., p. 493)

In the third *Listener* essay, 'The Meaning of a Poem', Orwell attempts to study the interaction of aesthetics and social or political imperatives in a page-long piece of literary criticism. He deliberately selects 'Felix Randal', by Gerard Manley Hopkins, on the grounds that, in criticism on Hopkins, the *Listener* reader 'will usually find all the emphasis laid on his use of language and his subject-matter very lightly touched on' (*CO, XII*, p. 497). While accepting that in poetry criticism, 'it seems natural to judge primarily by the ear', Orwell declares that a poem is

> moving because of its sound, its musical qualities, but it is also moving because of an emotional content which would not be there if Hopkins's philosophy and belief were different from what they were. (ibid., p. 498)

He goes on to detail how much of the emotional content derives from Hopkins's Catholicism, made more potent by the decline of the English rural life Hopkins mourns in 'Felix Randal'. Orwell considers that while the poem synthesizes these elements, it is something more, 'a sort of growing together – of a special vocabulary and a special religious and social outlook. The two fuse together, inseparably, and the whole is greater than the parts' (ibid., pp. 498–9).

The final *Listener* piece was 'Literature and Totalitarianism' a version of which had also been spoken to the students at Oxford University (one of whom was Philip Larkin). As published, it summarizes the present condition of literature, and projects its future. If indeed it has a future, Orwell asking that if totalitarianism triumphs 'can literature survive . . . ? I think one must answer shortly that it cannot' (*CO, XII*, p. 503). Orwell makes the crucial assertion that 'this is not a critical age'. He notes the invasion of literature by politics, to the extent that it has become difficult to write 'honest, unbiased criticism': detachment has been replaced by partisanship. This decline in the vigour and integrity of criticism has vital implications for society generally and literature specifically. In social terms, the failings of criticism signal something broader and more ominous: 'We live in an age in which the autonomous individual is ceasing to exist' (ibid., p. 502). The functioning totalitarian state already 'does not and probably cannot allow the individual any freedom whatever'. Orwell continues:

> When one mentions totalitarianism one thinks immediately of Germany, Russia, Italy, but I think one must face the risk that the phenomenon is going to be world-wide. (ibid., p. 503)

The key word here is 'risk', for clearly the possibility remains that totalitarianism might not triumph globally.

He cautions that such states have 'abolished freedom of thought to an extent unheard of in any previous age' (ibid.). What sets totalitarianism apart, he thinks, is that while previous orthodoxies circumscribed thought, restricting individuals between restrictive but relatively stable boundaries, totalitarianism

> though it controls thought . . . does not fix it. It sets up questionable dogmas, and it alters them from day to day. It needs the dogmas, because it needs

absolute obedience from its subjects, but it cannot avoid the changes, which are dictated by the needs of power politics. It declares itself infallible, and at the same time it attacks the very concept of objective truth. (ibid., p. 504)

These ideas germinate in *Nineteen Eighty-Four* eight years later, but in 1941 Orwell sees real world parallels in the past, most clearly in the Nazi–Soviet pact of 1939, after which ordinary Germans, taught to 'regard Russian Bolshevism with horror and aversion' suddenly were asked to look upon the same regime 'with admiration and affection' (ibid.). Such external control of the emotions necessarily undermines the autonomy of the writer. In the decline of literature in Germany, Russia and Italy, Orwell detects the outward manifestations of the triumph of totalitarianism.

He assesses the complex, contested and changing relationships between literature and politics, which gets focused in 'Wells, Hitler and the World State', published in *Horizon* in August 1941. The essay begins with Orwell criticizing H. G. Wells' doubt over the importance of Hitler and the strength of the German military. Wells is wrong, Orwell considers, in being too sensible, too logical, so that he fails to appreciate that the

energy that actually shapes the world springs from emotions – racial pride, leader-worship, religious belief, love of war – which liberal intellectuals mechanically write off as anachronisms. (*CO, XII*, p. 538)

This attack on liberal intellectuals, of course, incorporates *Horizon* readers. Employing Wells as a generative figure means that Orwell can visit the sins of the father upon his children. Like Dickens, Wells is a nineteenth-century liberal, but living in the new totalitarian age has been unable to adapt his binary thinking:

On the one side science, order, progress, internationalism, aeroplanes, steel, concrete, hygiene; on the other side war, nationalism, religion, monarchy, peasants, Greek professors, poets, horses. History as he sees it is a series of victories won by the scientific man over the romantic man. (ibid., pp. 538–9)

Although written off as anachronisms by the likes of Wells emotional aspects such as nationalism and leader-worship are manifest. These emotions have been harnessed to the very forces Wells was confident would lead to the construction of an ordered, scientific and enlightened World State. The proof for Orwell lies in the fact that

[m]odern Germany is far more scientific than England, and far more barbarous . . . The order, the planning, the State encouragement of science, the steel, the concrete, the aeroplanes, are all there, but all in the service

of ideas appropriate to the Stone Age. Science is fighting on the side of
superstition. (ibid., p. 539)

The partiality of this argument is obvious: steel, concrete and aeroplanes are
neither the sole possession of Nazi Germany, nor the necessary consequence of
totalitarian organization. Science can work against superstition. Nevertheless,
Orwell's main point, that such elements can be employed in the service of
totalitarianism, actively challenges Wells' utopianism. Science, concrete and
steel might usher in tyranny.

Wells misjudges the importance and the allure of totalitarianism, yet Orwell
indicates that certain writers are equipped to understand the dangers: 'Trotsky,
Rauschning, Rosenberg, Silone, Borkenau, Koestler and others.' Significantly,
Orwell notes, none of these is English, but

> nearly all of them have been renegades from one or other extremist party,
> who have seen totalitarianism at close quarters and know the meaning of
> exile and persecution. (ibid., p. 538)

Orwell's brief time in Spain was his closest direct experience of anything like
totalitarianism, but as one who put great store in the eyewitness account, the
importance of such writers for Orwell is unsurprising. He argues towards the
end of 'Wells, Hitler and the World State' that 'the people who have shown the
best understanding of Fascism are either those who have suffered under it or
those who have a Fascist streak in themselves' (ibid., p. 540). Writers are ideally
placed to transmit that understanding to the public. Wells fails by continuing to publicize a view of totalitarianism based on outmoded generalizations:
'since 1920 he has squandered his talents in slaying paper dragons' (ibid.).
By the time 'Wells, Hitler and the World State' appeared in *Horizon* Germany
had invaded the Soviet Union. One day enemies of the West, the next day the
Soviets were lauded for their resilient courage. Orwell wrote disparagingly:

> [O]ne could not have a better example of the moral and emotional shallow-
> ness of our time, than the fact that we are all now more or less pro-Stalin.
> This disgusting murderer is temporarily on our side, and so the purges etc.
> are suddenly forgotten. (*CO, XII*, p. 522)

Not forgotten by Orwell, clearly.

Orwell began working for the BBC in the same month that his essay on Wells
appeared. The enormous new workload, coupled with his commitments to
Partisan Review, new associations with *The Observer* and *Tribune* from 1942, his
work on *Animal Farm*, and less substantial but no less time-consuming reviews
and articles for newspapers and journals, would limit the amount of time he
could spend on creative work and essays for much of the rest of the war. At the

end of his time at the BBC late in 1943 he described his time there to *Partisan Review*'s Philip Rahv as 'two wasted years' (*CO, XVI*, p. 22). This did not mean that he stopped writing essays. The month after 'Wells, Hitler and the World State' appeared *Horizon* published 'The Art of Donald McGill', an essay that connects back to 'Boys' Weeklies' in examining the neglected shelves of popular culture, and echoes the nostalgia and sentimentality that activated George Bowling's doomed attempt to recapture his youth in *Coming Up for Air*. Orwell analyses and celebrates seaside postcards, trying to understand the larger cultural relevance of these ephemeral artefacts. Its appearance only a month after the essay on Wells underlines Orwell's eclectic interests and Connolly's willingness to publish extended examinations of the seemingly trivial, if they were of sufficient literary merit.

As with 'Boys' Weeklies' Orwell treats the postcards seriously, as valuable sociological evidence of ideas and cultural forces at work in society. The postcards reflect and reinforce certain stereotypes and conventions (marriage only benefits the woman; all drunken men have optical illusions) that individually might be dismissed as crass, but that collectively, especially given how popular they are, suggest unconsciously accepted customs and attitudes embedded in the national culture. Orwell begins with the question 'Who does not know the "comics" of the cheap stationers' windows, the penny or twopenny coloured postcards with their endless succession of fat women in tight bathing suits?' But while he thinks the question 'ought to be rhetorical', many people are unaware of their existence. Among these, we can assume, would be many of the middle-class readers of *Horizon*, and just as he had prodded the periodical's liberal intelligentsia in the H. G. Wells essay, here he hints that the *Horizon* readers are missing something vital and illuminating. He actively prompts his audience to

> get a hold of these things . . . and spread them out on a table. What do you see?
> Your first impression is of overpowering vulgarity. This is quite apart from the ever-present obscenity, and apart also from the hideousness of the colours. (*CO, XII*, p. 24)

Presumably, many who did not read *Horizon* might not be overwhelmed by hideousness and vulgarity, but Orwell 'knows' the average *Horizon* readers. He aims to open them up to the novelty as well as to the vulgarity of the cards. We might read this approach as a small equivalent to that of *Wigan Pier*, where he brings back information for a largely innocent audience; here, ironically, the exotica is banal and easily available. As well as this introductory class in social anthropology, the essay constitutes a loose sociological investigation, replete with 'a rough analysis of their habitual subject matter, with such explanatory remarks as seem to be needed' (*CO, XVI*, p. 25). Their most important feature is 'their obscenity' (*CO, XIII*, p. 26), their open depiction of sexual desire in a way that would be impossible in other art forms save the music hall. And in their predilection for cartoonishly shaped women they offer not 'pornography, but a subtler thing, the parody of pornography', so that the female figures portrayed are 'caricatures of the Englishman's secret ideal', not the ideal itself. This essentially humorous take on desire lifts 'the lid on a very widespread repression' (ibid., p. 27) part of a more general 'low' form of comedy that has parallels in the music hall ribaldry of Max Miller. Both the postcards and music hall, of course, primarily are working class forms of entertainment, expressing an earthy and open attitude to life's hardships.

More generally, Orwell argues, the cards 'give expression to the Sancho Panza view of life', the 'little fat man who sees very clearly the advantages of staying alive with a whole skin' (ibid., p. 29). If there is a Sancho there must always be a saintly and heroic figure, a Don Quixote, and this prompts the vaguely existential question that 'If you look into your own mind, which are you . . .? Almost certainly you are both' (ibid.). This move from seaside postcards to classic literature brings the discussion more obviously into the realm of *Horizon* readers, but the specific example Orwell chooses validates the lowly figure over the deluded romantic. The postcards and the music hall, the essay suggests, 'are a sort of saturnalia, a harmless rebellion against virtue' (ibid., p. 30) suggesting that 'human beings want to be good, but not too good, and not quite all the time' (ibid.). In a time of war this might seem an irrelevant thought, but for Orwell the postcards suggest a human quality strikingly at odds with the totalitarian mentality that hunts down the vulgar and outmoded before eradicating it. We can read the cards as equivalents to Winston Smith's paperweight, just-surviving symbols, whose very existence offends the orthodoxy sniffers and has a subtle political import. For, as Shelden astutely observes, 'Winston Smith's attachment to his glass paperweight is a revolutionary act because it is the expression of an individual mind which is capable of being sentimental, unpredictable and willful' (Shelden, 1991, p. 389). Seaside postcards, on this reading, are equally subversive.

The role for writers generally in war-time Britain was ambiguous and troubled. Orwell's own activities in the early part of the war included fruitless attempts to sign up for military duties, editing the Searchlight Books series, work on *Animal Farm*, reviews and essays for periodicals, papers and magazine, work as a BBC Talks Producer and membership of the Home Guard. In an effort to clarify the place and value of writers in this charged environment Orwell supported a *Horizon* manifesto, 'Why Not War Writers' prepared by young writers 'both in the Forces, and in other work of national importance'. It appeared in the journal's October 1941 number. The young writers went unnamed, and the manifesto was 'published on their behalf' by established writers including Connolly, Arthur Koestler, Spender and Orwell. It aimed to publicize the argument that '[t]he role of writers to-day, when every free nation and every free man and woman is threatened by the Nazi war-machine, is a matter of supreme importance' (*CO, XII*, p. 44) calling the government to support literature. Proposing the formation of an official group of war writers, it argues that the 'international exchange of writers to be encouraged and accelerated' (ibid., p. 46). But the manifesto had no effect, Connolly describing it as '*Horizon*'s most lost of lost causes' (cited in Fisher, p. 220). A *Horizon* reader responded in derisive terms, and Connolly published the response. Adopting the neatly belligerent pseudonym 'Combatant', the writer – a soldier – assaults the 'preposterous document' and its authors (*CO, XII*, p. 47). Rather than forming official groups, 'Combatant' declares, the writers should fight, for though the 'atmosphere is uncongenial for writing . . . that is all to the good . . . Genius overcomes privation and inferiority'. He remarks acidly: 'I am afraid that I do not believe for a moment that these young men want to write: they want to be writers' (ibid.). Given the measured force and brilliance of this group character assassination Clive Fisher's revelation of 'Combatant''s identity does not surprise – it was Evelyn Waugh (Fisher, p. 221).

A Choice of Kipling's Verse, a collection put together and introduced by T. S. Eliot, provided the spur for Orwell's assessment. Kipling would likely be dismissed or abhorred by readers of *Horizon*, and while he critically examines Kipling's qualities he also castigates Eliot for misjudging those qualities, or for defending Kipling 'where he is not defensible'. Orwell states baldly that 'Kipling *is* a jingo imperialist, he *is* morally insensitive and aesthetically disgusting', and that '[i]t is better to start by admitting that, and then try to find out why it is that he survives while the refined people who have sniggered at him seem to wear so badly' (*CO, XIII*, p. 151). The 'refined people' are those amenable to *Horizon* readers (and possibly incorporate those readers), so that the essay performs a complex set of tasks: criticizing Eliot's defence of Kipling; passing judgement on Kipling's faults; castigating *Horizon* readers who dismiss Kipling without fully understanding him and analysing particular facets of Kipling's attitudes and writing that warrant reconsideration. The 1942 'Rudyard Kipling' has points of overlap with the brief 1936 essay written just after Kipling's death, most clearly in its examination of the 'vulgarity' of Kipling's work. In both essays Orwell notes that Kipling is a byword for badness, but he calls Eliot to task for trying to validate Kipling by labelling him a 'great verse writer' rather than a great poet. Orwell thinks it truer to describe him 'simply as a good bad poet'. What seems a damning phrase is more nuanced, for Kipling is 'as a poet what Harriet Beecher Stowe [the author] of *Uncle Tom's Cabin*] is as a novelist' (ibid., p. 158). Such good bad poetry (Orwell gives 'The Charge of the Light Brigade' as one example) can be seen as 'a graceful monument to the obvious. It records in memorable form . . . some emotion which nearly everyone can share' (ibid., p. 159).

Kipling's aesthetic qualities suggest the reason for his power, and are linked to his 'world-view, even though it happened to be a false one'. Kipling is no Fascist in Orwell's eyes because his Victorian perspective could not comprehend the power worship of totalitarianism. He was a Conservative in the antiquated sense of identifying with the British governing class, not financially but emotionally, a move that led him 'into abysses of folly and snobbery' (ibid., p. 160). Kipling's attitude to imperialism was also blind to the reality that imperialism is 'primarily a money-making concern. Imperialism as he sees it is a type of forceful evangelising' (ibid., p. 152). This reading of Kipling marks a substantial change from Orwell's 1936 analysis, but it also allows Orwell to launch a surprise attack on 'the middle-class Left' (including *Horizon* readers and Orwell himself) who, though they profess internationalist aims and an abhorrence of imperialism, live as they do in a system underpinned by exploitation, by 'robbing Asian coolies' (ibid., p. 153):

> A humanitarian is always a hypocrite and Kipling's understanding of this is perhaps the central secret of his power to create telling phrases. It would be difficult to hit the one-eyed pacifism of the English in fewer words than in the phrase, 'making mock of uniforms that guard you while you sleep'. (Ibid.)

For all his aesthetic vulgarity and his political deficiencies, then, Orwell thinks Kipling worth defending, although in a different way than from Eliot. Orwell's defence is moderated by a recognition of Kipling's shortcomings, but he ends the essay with a parting shot at its initial *Horizon* readers: '[even] his worst follies seem less shallow and less irritating than the "enlightened" utterances of the same period, such as Wilde's epigrams or the collection of cracker-mottoes at the end of [Shaw's] *Man and Superman*" (ibid., p. 160). Cyril Connolly, *Horizon*'s editor and himself a self-criticizing provocateur, might well have approved of Orwell's tactic here, even if he disagreed with the argument Orwell propounded. Certainly the essay operates as another instance of Orwell writing against the grain of a periodical's assumed audience.

If, as Orwell told Philip Rahv, his work for the BBC did constitute two wasted years, the series and programmes he produced brought him into contact with some of the major literary and critical figures of the day (one photo has him with T. S. Eliot, William Empson, Tambimuttu, Mulk Raj Anand and others). But it raised his public profile only in India, and, given the poor quality of radio reception, perhaps very little there. Soon after leaving the BBC late in 1943, he began work as literary editor of the leftwing weekly *Tribune*, a post that in time would establish his reputation as a perceptive and provocative writer and commentator. He had written occasional unpaid reviews for *Tribune* in 1940, when, as he recalled in 1947

> it was still a threepenny paper aimed primarily at the industrial workers and following more or less the Popular Front line which had been associated with the Left Book Club and the Socialist League [a radical Labour Party faction].

> With the outbreak of war its circulation had taken a severe knock, because
> the Communists and near-Communists who had been amongst its warmest
> supporters now refused to help in distributing it . . . After that *Tribune* passed
> out of my consciousness for nearly two years. (*CO, XIX*, pp. 35–6)

BBC work reacquainted him with *Tribune*, by which time it 'was an almost completely different paper . . . Its prestige among the BBC personnel was very striking', he observes, adding that 'it was one of the most sought-after periodicals,
not only because it was largely written by people who knew something first
hand about Europe, but because it was the only paper of any standing which
criticized the Government' (*CO, XIX*, p. 36). His new job for *Tribune* left him
'a little spare time', he explained to Rahv in the 'wasted years' letter, 'so I have
got another book under weigh which I hope to finish in a few months if nothing intervenes' (*CO, XVII*, p. 22). That book was *Animal Farm*, making the move
to *Tribune* massively consequential for his career and reputation.

As well as editing the literary section of *Tribune* from November 1943 until
February 1945, Orwell wrote reviews and occasional short pieces on topics of interest. The freedom to express his ideas and enthusiasms regularly
was given official sanction in his 'As I Please' column that he wrote from
December 1943. The first of what would eventually amount to 59 articles in
the first instance (Orwell resumed the column when he returned to *Tribune*
in 1946) welded together thoughts on anti-American sentiment, Fascism and
the largely forgotten writer Mark Rutherford in around 1,000 words. This
list suggests something of the column's format, although other pieces were
shorter and dealt with only one or two issues, or tackled an array of topics, as
in the one for New Years Eve 1943 which touched upon Hitler's war guilt, ugly
buildings and monuments, George Bernard Shaw's plan to rewrite the second
verse of the National Anthem, *Old Moore's Almanac* and Orwell's acquisition of
'Chronological Tablets' proving that the world was created in September 4004
BC (*CO, XVII*, pp. 45–7). As their title indicates, the columns are expressions
of Orwell's own interests, views and whims, although as Davison points out,
'from the outset . . . [columns] attracted letters from many readers' which
Tribune printed and to which Orwell replied. 'The result is a genuine dialogue'
(*CO, XVII*, p. 14) Davison suggests, with occasionally hot debate, such as the
first column on American soldiers that drew several agitated responses disagreeing and agreeing with Orwell's position. More substantially, his interpretation of James Burnham's *The Managerial Revolution* in January 1944 drew a
belligerent response from Burnham himself, who wrote that 'perhaps because
[Orwell] had not read my book, [he] makes a number of mis-statements of fact
on matters of some consequence' (*CO, XVII*, p. 62). Orwell responded forcefully to Burnham's response, ending with the barbed comment that 'We could
all be true prophets if we were allowed to alter our prophecies after the event'
(ibid., p. 64).

The first person pronoun is central to these pieces, and the original articles coupled with Orwell's responses did a great deal to fashion his profile among *Tribune* readers, Crick noting that the column 'gained him fame and notoriety throughout the Labour movement' (Crick, p. 444). He adds that without editor Aneurin Bevan's support 'Orwell (despite his growing fame) might not have lasted' (ibid., p. 446). But while the personal voice and the array of topics chosen by the author approximate the essay form, do the columns constitute essays? John Hammond suggests that they do, seeing them 'as a fascinating exercise in the now unfashionable genre: the causerie' (Hammond, p. 225), a form sometimes defined as 'a short, informal essay, often on a literary topic', or as a 'chatty article'. The fact of the causerie being out of fashion perhaps indicates that it has been superseded by the column, a term that better describes the form and tone of 'As I Please', which range well beyond the literary. 'Before "As I Please" came along,' Shelden observes usefully, any one of the 'stray thoughts' that made up the column

> could have been the beginning of a long essay, but only so many long essays can be turned out in an average year, and during that time a lot of stray thoughts can come and go without ever being captured on paper.

Should this seem to write off the columns as literary mayflies Shelden adds persuasively that ' "As I Please" allowed him to increase his catch in a dramatic way, and as a whole, the many columns he wrote for *Tribune* in the 1940s form a splendid monument to his literary powers and dynamic character' (Shelden, 1991, p. 388). 'Viewed in their entirety', Hammond writes, 'these short pieces are among the finest contributions to the English essays written in [the twentieth] century' (Hammond, p. 25). But the columns by their nature remained separated, and while they provide a detailed catalogue of Orwell's interests and responses to events, they are passing observations, enlightening at times but never building to a more sustained reflection. This is not damning criticism; they are what they are. But they are not essays.

A point of comparison illustrating this is 'Raffles and Miss Blandish', an essay that resulted from Dwight Macdonald's request for material for *Politics*, a new journal he set up in 1943 after leaving *Partisan Review* acrimoniously. Orwell was reluctant to supply anything political because of his established arrangement with *Partisan Review* but offered to write a cultural piece 'on the change in ethical outlook in the crime story during the last 50 years or so'. He explained that he had recently written a 'short thing for a French magazine [*Fontaine*] on the English detective story' and that this had prompted his interest in something more substantial that would compare British and American versions of the crime story. As with his earlier essays on popular culture 'Raffles and Miss Blandish' looks to discover the hidden depths and cultural markers usually left slightly undetected. The subject matter ostensibly sets this essay apart from

'Boys' Weeklies' or 'The Art of Donald McGill', for here the crime novels deal with different cultures and traditions: British (*Raffles*) and American (*No Orchids for Miss Blandish*).

The two novels suggest transatlantic differences, but they also register the social codes and expectations of two distinct times: the turn of the twentieth century in the case of E. W. Hornung's *Raffles* and the cusp late 1930s with James Hadley Chase's *Miss Blandish*. Orwell states that he is comparing the two 'for sociological purposes', particularly what they reveal about the 'immense difference in moral atmosphere . . . and the change in the popular attitude that this probably implies,' including the potential Americanization of British culture. Orwell had touched on this in 'Boys' Weeklies' in his discussion of the new 'he man' or 'tough guy' wielding a rubber truncheon, with (for him) the Fascist symbolism of that weapon. Here the comparison takes place in the essay itself, the world of Raffles explored as a way of highlighting the very different moral, cultural and political world reflected in *No Orchids for Miss Blandish*. So, where Raffles is a gentleman, exuding personal charm, and supposedly held to concepts and codes such as the need to observe 'good form', the world inhabited by Chase's characters is one in which might is right, where sadism and masochism are rife, and in which weakness is despised. The type of crime and their quantity are also indicative: Raffles is essentially a 'very petty' criminal, a thief, using charm and deft skills in a series of thefts, but the *Miss Blandish* criminals are machinegun-wielding thugs and sadists, insatiable and amoral, who delight in torture, rape and murder. This, to Orwell, points to an illuminating difference between British and American attitudes to crime, in that in the latter country, built rapidly on the capitalist model, 'success' is considered sufficient reason to ignore the means of origin of that success. If successful, the criminal is tolerated, even admired. In Raffles' world, certain things are simply 'not done', and when he is exposed as a criminal he 'belongs irrevocably to the "cohorts of the damned"' (*CO, XVI*, p. 348), and so does the only honourable thing available to an upper middle class Englishman – he dies in battle. No such expectation attends the criminals in Miss Blandish, who not only actively enjoy their perversion, but who draw their victims into the same mindset – Miss Blandish, having been brutally treated by the gangster Slim but unable to live without him, throws herself from a skyscraper when he dies.

The obvious differences in the moral worlds depicted have something to do with class (Raffles is a gentleman, Slim a common thug) and place, but also, as Orwell sees it, with distinct moral codes that reflect larger social changes between 1900 and 1939. The contemporary world is modelled by power, and *No Orchids for Miss Blandish*'s huge popular success derives from the fact that it 'is aimed at the power instinct, which *Raffles . . .* is not'. To some degree, the distinction comes from the differences between British and American societies, but Orwell reveals that Chase is English, and has merely absorbed the argot and atmosphere of American gangsterism. This suggests the attraction of American culture for British readers, part of a broader if low-intensity Americanization of Britain. But something looms larger, for *Miss Blandish*

> is a daydream appropriate to a totalitarian age. In his imagined world of gangsters Chase is presenting . . . a distilled version of the modern political scene, in which such things as the mass bombing of civilians, the use of hostages, torture to obtain confessions, secret prisons, executions without trial, floggings with rubber truncheons, drownings in cesspools, systematic falsification of records and statistics, treachery, bribery and quislingism are normal and morally neutral, even admirable when they are done in a large and bold way. (ibid. p. 355)

The hyper-extended list functions as an index of the scale and depth of the deprivations that Orwell argues have been normalized between the age of Raffles and Miss Blandish. In Chase's books, Orwell writes: 'Emancipation is complete. Freud and Machiavelli have reached the outer suburbs' (ibid., p. 356). The daydream and the nightmare become indistinguishable.

With a sad irony, Orwell's last published essay during the war was the April 1945 piece 'Anti-Semitism in Britain', which he contributed to the New York-based journal *Contemporary Jewish Record*, set up by the American Jewish Committee as part of its advocacy of Jewish interests generally. (Orwell would also contribute a piece on the 1945 British election to its successor, *Commentary*.) Presumably contacted by the journal, which had associations with *Partisan Review*, Orwell used the topic to present a personal take on the state and significance of anti-Semitism in Britain. The essay begins by establishing certain facts that prove there is no actual Jewish 'problem' in Britain, playing this reality against the general proposition that 'anti-Semitism is on the increase' in Britain, 'that it had been greatly exacerbated by the war, and that humane and enlightened people are not immune to it' (*CO, XVII*, p. 64). As with British citizens generally, Orwell had no sense, when he wrote the essay early in 1945, of the horrors soon to be exposed, although of course he was aware of Nazi persecution of Jews from 1933. He personalizes the essay's perspective by recounting a set of anti-Semitic remarks heard by him in the previous few years, adding that 'I could fill pages with similar remarks' (ibid., p. 65). For readers of *Contemporary Jewish Record* these comments probably, and regrettably, were unsurprising, Orwell revealing that when he has touched upon the subject in newspaper articles 'I have always had a considerable "come-back"' (ibid., p. 66) from readers challenging his views. The essay concentrates and comments on these entrenched and barely hidden attitudes rather than on any instances of actual physical abuse or institutional discrimination in Britain, Orwell being interested in a phenomenon that is irrational and internally inconsistent, but also persistent and pervasive. Anti-Semitism might require 'an ability to believe stories that could not possibly be true' (ibid.) (or be felt publically to be sinful and disgraceful) (ibid., p. 67) but it transcends class, even if expressed in different ways. The 'common man', he suggests, rationalizes the Jew as 'an exploiter', while those higher up the intellectual scale claim that the Jew 'spreads disaffection and weakens national morale' (ibid., p. 69). But these are merely variations on a theme.

While he notes examples of anti-Semitism, Orwell admits to having 'no hard and fast theory about the origins of anti-Semitism' (ibid.). He does, however, place it in the context of British cultural history, recognizing the 'perceptible anti-Semitic strain in English literature from Chaucer onwards' and adding that without leaving his chair he 'could think of passages which *if written now* would be stigmatized as anti-Semitic in the works of Shakespeare, Smollett, Thackeray, Bernard Shaw, H.G. Wells, T.S. Eliot, Aldous Huxley and various others' (ibid., p. 68). He mentions Dickens as one writer he would not put on that list, a curious omission given the controversial portrait of Fagan in *Oliver Twist*, but in line with his debatable argument in 'Charles Dickens' that Dickens 'shows no prejudice against Jews'. He had admitted in that essay that Dickens 'takes it for granted (*Oliver Twist* and *Great Expectations*) that a receiver of stolen goods would probably be a Jew, which at the time was probably justified' balancing this dubious piece of sociology with the claim that the 'Jew joke' never appears in Dickens, and that the great writer also 'makes a pious though not very convincing attempt to stand up for Jews' (*CO, XII*, p. 35). Unless they had read 'Charles Dickens' the essay – and even if they had – his absence from the roll call of anti-Semitic English writers might have troubled *Contemporary Jewish Record* readers. But Orwell accepts the prospect that his views will be rejected by the journal's readers, acknowledging that 'in this essay I have relied almost entirely on my own limited experience, and perhaps every one of my conclusions will be negatived by other observers' (*CO, XVII*, p. 69). This open admission does not weaken the essay's argument so much as expose its limitations, gaps and biases. It could apply to many of Orwell's essays, and indeed to the essay form itself, revealing the peculiar interactivity the essay promotes, the call to engage actively with arguments that, whether admitted or not, remain merely attempts at fashioning a position.

'Anti-Semitism in Britain' contains several openly provocative assertions, including that had intellectuals done what in Orwell's eyes is 'mischievous' work 'a little more thoroughly, Britain would have surrendered in 1940' and that because a large number of the disaffected intelligentsia are Jews, some claim that 'Jews are the enemies of our native culture and our national morale' (ibid.). This assessment hangs ominously in the air until Orwell deflates it with the follow-up statement that 'carefully examined, the claim is seen to be nonsense', but the essay as a whole suggests that in Britain the careful examination of anti-Semitism rarely takes place. Indeed the essay takes up this very point, arguing that 'one effect of the persecution in Germany has been to prevent anti-Semitism from being seriously studied' (ibid., p. 66). In this way the essay gestures beyond itself, for as well as admitting that his views might be rejected by other observers, Orwell argues that because there 'are almost no data on this subject' it 'needs serious investigation'. Yet that investigation cannot simply be an exercise in data collection and analysis. Any 'post-Hitler investigation of anti-Semitism' must begin not by 'debunking anti-Semitism, but by marshalling all the justifications that can be found for it in one's own mind or anybody else's' (ibid., p. 70). That line could have read oddly to the readers of *Contemporary Jewish Record*, but the strategy suggested obviously applies more readily to non-Jews. Orwell asserts that for him anti-Semitism is a manifestation 'of the larger disease loosely called nationalism', a view that sets up the ungainly final sentence: 'But that anti-Semitism will be definitely *cured*, without curing the larger disease of nationalism, I do not believe' (ibid.). This gloomy but realistic conclusion, placing anti-Semitism in the larger context of nationalism, argues the need for a study of the phenomenon but also hints at the difficulties until the problematic term 'nationalism' has been defined. The essay does not try to do so, but the topic of nationalism and its relation to patriotism would continue to trouble and stimulate Orwell.

The war years were largely a time of frustration for Orwell's ambitions as a fiction writer, but proved vital for his development as an essayist. The *Inside the Whale* collection announced him as an astute and independent critic, an inquisitive student of popular culture and an informed and provocative commentator on the fraught and immensely complex interactions between literature and politics that continued to morph and warp as the conflict played out. Contributions to *The Betrayal of the Left* along with essays such as 'My Country Right or Left' and especially 'The Lion and the Unicorn' helped cultivate and publicize his own take on the political situation and his always-evolving sense of what a democratic Socialist Britain might look like and require. His interest in what made British culture distinctive and worth defending and celebrating manifested itself in a rich miscellany of essays that looked back with clear-eyed nostalgia, around at underlying and often forgotten cultural forces at play, and forward to possibilities once the world had 'shaken itself into a new shape'. That phrase from 'Inside the Whale' often has been misinterpreted to suggest that Orwell was advocating Henry Miller's brand of quietism. But readers of the collection only had to read 'Charles Dickens' to see a far more active model of literary engagement. Miller's position was at best a temporary option, not a long-term strategy (Connolly's point about civilization temporarily being on the operating table takes a similar line). Orwell's substantial literary output, his work for the BBC and for *Tribune*, hardly suggest a writer withdrawing from the political fray, and while there is a definite move from the anti-imperialist, anti-war position of 1939, the war years saw him produce a more sustained argument for some form of revolutionary transformation. Orwell's belief that without such transformation Britain was doomed was disproved by the facts, a reminder that forceful, independent thought clearly expressed does not insure against error. Much of

Orwell's political work was fashioned in response to fresh changes, projecting into the short and medium term future, a situation that increased the likelihood of fallibility, but did not remove him from political engagement.

Despite the 'slaughter of the magazines' recorded by Hewison, and regardless of the undoubted difficulties that war created, it was also a period in which Orwell established substantial and sustaining connections with a range of periodicals, reviews and papers in Britain and the United States. Although he published no fiction during the war, essays and journalism materially improved his public profile, extended the number of periodicals in which he published and added to the range of topics addressed. As well as the essay collection *Inside the Whale* and his extended essay 'The Lion and the Unicorn', contributions to *The Betrayal of the Left* and the 'As I Please' columns in *Tribune* presented him as an engagingly independent left-wing commentator. Journals supplied diverse platforms for his arguments and interpretations. His *Horizon* work particularly displayed his abilities as an imaginative and incisive critic of literature and popular culture. Reports on conditions in Britain for *Partisan Review* opened a connection to the Left intelligentsia in the United States, as did occasional pieces for *Politics* and *Contemporary Jewish Record* (although the readership of these New York- based journals was relatively small). That said, the sheer variety of journals in which his essays appeared meant that while an assortment of people read his work, no individual was likely to have read all his essays; *Tribune* and *Partisan Review* spoke to different constituencies, and even in Britain few people read both *Tribune* and *Horizon*. There were overlapping subsets of readers but also discrete groups to which individual journals consciously catered. His work appeared in a complex, vital and interactive periodical culture of writers, journals and readers. This arrangement suited Orwell's eclectic and evolving interests as well as providing necessary income before, during and after his job at the BBC: his Payment book indicates, for example, that he earned £586 from articles and essays in 1944 (*CO, XVII*, p. 464). Periodicals gave him access to different audiences that for the most part he knew in advance and could address specifically. Consequently he was able to deliver energetic observations on the opportunities of Socialist revolution to *Left News*, subtle and amused readings of seaside postcards to *Horizon*, a provocative take on trends in modern crime fiction for *Politics* and a personal evaluation of anti-Semitism in Britain for the audience of *Contemporary Jewish Record*. Examples such as these signal the broadening range of subject matter Orwell dealt with from different zones of literature, culture and politics. In many cases their only real connection was his interlaced enthusiasm. His politically engaged and sharply focused essays of the late 1930s had been supplemented by new concerns and interests, some (such as 'Marrakech' and 'Raffles and Miss Blandish') prompted by periodical editors. Orwell produced distinct types of essays depending on the subject matter and the expected audience, from the vigorous polemic to the measured account of social conditions, from extended literary-sociological analysis to detailed personal takes on ignored or commonplace cultural artefacts. By war's end, despite having published no fiction, he had a far greater claim to the label 'man of letters' that Q. D. Leavis had proposed for him in 1940. Tosco Fyvel, who had helped Orwell edit the Searchlight series before heading off to war, registers this change, noting that when he left to fight Orwell 'was becoming an established writer and journalist' but that Fyvel returned after two years in 1945 to discover 'what a leading essayist and journalist he had become' (Fyvel, p. 129).

Chapter 4

Orwell and the Uncertain Future
(1946–50)

By the time the conflict ended Orwell had left his job as Literary Editor for *Tribune* and was in Europe as a correspondent for *The Observer* and the *Manchester Evening News*, obtaining and transmitting a necessarily limited but still highly informative eyewitness accounts of the physical devastation and of emerging political and ideological forces. His own views had changed more than once since 1939, and the surprise electoral victory of the Labour Party in July 1945 once again transformed the political habitat. As he wrote in a November 1945 piece for the American journal *Commentary* (the successor to *Contemporary Jewish Record*): 'So far as I know, not a soul in England foresaw any such outcome. Before the election my own forecast had been a small Tory majority' (*CO*, *XVIII*, p. 335). He added that although the result revealed a national drift leftward '[i]t would be absurd to imagine that Britain is on the verge of violent revolution, or even that the masses have been definitely converted to Socialism'. By late 1945 Britain was governed by a party ostensibly committed to nationalizing key industries and utilities, proposals close to many of Orwell's own views, and while he never abdicated his role of caustic critic, he remained in general a supporter of its actions. Democratic Socialism might be achieved through the ballot box rather than through revolution. What had not changed was his sense that a totalitarian future, while not inevitable, was still possible. The defeat of Fascism did little to neutralize this fear, given his long-term antagonism to the Soviet Union and his view that sections of the Left intelligentsia were still susceptible to 'Russian' totalitarianism. The need to undermine the mythology of the Soviet Union and combat the threat of totalitarianism had become more prominent, more pressing, and it proved a dominating theme in the post-war years.

The end of the Second World War marks a slightly arbitrary boundary by which to consider Orwell's work. Some of his 'postwar' writing (most obviously *Animal Farm*) was completed while the war ground on to its cataclysmic end in Hiroshima and Nagasaki. But the cessation of war did have particular relevance for Orwell's career: it meant that when *Animal Farm* was published in August 1945 in Britain (it was not published for another year in the United

States) the war-time alliance with the Soviet Union already was being questioned; publication roughly coincided with the first substantial period of left-
wing rule in Britain; the dropping of the atom bombs on Japan prompted
the reconfiguration of the balance of political, military and economic power.
From the middle of 1945 people and nations began experiencing the emerging 'cold war', a term Orwell coined in his essay 'You and the Atom Bomb'.
While the end of the 'hot war' signalled the termination of old political hos-
tilities and the readjustment to implicit new ones, politics was not enveloping,
and Orwell continued to examine the less momentous aspects and pleasures
of life: the competing attractions of cigarettes and books; the decline of the
English murder. Nevertheless the potential suppression of original literature
and the control of language remained a genuine concern.

The war had started disastrously for periodical culture with the winding up
of many influential journals (most notably *Criterion*), but despite the tough economic and cultural pressures during the war that toughened up many which
managed to survive, so that there was no 'slaughter' of magazines at the end
of the war comparable to its beginning. Even so, the pressures on periodicals
in the post-war period still were considerable, as Orwell revealed in a letter
to Dwight Macdonald about a new British venture, *Polemic*. Orwell explained
that

> they only did 3,000 of the first number. The second number will be 5,000
> and they hope to work it up to 8,000, but they can only become a monthly by
> stealth. One is not allowed to start new periodicals [because of paper short-
> ages] but you can get hold of a little paper if you call yourself a publisher,
> and you have to start off by pretending that what you are publishing is a book
> or pamphlet. (*CO, XVIII*, p. 12)

War-time rationing was still in operation across most sectors of economic and
cultural life, severely constraining the potential for new and unorthodox views
to enter the public arena. New journals such as *Polemic, Gangrel* and *Politics and
Letters* were established in the post-war years, and Orwell wrote for them and
for others. But it says much for the tough environment of the period that none
survived more than a few years.

1945 proved momentous for Orwell in two strikingly different ways – his
wife Eileen died unexpectedly in March, and *Animal Farm* was published
in August. While the first of these was personally shocking, the later event
proved critical to the rest of his career and to his posthumous legacy, transforming him (especially once the book was published in the United States)
from a respected but marginal British writer to an international literary
figure. The postwar period in some ways can be seen as bookended by the
two fictions (*Animal Farm* and *Nineteen Eighty-Four*) that ensured Orwell a
global following for decades to come. But in the five years between those

works Orwell published some of his most enduring and representative essays, including 'Notes on Nationalism', 'Politics and the English Language', 'Why I Write', 'The Prevention of Literature', 'Thoughts on the Common Toad' and 'Reflections on Gandhi'. Each was published in a different periodical, demonstrating his broad reach as well as the recognized quality of the work. Graham Good makes the illuminating if contestable claim that '[t]he effect of the war years and their immediate aftermath was clearly to make the essay his main form of expression' adding that Orwell's 'production in it certainly bears the pressures of the time and its issues' (Good, p. 152). One purely pragmatic reason for the sustained production of essays was that from 1945 until his death in 1950 Orwell was ill or hospitalized for long periods, making it close to impossible to begin major novels he had planned. *Nineteen Eighty-Four* was the notable exception to this, but as all his biographers have recorded, and as his own correspondence makes plain, that novel – begun in 1945 and not completed until 1949 – was written under enormous physical hardship. That said, his established facility as an essayist and the essay's flexibility, which allowed him to write on political language, toads and Gandhi, continued to make it a hugely attractive form. Essays in fact made up the third book Orwell published in the post-war period – *Critical Essays* – a collection whose variety and excellence established him on both sides of the Atlantic as one of the most interesting contemporary essayists.

Orwell began planning *Critical Essays* in 1944. Fenwick records that in January 1945 'he sent the manuscript to Leonard Moore, except for the essay, "In Defence of P.G. Wodehouse", which he completed and sent off by early February' (Fenwick, p. 244). Due to various delays – including lack of paper – Secker and Warburg did not publish *Critical Essays* until February 1946, by which time the Wodehouse essay had already appeared (July 1945) in *The Windmill,* initially edited by Kay Dick (who went under the pseudonym of Edward Lane) and Reginald Moore. As Jefferson Hunter explains, *The Windmill* initially appeared as a one-off miscellany published by Heinemann in 1923, the next number under that title not appearing until 1944. Orwell's essay was published in the second (1945) number, after which *The Windmill* came out three or four times a year until 1948. This rather casual publication schedule is in line to some degree with an 'Argument' that led off the second number, Hunter noting that it committed the journal 'only to catholicity – the encouragement of diverse points of view and interests, as expressed by known and unknown contemporary writers'. Hunter adds that

> *Windmill* sought to avoid the tendentiousness, aesthetic theorizing, and political factionalism characteristic of so many little magazines of the forties. It was deliberately bookish and somewhat old-fashioned, in the tone of the best-known essay to appear in its pages, George Orwell's 'In Defence of P.G. Wodehouse'. (Hunter, p. 500)

Orwell had reviewed Wodehouse's *My Man Jeeves* for the *New English Weekly* nearly a decade earlier, but his defence of the famous comic writer was prompted by the massive political changes since then. Wodehouse had been living in Belgium when the Second World War began, been captured by the advancing Germans in 1940, interned, and then taken back to Germany. The following year he made a series of radio broadcasts that for many in Britain showed he was collaborating with the Germans or was a Fascist sympathizer. Wodehouse was heavily criticized in the British press and in parliament; some libraries withdrew his books, and the BBC for a time banned his lyrics. 'In Defence of P.G. Wodehouse' opens with a quick account of the facts of the writer's situation, along with a summary of the evidence against him, before Orwell begins to make the case that 'the events of 1941 do not convict Wodehouse of anything other than stupidity' (*CO, XVII*, p. 53). He develops this argument by examining Wodehouse's novels for Fascist tendencies and by arguing that the writer's attitudes and actions reflect a mindset locked in conventions and assumptions that far predate the Fascist ascendancy.

To a point 'In Defence of P.G. Wodehouse' resembles Orwell's analysis of Rudyard Kipling, for although he remains critical of Wodehouse's general position, he views him as a writer whose work reveals some larger insights into aspects of British culture. Rather than simply dismiss or denigrate Wodehouse and his work, Orwell tries to divine what those aspects might be, in the way that he treated Kipling's verse, seaside postcards and boys' weeklies as indicative of powerful conservative forces. Much of the essay examines Wodehouse's novels, breaking them into 'three fairly well-marked periods' (ibid., p. 54): the school-story period, beginning in 1902; the American period (prompted by Wodehouse living in the United States from 1913 to 1920); and the country-house period, from the 1920s onwards. The first group celebrates and does not advance much beyond the English public-school system, the second shows how Wodehouse became 'Americanised in idiom and outlook' (ibid., p. 55) while the third (especially the Jeeves and Wooster novels) in part explores the 'comic possibilities of the English aristocracy' (ibid., p. 57). Orwell develops two important lines of argument from this: that Wodehouse is no satirist of the English – 'no one who genuinely despised titles would write of them so much' (ibid.) – and that Wodehouse characters, and indeed many of the books that made him famous, represent a world frozen in 1915 at the latest. The first point has several consequences, for it disputes the accusation that Wodehouse's broadcasts reinforce the anti-British sentiment of his novels, and suggests how Wodehouse might be misinterpreted by those unable to comprehend the nuances of his comic approach. More importantly for Wodehouse's defence, his most famous creation Bertie Wooster inhabits an Edwardian world (even when the setting is more modern) and that 'Wooster, if he ever existed, was killed around 1915' (ibid., p. 59). Here the argument connects to that presented in 'Boys' Weeklies', 'Rudyard Kipling' and 'Raffles and Miss Blandish',

which present a set of codes that are substantially different to those dominating the totalitarian age. Wodehouse essentially remains a comedian foolishly
playing for laughs in a time of grave danger, a political naïf, a puppet for the
cynically manipulating German propaganda machine and someone unable to
fathom the new world order at play.

For Orwell, as a consequence, Wodehouse's mentality made it 'untenable
and even ridiculous' that he 'consciously aided the Nazi propaganda machine'
(ibid.). He asks rhetorically: 'how could he fail to grasp what he did would be a
big propaganda score for the Germans?' Part of the answer lies in Wodehouse's
political innocence, the other in an intriguing reading of the British public's
attitude to political developments in the late 1930s and early 1940s. Orwell
judges that the 'bulk of the British people' were 'anaesthetic' to the ideological struggle against Fascism in the 1930s:

> Abyssinia, Spain, China, Austria, Czechoslovakia – the long series of crimes
> and aggressions had simply slid past their consciousness or were dimly noted
> as quarrels occurring among foreigners and 'not our business' . . . [T]he
> ordinary Englishman thought of 'Fascism' as an exclusively Italian thing and
> was bewildered when the same word was applied to Germany. (ibid.)

As with so many of Orwell's contentious generalizations the impossibility
of proving the proposition right or wrong generates an argumentative tension, but his main point is that whereas the war itself rapidly focused the
attention of the British public from late 1940, Wodehouse was at that point
interned, and so had no awareness that the war had 'reached its desperate
phase' (ibid., p. 60). His remarks, then, were doubly innocent, the combination of a fundamental lack of a political consciousness and an ignorance of
new conditions.

This larger sense of the context in which Wodehouse made his comments
and in which they were received in Britain prompts a broader reading of why
'a few rather silly but harmless remarks by an elderly novelist' (ibid.) provoked
such hostility. Orwell compares those remarks with the powerful and then
still-developing myth of the war as one 'which the common people had to win
by their own efforts' (ibid., p. 61). In this environment

> [t]he upper classes were discredited by their appeasement policy and by the
> disasters of 1940, and a social leveling process was taking place. Patriotism
> and left-wing sentiments were associated in the popular mind, and numer-
> ous able journalists were at work to pull them together. (ibid.)

One of those, he might have added, was George Orwell, although his own
version of patriotism and left-wing sentiment in 'The Lion and the Unicorn'
was more sophisticated than a simple social levelling. Given these conditions,

though, Wodehouse's foolish statements made him 'an ideal whipping boy', a rich writer when 'it was generally felt that the rich were treacherous' and a figure for distracting attention from real parasites such as the press baron Lord Beaverbrook. Orwell's belief that the continued hounding of Wodehouse for undoubtedly lamentable acts distorts an awareness of the truly treacherous feeds into a final barrage, that 'if we really want to punish the people who weakened national morale at critical times, there are other culprits who are nearer home and better worth chasing' (ibid.). By failing to name those culprits, the essay consciously prompts readers to consider possible candidates, but the upper classes loom large. Kay Dick would later try unsuccessfully to procure other contributions to *Windmill* from Orwell (*CO, XVII*, p. 290), although a more interesting consequence of 'In Defence of P.G. Wodehouse' (whom Orwell met while a war correspondent in Europe) was that Wodehouse would write thanking Orwell for his support. There was a final twist: after Orwell's death Wodehouse complained about what he saw as Orwell's falsification of facts 'to make a point' (*CO, XVII*, p. 63).

The publication of *Animal Farm* in August 1945 was the first of the two great changes in Orwell's reputation, the other of course being *Nineteen Eighty-Four*. Given the fiction Orwell had written up until then, *Animal Farm* is an oddity. Its fusion of allegory and fairy story marks a substantial departure from the comic bumbling of George Bowling or the unrelenting cynicism of Gordon Comstock. Yet, while it might easily and instructively be read to young children, it created more problems for Orwell than any of his realist novels for adults. The difficulties getting *Animal Farm* published during the Second World War when its suposedly anti-Soviet message was thought to be problematic added to Orwell's sense of how unorthodox ideas could be delayed and potentially eradicated, as had been true with *Homage to Catalonia*. The convoluted story of *Animal Farm*'s publication needs no rehearsing here, except to note the reality that writers did not need to live in outwardly totalitarian nations to experience totalitarian pressures. Orwell's fear from the late 1930s – captured in essays such as 'Inside the Whale' – that a British form of Fascism was at least possible and perhaps under certain circumstances likely seemed once again enacted in *Animal Farm*'s rejection on political rather than aesthetic grounds.

Ironically, although it was published to wide and almost immediate acclaim in Britain, and although its clarity and political insight were praised (reviewers seeming sure that they fully understood its vivid simplicity), Orwell's friend and former BBC colleague, the brilliant literary critic William Empson, warned him that 'you must expect to be misunderstood on a large scale about this book; [allegory] is a form than inherently means more than the author means, when it is handled sufficiently well' (cited in Crick, p. 492). Empson's caution was well-founded, for readers can too easily fall into a two-level model for reading allegory, in which once the surface narrative has been connected to a subterranean equivalent, the search for alternative interpretations halts. Episodes or

characters that are difficult to fit into the supposed reference points of the text
are discarded or downgraded. For *Animal Farm* this means only recognizing or
validating Soviet parallels, ignoring the fact that an allegory on the betrayal of a
revolution which has a major figure named Napoleon, occurs on Midsummer's
Eve in England, has a unifying song 'with a stirring tune, something between
"Clementine" and "La Cucuracha"' (*CO, XVIII*, p. 7) – that roughly alludes to
Shelley's 'To the Men of England' – might have references, subtleties and ambiguities beyond the obvious.

An overt criticism of intellectuals plays a crucial part in *Animal Farm*'s critique: not only are the ruthless and power-obsessed pigs the self-proclaimed
'brain workers', but the refusal by Benjamin – the only other animal who can
read – to reveal the adulteration of the Seven Commandments constitutes a
crucial failure by a figure who is not part of the ruling elite. Orwell had regularly criticized intellectuals from at least as far back as *Wigan Pier*, especially
those on the Left who he felt were power hungry, self-serving and slavishly
devoted to the Soviet model of Communism that he abhorred. Intellectuals,
however, need not support the Soviet Union as such to attract his denigration.
What was reprehensible was intellectual dishonesty, as he saw it. But in the
post-war period especially, the prominence of the Soviet Union as a global –
and, for Orwell, a totalitarian – power, coupled with its continuing attraction
for certain sections of the British (and American) Left made them the primary
target for many of his most forceful attacks.

A year after he completed *Animal Farm* in May 1944, but several months before
it was printed, Orwell had written 'Notes on Nationalism' for the first number
of *Polemic*, a periodical edited by his friend Humphrey Slater. Orwell would later
suggest to *Partisan Review*'s Philip Rahv that Slater replace him as the author
of the 'London Letter' (*CO, XVIII*, p. 397). The philosopher A. J. Ayer, whom
Orwell met in Paris while working as a war correspondent and with whom he
became close friends – Ayer also happened to be another old Etonian who had
written for *Horizon* – also contributed four times to the journal's eight issues. As
before, the relatively small but interactive networks to which Orwell was connected gave him the opportunity to expand his cultural and political reach and
gave him access to journals that enabled him to publicize his views. Slater had
been a Communist, but *Polemic*'s political stance essentially reflected his rejection of that ideology. As Ayer recounts, Slater's 'political position was similar to
that of George Orwell. [Slater] had, however, developed a greater interest in
philosophy than in politics and sought to make *Polemic* as much a philosophical
as a political or literary magazine' (Ayer, p. 300). John Newsinger notes that

> The editorial in the first issue emphasized that the journal's intention was
> not to 'indoctrinate the public with any ready-made ideological system' but
> rather to emphasise 'the value of an exchange of different opinions . . . that
> from conflict of opinion truth arises.' (Newsinger, p. 142)

These values roughly equate to the essay's general approach and to the public sphere's activation of debate through periodicals. *Polemic* itself specified interest in

> four crucial areas in which it proposed to intervene: (1) The discovery of the Unconscious; (2) The evolution of the problem of verbal meaning; (3) The success of Marxism; (4) The fundamental significance of the arts. (ibid.)

While Orwell's direct interest in the discovery of the unconscious was negligible, he had obvious concerns with the other advertised areas. Stefan Collini observes that *Polemic*'s aspiration was to 'occupy the classic space of the "general" or non-specialist intellectual periodical', and he quotes from the second editorial, which declared: 'From the beginning our intention was to print essays about ideas, written from a more general point of view than that of the popular sciences or of politics' (Collini, p. 396). By the third issue *Polemic* had acquired a subtitle – *A Magazine of Philosophy, Psychology and Ethics* – that advertised its scope. As such it was notably different from journals such as *Horizon* or *New Writing*, where literature and culture more generally were the principal topics of interest. There were points of overlap – Henry Miller and Stephen Spender contributed to the first number – along with Orwell, but so also did the philosophers Bertrand Russell (who wrote on Logical Positivism), C. E. M. Joad and Ayer, who supplied an essay on 'Deistic Fallacies' (Ayer, p. 300).

Orwell's commitment to *Polemic* was more substantial than that to any other journal in the post-war period. By July 1945, before the first number appeared, he had signed a contract for another four essays and in May 1946 would write the journal's third editorial. In an April 1946 letter to his old Eton tutor Andrew Gow (who had also taught Ayer) written after the second number he admits that 'I have great hopes that it will develop into something good. Bertrand Russell is of course the chief star in the constellation' (*CO, XVIII*, p. 242). Orwell's five essays for the journal would make him its major contributor, ahead of Ayer and Russell. He eventually (1947) joined its Editorial Board with Ayer, Russell and others (Ayer in Hahn, p. 22). He did more than just provide content, Collini judging that

> Orwell and Ayer, in particular, did much to set the tone, and the magazine developed a distinctive identity – in favour of a cool, liberal rationalism, sympathetic to science, hostile to the intellectual manifestations of romanticism, and markedly anti-Communist. (Collini, p. 396)

Given its motivating ideas and its main contributors, Orwell's association with the journal challenges the view that he was irrevocably opposed to intellectuals per se. His ongoing connections to other 'highbrow' journals and figures such as Connolly, Koestler and Macdonald bolster this counter-argument.

Still, Orwell's attacks upon certain classes of intellectuals were unrelenting and potentially distorting.

Polemic's brief as a magazine of ideas meant that it offered contributors space in which to develop their own arguments. Orwell's first contribution, 'Notes on Nationalism', extends points he had made in such war-time essays as 'My Country Right or Left' and 'The Lion and the Unicorn'. In these earlier pieces he compared patriotism with nationalism, proposing that while the latter involved the celebration of one's native culture and the denigration of another to the point of potentially trying to impose your own system upon it, patriotism was essentially defensive, operating as an awareness of and allegiance to a nation's ongoing cultural identity. The title 'Notes on Nationalism' advertises an essayistic incompleteness, and Orwell employs the word 'Nationalism' in an ambiguous and potentially confusing manner. He begins obliquely by drawing on a thought advanced by Byron 'somewhere or other' that while the English language has no equivalent for the French term '*longueur*' the thing itself exists 'in profusion'. This opening allows Orwell to consider a comparable 'habit of mind which is now so widespread that it effects our thinking on nearly every subject, but which has not yet been given a name' – nationalism (*CO, XVII*, p. 141). Admitting from the outset that he is 'not using it in quite the ordinary sense' he adds that nationalism can be employed positively or negatively, to argue for or against a nation, an idea or a movement. This identification with a particular position entails 'placing it beyond good and evil and recognizing no other duty than advancing its interests' (ibid.). Orwell distinguishes nationalism from a defensive patriotism, asserting that nationalism 'is inseparable from a desire for power'. As such it is not confined to a specific set of beliefs or zone of human activity but can encompass 'such movements and tendencies as Communism, political Catholicism, Zionism, anti-Semitism, Trotskyism and Pacifism' (ibid., p. 142). This capacious list of potential forms of nationalism uncouples the term from any ideology, religion or philosophy, linking it instead to a habit of mind that surrenders the potential for critical and self-critical thought for the sake of insistent dogma, the very opposite of *Polemic*'s attempt to sponsor truth through the conflict of opinion. Essentially, Orwell argues, 'Nationalism is power-hunger tempered by self-deception' (ibid.). We might see in this formulation the rudiments of Party control in *Nineteen Eighty-Four*. Even so, the oddity of labelling power-hunger tempered by self-deception as 'nationalism' creates an unresolved ambiguity in the essay, if only because the term has obvious value in terms of nations rather than simply to potentially transnational movements and tendencies. Ayer judges that Orwell in this essay understands ' "nationalism" in the broad sense in which it covered uncritical devotion to any sort of creed' (Ayer, p. 300), which might suggest that 'partisanship' or 'bias' would be adequate substitutes. But these terms perhaps do not in themselves carry sufficient ballast to convey the large-scale adherence Orwell thinks that 'nationalism' conveys.

Adding to the tendentiousness of the essay's argument, Orwell makes a series of large claims: 'I think it will be admitted that the habit of mind I am talking about is widespread among the English intelligentsia, and more widespread there than among the mass of the people' (*CO, XVII*, p. 142). As we might now expect, no evidence is produced to substantiate the accusation, nor the followup declarations that '[a]mong the intelligentsia it hardly needs saying that the dominant form of nationalism is Communism' and that 'obviously such people abound and their direct and indirect influence is very great' (ibid., p. 144). The question of Communist influence in postwar Britain is complex, as two conflicting examples show: in parliamentary terms the Communists had polled poorly in the 1945 election, receiving less than half a percent of the popular vote, while around the same time Communist double agents such as Kim Philby and Donald McLean were advancing towards the top of British intelligence. As we will see, Orwell's target in the essay is not specifically Communism, and he admits that 'other forms of nationalism also flourish'. In fact he declares that 20 years earlier Catholicism was the dominant form of nationalism. His key purpose remains exposing the general habit of mind that he sees as fundamental to nationalism.

His definition of nationalism comprises three 'principle characteristics': obsession, instability and indifference to reality. Obsession, not surprisingly, involves the adherent only ever thinking, talking or writing about 'anything except the superiority of his own power unit' (ibid., p. 145). G. K. Chesterton's Catholicism provides an example from a previous age. Instability involves the capacity of the nationalist to transfer allegiance from one idea to another without any loss of intensity, so that bigoted Communists can become bigoted Trotskyites or bigoted Fascists in a very short time. Indifference to reality allows the nationalist to ignore facts, or not to see resemblances between facts, so that atrocities committed by one's own side are ignored, as are facts that don't accord with one's world view. Consequently, the 'English admirers of Hitler contrived not to learn of the existence of Dachau and Buchenwald', while Russophiles ignored the 1933 famine in Ukraine (ibid., p. 147). This capacity to ignore inconvenient facts had a disturbing implication: 'Every nationalist is haunted by the belief that the past can be altered' (ibid., p. 148). Orwell expands on this idea with a proposition that connects back to what he had experienced in the Spanish Civil War and tried to counteract with his essays and articles:

Much of the propagandist writing of our time amounts to plain forgery. Material facts are suppressed, dates altered, quotations moved from their contexts and doctored so as to change their meaning. Events which, it is felt, ought not to have happened are left unmentioned or utterly denied. (ibid.)

Equally, and more importantly for his eventual reputation, this argument projects forward to the ruling ideology and practices of *Nineteen Eighty-Four*, which he had begun writing.

But 'Notes on Nationalism' explores beyond the mindset of one particular party or group, and perhaps in line with *Polemic*'s more philosophical bent Orwell offers a rough taxonomy of nationalism under the categories of 'Positive Nationalism', 'Transferred Nationalism' and 'Negative Nationalism'. These headings allow a more fine-grained analysis. Neo-Toryism, Celtic Nationalism and Zionism are labelled Positive Nationalism. Transferred Nationalism (the devotion to something other than one's own group) gets exemplified by those who advocate for Soviet Communism, by intellectuals who believe in the innate superiority of the 'coloured races' or the working class, and by pacifists 'whose real but unadmitted motive appears to be hatred of western civilization and admiration for totalitarianism' (ibid., p. 151). Anglophobia, Anti-Semitism and Trotskyism (personified in 'the doctrinaire Marxist whose main motive is hostility to the Stalin regime' [ibid., p. 152]) make up the varieties of Negative Nationalism. Explaining these different forms of nationalism with examples produces a more detailed account of how Orwell understands nationalism for the purposes of this essay, but the often provocative and unsubstantiated claims to some degree undermine their explanatory potential: how to deal with the assertion that those who think the 'coloured races' superior also think that those races' 'sex lives are superior, and [that] there is a large underground mythology about the sexual prowess of the Negroes'; or that 'pacifism, as it appears among the intelligentsia, is secretly inspired by an admiration for power and successful cruelty' (ibid., p. 151)?

Orwell saves his tripartite classification from being dismissed as a set of extreme overstatements by a massive qualification that requires extensive quotation:

> In the classification I have attempted above, it will seem that I have often exaggerated, oversimplified, made unwarranted assumptions and left out of the account the existence of ordinary, decent motives. This was inevitable, because in this essay I am trying to isolate tendencies which occur in all our minds and pervert our thinking, without necessarily existing in a pure state. To begin with, no one has the right to assume that everyone, or even every intellectual, is infected by nationalism; secondly, nationalism can be intermittent and limited . . . Thirdly, a nationalist creed may be adopted in good faith from non-nationalist motives. Fourthly, several kinds of nationalism, even kinds that cancel each other out, can co-exist in the same person. (ibid., p. 152)

Although in some ways this extended apology threatens to undermine the rough theoretical edifice Orwell has constructed, this overt consideration of the essay's own partiality and incompleteness clearly is meant to salvage the argument, positioning the essay itself as a dynamic and suggestive effort at exploring an important if undetected intellectual habit. 'Notes on Nationalism' is unusual in pointing openly to its status as an essay, emphasizing through terms such as 'attempted' and 'trying' that Orwell is offering a way of thinking about the problem without having resolved that problem. In presenting this case Orwell actively exempts 'Notes on Nationalism' from the requirements of proof that would be expected of a more sustained thesis. Simultaneously, he demonstrates the value of self-critical thinking to an awareness of personal bias, without abandoning the main rhetorical thrust of the argument. He chooses his examples and additional comments for maximum impact, and whether readers think that the subsequent self-criticism invoked by the lengthy statement above goes far enough to retain the explanatory force of the general argument remains a question for the individual.

Having already made an attempt to define nationalism, sketch an approximate catalogue of its varieties, and justify the excessiveness of some of his claims, Orwell ends by considering the potential effects. What becomes clear here is that, as with *Nineteen Eighty-Four*, the argument of 'Notes on Nationalism' functions as a warning of what might happen if such patterns of thought were to become pervasive in their pure form: 'it can be argued that *no* unbiased outlook is possible, that *all* creeds and causes involve the same lies, follies and barbarities, and this is often advanced as a reason for keeping out of politics altogether' (ibid., p. 154). That stance would run counter to *Polemic*'s very rationale, that argument can lead to some form of truth, and Orwell rejects political quietism in favour of engagement. And yet by the nature of nationalism as he defines it in this essay, that engagement is not solely or even primarily political: 'one must have preferences: that is, one must recognize that some causes are objectively better than others, even if they are advanced by equally bad means' (ibid., p. 155). Here is the cool, liberal rationalism detected by Collini. Beyond that Orwell argues that whether it is in fact possible fully to rid yourself of 'nationalistic loves and hatreds' he does believe 'that it is possible to struggle against them, and that this is essentially a *moral* effort'. The italicizing of 'moral' is instructive, especially as it gets reiterated and expanded in the concluding statement, where he asserts that balancing undeniable emotions with an 'acceptance of reality . . . needs a *moral* effort, and contemporary English literature, so far as it is alive to the major issues of our time, shows how few of us are prepared to make it' (ibid., p. 154). Moral effort becomes a recurrent theme in his post-war essays, part of an attempt to call to account the self-serving rationalization by intellectuals.

Orwell had begun writing again for *Tribune* late in 1945, producing as a series of short essays that touched on topics of current or personal interest: 'You and the Atom Bomb', 'Good Bad Books' and 'Revenge Is Sour', among others. In a way they are extensions of his 'As I Please' columns, but by focusing on a particular topic (and at greater length) they supply Orwell opportunities to develop single themes or observations. Certainly they are slight pieces compared to the serious and rather more abstract work Orwell had contributed and would contribute to *Polemic*, and it reflects generously on the periodical culture that even in an austere era Orwell was able to address distinct readerships, changing gear and direction easily and frequently in terms of tone and subject matter to suit specific journals. Having different types of material published almost simultaneously with separate audiences further increased his readership and literary profile as well as extending the range of his literary voice. The *Tribune* essays present an assortment of material and comments that reveal the light and the shade of Orwell's concerns and personality. This more revealing or more rounded sense of Orwell also registers how, more than any other paper, review or periodical, Orwell had established and cultivated an intimate relationship with *Tribune* readers. To a considerable extent the more personal, and often light-hearted essays he wrote for the paper required that intimacy in order to work; they might not have done so in journals where Orwell was not well known. The relationship also meant that he could incorporate a whimsically skewed observation or an actively provocative statement, knowing the response that might be triggered. But the same intimate situation between writer and readers also meant that only *Tribune* readers of the time gained a multifaceted understanding of Orwell. The Orwell heard in *Polemic* essays often was stern and sometimes hectoring, the *Partisan Review*'s Orwell was informative and balanced, while the *Horizon* Orwell was astute and idiosyncratic. To some extent, the different journals in which Orwell had a sustained presence heard from different 'Orwells'. Most readers while he was alive only read one or perhaps two of these journals and so saw just a small sample of his essays. Only after his death did the full array of essays begin to appear to a general readership.

The *Tribune* essays often reveal Orwell's more playful side. 'Good Bad Books', for example, draws its title from an idea by G. K. Chesterton and refers to 'that kind of book that has no literary pretensions but which remains readable when more serious productions have perished' (*CO*, *XVII*, p. 348); *Raffles* and the Sherlock Holmes books are proclaimed 'outstanding books in this line'. Orwell had already shown a serious interest in the appeal and the sociological forces of these popular works, reiterated in his assessment of Kipling, but in this case the thoughts that triggered the essay came as the result of a publisher commissioning him 'to write an introduction for a reprint of a novel by Leonard Merrick' (ibid., p. 347). The enthusiasm with which he writes about authors of the good bad book – some of them already obscure in 1945 – invigorates the essay, indicating someone with an informed and genuine interest in the novels and writers being considered. The tone is light, amused and energetic, Orwell eager to persuade readers about the value of books neglected by academics or literary purists. He aims to make instructive comments, distinguishing primarily escapist works from those with a serious intention but poor in aesthetic terms. More generally, he argues that the existence of such literature 'is a reminder that art is not the same thing as cerebration', so that while Carlyle is more intelligent than Trollope, the latter survives, Carlyle's 'cleverness' working against him (ibid., p. 349). (Wyndham Lewis provides Orwell a more contemporary version of the same failing.) So, the category of the good bad book acts as a rough guide not to literary quality but to literary longevity, identifying works that find and keep an interested readership. This despite the fact that perhaps 'the supreme example of the "good bad book", *Uncle Tom's Cabin*, . . . is an unintentionally ludicrous book, full of melodramatic incidents; it is also deeply moving and essentially true' (ibid.). The paradox that a piece of literature can have substantial aesthetic deficiencies but still be effective and true leads to the personal revelation that Orwell would rather have written great music hall songs than some of the poetry published in anthologies. And it drives his last point that he 'would back *Uncle Tom's Cabin* to outlive the complete works of Virginia Woolf or George Moore, though I know of no strictly literary test which would show where the superiority lies' (ibid., p. 350). Time has proven him right as regards George Moore, who is now little read. Woolf, though, while still a minority taste, is now better regarded than she was in her own day. The point, of course, is not so much that Orwell was right or wrong in particular instances as that his general argument makes a case for books whose value is weighed on the scale of public opinion.

'Revenge Is Sour' is more serious, dealing with the paradox that the thought of revenge against a foe (in this case the German enemy) is more exhilarating and satisfying when the person wanting revenge is powerless, and that once the victim is able to take revenge the exhilaration or even the desire disappears or diminishes. In this short piece Orwell returns to an old rhetorical strategy, basing his argument on the eyewitness experience of inspecting a prisoner-of-war camp while a correspondent in Europe. In this instance Orwell is not an active participant, as in 'Shooting an Elephant', nor is he exposing suppressed facts, as in 'Spilling the Spanish Beans'. Instead he remains a perceptive and sympathetic onlooker who suspects that a Jewish guide showing him through the camp, and briefly brutalizing a Nazi officer, was not really enjoying himself but rather was '*telling* himself that he was enjoying it, and behaving as he had planned to behave in the days when he was helpless' (*CO, XVII,* p. 362).

More significant than this brief rumination on one of the consequences of war is 'You and the Atom Bomb'. Its importance lies not so much for its qualities as an essay as in its reference to James Burnham's *The Managerial Revolution* and for the fact that here Orwell coins the phrase 'cold war' to describe a plausible scenario to come. 'You and the Atom Bomb' is interesting for another reason; several of Orwell's essays were written as the result of an editor requesting material for a periodical, but in this case the prompt for the essays appears to be a letter to *Tribune* by a reader – Miss S. D. Wingate – who wondered what a nuclear-armed world entailed. Orwell's essay was one of several responses that included other readers' letters (ibid., pp. 316–23) and it begins with characteristic energy: 'Considering how likely we are to be blown to pieces by it in the next five years, the atomic bomb has not roused so much discussion as might have been expected' (ibid., p. 319). Orwell's response to this is that the cost and technological difficulty of manufacturing such a bomb means that only a very few richest and technically advanced would be able to construct one. He plays off this potentially comforting thought (no crazed boffins could make one on their own) against the most likely consequence that the limited number of nations capable of manufacturing the weapon will leave the concentration of power in fewer hands. This imagined scenario enables him to draw upon Burnham's book, which though it assumed that Germany would win the Second World War, still proposed a post-war world dominated by 'three great empires, each self-contained and cut off from contact with the outer world, and each ruled . . . by a self-elected oligarchy' (ibid., p. 320). Clearly, elements of Burnham's view would appear in modified form in *Nineteen Eighty-Four*, with the atom bomb supplying the transformative difference. Orwell predicts that those nations who possess the bomb, and who realize its destructive capacity may 'make a tacit agreement never to use the bomb against one another' (ibid.). He argues that while Burnham's theory has been discussed

> few people have considered its ideological implications – that is, the kind of world-view, the kind of beliefs, and the social structure that would probably prevail in a State which was at once unconquerable and in a permanent state of 'cold war' with its neighbours. (ibid., p. 321)

The inverted commas around 'cold war' register it as a neologism, but equally significant are the parallels between Orwell's reading of the consequences of the atom bomb and the scenario of his still-embryonic dystopia. Admittedly in *Nineteen Eighty-Four* there are ten years of atomic war before a state of equilibrium is reached, but the essential conditions apply. With a wonderful circularity, the eventual success of *Nineteen Eighty-Four* probably explains why the OED later would credit Orwell with inventing the term. 'You and the Atom Bomb' initially was only read by subscribers to *Tribune*, who were unlikely to remember the odd phrase from an obscure essay. It was reprinted in a collection of *Tribune* pieces in 1958 (Fenwick, p. 169) but this also would have enjoyed only a small audience. The essay would not be published again until the *Collected Essays, Journalism and Letters of George Orwell* in 1968, which caused scholars and the public to consider work that essentially had disappeared for nearly twenty years or more, including 'You and the Atom Bomb'. Orwell's posthumous claim to the phrase 'cold war' rested, ironically, on the global success of *Nineteen Eighty-Four*, that prompted the collection.

'Books vs Cigarettes', another *Tribune* piece, provides an instance of Orwell exploring everyday assumptions, this time the view that given a choice between the two the average worker will spend money on cigarettes. A newspaper editor friend had picked up this insight while fire-watching during the war with some factory workers, and while the incident took place 'a couple of years ago' it stuck in Orwell's mind sufficiently to suggest a short follow-up study: 'The idea that the buying and even the reading of books is an expensive hobby and beyond the reach of the average person is so widespread that it deserves some attention' (*CO, XVIII*, pp. 94–5). The bulk of the essay comprises Orwell's rough attempt to analyse the proposition, beginning with him quantifying how many books he has and how much he has spent over his adult reading life. He counts his personal collection, including books he has 'here, in my flat' and those 'stored in another place', breaking these down into categories of books bought, given to him, review copies, those temporarily on loan and those 'Borrowed and not returned'. This is presented as an inventory, the semi-comic seriousness of the exercise apparent in the 'Borrowed and not returned' category. He wants to give the subject sufficient attention without being po-faced. This leads to a consideration of how much these books have cost him, before he adds other books and subscriptions to newspapers and periodicals, estimating that 'my total reading expenses over the past fifteen years have been in the neighbour-hood of £25 a year' (ibid., p. 96). That factual point established, he compares the amount spent on beer and drink by the average adult, drawing on a few national statistics and his own habits to reach the pseudo-sociological conclu-sion that 'it looks as though the cost of reading . . . does not amount to more than the combined cost of smoking and drinking' (ibid.).

Having established these rough and ready facts, somewhat in the manner of the lists of costs and expenses for miners in *Wigan Pier*, Orwell makes the much wider social point that 'this is not a proud record for a country which is nearly 100 per cent literate and where the ordinary man spends more on cigarettes than an average Indian peasant has for his whole livelihood' (ibid., p. 97). Given the domestic or at least national focus of the essay to this stage, this brief interna-tional comparison in the penultimate sentence is both unexpected and admoni-tory, but he leaves it as a slightly shameful reproach. Not that Orwell develops the insight in any way, finishing with a double-headed assertion that in a sense damns writers as well as non-readers: that if book consumption is as low as he has estimated 'let us admit that it is because reading is a less exciting pastime than going to the dogs, the pictures or the pub, and books, whether bought or bor-rowed, are too expensive' (ibid.). The first item in the list of pastimes, going to the dogs, is an index of *Tribune*'s audience; greyhound races were unlikely to be a high priority for the predominantly middle-class readers of *Horizon* or *Polemic*. But if the essay ends somewhat critically of the ordinary reader, the voice mak-ing the criticism criticizes gently, ending almost apologetically by insinuating that writers are not providing sufficiently exciting material. Short and quirky,

'Book v. Cigarettes' deftly employs for comic and illustrative purposes the humane intimacy allowed the personal essayist.

Orwell's second contribution to *Polemic* deals with far weightier material. 'Notes on Nationalism' had warned of the dangers of unthinking adherence to a cause, while 'You and the Atom Bomb' speculated on the possibility of superstates perpetually at war with each other. 'The Prevention of Literature', published in January 1946, adds other components that in modified form find places in *Nineteen Eighty-Four*: the view that 'history is something to be created rather than learned' (*CO, XVII*, p. 374); that a totalitarian state was 'in effect a theocracy, and its ruling caste, in order to keep its position, has to be thought of as infallible'; that the state would produce pulp literature for the masses; that 'so long as two plus two have to make four' (ibid., p. 379) some sense of reality has been preserved; that the literature of the past 'would have to be suppressed or at least elaborately rewritten', and that freely created literature would be eradicated (ibid.). These intimations of ideas that emerge in *Nineteen Eighty-Four* suggest an obvious continuity of thought between the essay and the novel, which due to Orwell's dire health would take more than three years to complete. While 'The Prevention of Literature' is not a dry run for the novel, both are warnings about what might happen rather than predictions of what will happen. In essence 'The Prevention of Literature' warns of contemporary dangers in a British context, Orwell declaring that

> to be corrupted by totalitarianism one does not have to live in a totalitarian country. The mere prevalence of certain ideas can spread a kind of poison that makes one subject after another almost impossible for literary purposes. (ibid., p. 376)

The central concern with literature ensures that, despite the crossovers, 'The Prevention of Literature' address different concerns from 'You and the Atom Bomb' and 'Notes on Nationalism'.

Being an eyewitness to events had repeatedly spurred Orwell to report back, often from unknown or dangerous locations (at least to his readers). In this instance the prompt had occurred a year before and was dramatically less exotic – a meeting of the writers' association PEN to mark the tercentenary of Milton's *Areopagitica*, his famous seventeenth-century defence of intellectual liberty in which he asserts that 'he who destroys a good Book kills reason itself'. None of the four speakers Orwell heard considered in detail Milton's forceful prose and trenchant argument, and only one considered the freedom of the press – in relation to India. And out of the several hundred people in the audience, none pointed out something Orwell felt essential, 'that freedom of the press, if it means anything at all, means the freedom to criticise and oppose' (ibid., p. 370). He admits that, as any eyewitness might, he struck a bad day in a PEN gathering that went on for a week, but he draws from what he did experience and from other speeches from the gallery he had read the worrying conclusion

> that almost nobody in our day is able to speak out as roundly in favour of intellectual liberty as Milton could three hundred years ago and this in spite of the fact that Milton was writing in a time of civil war. (ibid., p. 371, note)

The key point about this inability to speak out in Britain is that it is not a situation imposed by a totalitarian authority but rather one that depends on a failure by contemporary writers 'to report what one has seen, heard, and felt, and not to be obliged to fabricate imaginary facts and feelings' (ibid., p. 372). The problematic verb 'to fabricate', with its strong suggestion of artificiality and connivance, contrasts instructively with the more empirical and favoured 'report'. 'Indifference to reality' had been used as a principal characteristic in 'Notes on Nationalism'. Here, Orwell emphasizes the impact this conscious indifference has, particularly on fiction and non-fiction, broadly conceived, but with crucial stress on history and the novel.

History, ideally, offers a true and detailed account of reality. Orwell was no innocent about the partiality of written history, but his experiences, primarily in Spain, had alerted him to something other than different interpretations. These experiences, and his subsequent reading of the ways in which various important 'facts' and historical data had been misreported, or reconfigured when circumstances changed, promoted a critical scepticism about the motives and malleability of historians and other writers who adopted the type of 'organized lying practiced by totalitarian states' (ibid., p. 373). This he sees as 'integral to totalitarianism', a position that leads to the belief that history is something to be created rather than learned. A primary condition of the totalitarian state, though, is that the ruling caste has to be thought infallible, and this makes it 'frequently necessary to rearrange past events in order to show that this or that mistake was not made, or that this or that imaginary triumph actually happened' (ibid., p. 374). This approximates the nightmare world of Oceania, but Orwell finds a test case for this perverse requirement from recent history: the Nazi–Soviet non-aggression pact of September 1939, later tossed aside once Germany had attacked the Soviet Union in mid-1941. He had used the same example in 'Literature and Totalitarianism'. This regular reworking of facts and of history to suit an ideologically determined narrative probably requires, he suggests, 'a disbelief in the very existence of objective truth'. Emmanuel Goldstein's Theory and Practice of Oligarchical Collectivism in *Nineteen Eighty-Four* reveals that 'The mutability of the past is the central tenet of Ingsoc. Past events, it is argued, have no objective existence' (*CO, IX*, p. 222). In a sense 'The Prevention of Literature' hints at Goldstein's analysis, but one where the dangers are located firmly within Orwell's contemporary moment.

Crucially, the writers of history are likely to be intellectuals, broadly conceived, and so '[i]t is at the point where literature and politics cross that totalitarianism exerts its greatest pressure on the intellectual' (*CO, XVII*, p. 374). Naturally, this places an enormous load on intellectuals to withstand and actively resist that pressure, but Orwell's entrenched suspicion of intellectuals, coupled with the failings demonstrated by the PEN audience, bode ill for the future, as it were, of history. Literature also clearly encompasses creative writing, and here too the pressures were considerable. At least as far back as 'Inside the Whale' Orwell had argued that the key elements of totalitarianism were toxic to creative writers who wanted to maintain their intellectual freedom. By way of a challenge he invokes the Revivalist hymn 'Dare to be Daniel/ Dare to stand alone/ Dare to have a purpose firm/ Dare to make it known', presenting the situation as a moral as well as an aesthetic or political problem, and by implication negatively comparing an earlier age when independent thought and expression were encouraged. In contrast, too many modern writers have given up their freedom of expression, falsifying or suppressing their true ideas and feelings. In the context of Orwell's contemporary Britain, the central motivating force for failing the Revivalist test is less external than internal, manifesting itself both in content and in expression. Adulterating one's ideas to fit an ideological template destroys the creative writer's creative 'dynamo', so that '[n]ot only will ideas refuse to come to him but the very words will seem to stiffen under his touch'. This danger extends to a larger argument that

> Political writing in our time consists almost entirely of prefabricated phrases bolted together like the pieces of a child's Meccano set . . . To write in plain, vigorous language one has to think fearlessly, and one cannot be politically orthodox. (*CO, XVII*, p. 376)

Orwell would develop this argument in 'Politics and the English Language', while in a more extreme form the notion of prefabricated phrases returns in the way Newspeak functions in *Nineteen Eighty-Four*. What distinguishes his argument here from those later works is the essay's open call for intellectuals generally and creative writers specifically to think and write fearlessly. Orwell had attributed fearlessness to Charles Dickens and in this instance uses Milton as the model of a writer brave enough to utter the unorthodox thought. He offers no contemporary equivalent.

The essay asserts that the situation, while dire, is not terminal:

> [T]otalitarianism has not fully triumphed everywhere. Our society is still, broadly speaking, liberal. To exercise your right of free speech you have to fight against economic pressure and against strong sections of public opinion, but not, as yet, against a secret police force . . . But what is sinister . . .

is that the conscious enemies of liberty are those to whom liberty ought to mean most . . . intellectuals. (*CO, XVII*, p. 379)

By now the target of this attack should come as no surprise, and Collini (pp. 350–74) is not the only commentator to criticize Orwell's near-obsession with the supposed duplicity and deficiencies of intellectuals, and his encouragement of 'an undiscriminating hostility to intellectuals' (Collini, p. 372) as distorting and self-contradictory given that he easily might be considered an intellectual. Repetitive though it undoubtedly is, his attack on intellectuals does have gradations and variations – in 'The Prevention of Literature' the accusation that intellectuals have failed in a primary duty operates more as exhortatory criticism than simplistic condemnation. As before, the journal in which the essay appears, and the specific audience that it addresses, need to be considered. Readers of *Polemic* were more likely to see themselves as intellectuals than, say, the readers of *Tribune*. Those who read other contributors to the journal such as Bertrand Russell and A. J. Ayer, even when these eminent philosophers were writing in their public voice, presumably were interested in the type of open, liberal and rational discussion characteristic of both. Orwell's charge is not that intellectuals are incapable of such discussion, but that in unthinkingly adulterating their ideas – particularly those who have indulged in mindless Russophilia – they have failed to participate actively and productively in those discussions. One problem with the accusation, of course, is, as Collini argues, its undiscriminating nature. And in fixating on Communists and fellow-travellers, it gives other dissembling or timid intellectuals a free pass.

As an alternative to the interplay of freethinking intelligences, especially in terms of creative literature, Orwell raises the prospect that 'if the liberal culture that we have lived with since the Renaissance actually comes to an end, the literary art will perish with it' (*CO, XVII*, p. 378). Again, this remains a projection rather than something inevitable, but Orwell speculates (fallaciously, as it happens) that in that scenario 'probably novels will be completely superseded by film and radio productions'. What literature that might be fabricated by bureaucrats, machines and formulas, and while this process would produce 'rubbish', by the logic of totalitarian infallibility 'anything that was not rubbish would endanger the structure of the State. As for the surviving literature of the past, it would have to be suppressed or at least elaborately rewritten' (ibid., p. 379). While these observations gesture towards *Nineteen Eighty-Four*, the essay directs its main attention on the present, using the Soviet writers Ilya Ehrenburg and Alexei Tolstoy as examples of writers who are not – as other Soviet writers are – 'viciously prosecuted', but who have had taken away from them 'the only thing which is of any value to the writer as such – his freedom of expression' (ibid.). This example simultaneously functions as a warning to British writers and as an assault on the Soviet 'myth', but again where in the

Soviet Union a malevolent state apparatus operates to enforce totalitarianism, in Britain writers themselves abdicate responsibility. And

> literature is doomed if liberty of thought perishes. Not only is it doomed in any country which retains a totalitarian structure, but any writer who adopts the totalitarian outlook, who finds excuses for persecution and the falsification of reality, thereby destroys himself as a writer. (*CO, XVII*, p. 380)

Although Orwell's insistent attacks upon the shortcomings of intellectuals might appear excessive, 'The Prevention of Literature' explains what he felt was at stake in the developing British context. That liberty of thought did not perish does not in itself invalidate the argument he makes in the essay. Indeed, one could argue that warnings such as 'The Prevention of Literature' promote thinking about liberty of thought. Against this grand claim could plausibly be counterpoised the relatively small *Polemic* audience. (But as the next chapter details, Orwell's essays generally were to have an afterlife far more influential than anything he would ever experience.) 'The Prevention of Literature' did, however, provoke the writer, editor and Communist Randall Swingler to a sustained, detailed and forceful attack on Orwell that *Polemic* printed (along with Orwell's annotated reply) later in the year (*CO, XXIII*, pp. 432–45). At least one intellectual was prompted to respond.

Critical Essays, his major essay collection, was published in February 1946. The delay between the planning and the publication was considerable – over 18 months – which gave Orwell time to write 'In Defence of P.G. Wodehouse' and other new material. But the collection also included essays from as far back as *Inside the Whale*; two of its three essays were reprinted, excepting the title essay, which was somewhat dated by 1946. *Critical Essays* also resurrected *Horizon* pieces (including 'Wells, Hitler and the World State', 'The Art of Donald McGill', 'Rudyard Kipling', 'W.B. Yeats' and 'Raffles and Miss Blandish') as well as the Wodehouse essay, a brief study of Arthur Koestler and, surprisingly, an essay on Salvador Dali. Where Gollancz had printed only 1,000 copies of *Inside the Whale*, Secker and Warburg published over 3,000 copies of *Critical Essays*, suggesting Orwell's increased pulling power after *Animal Farm*. A reissue of over 5,500 copies followed in May 1946, making it more successful than any piece of Orwell's 1930s fiction. Evelyn Waugh in the Catholic journal *Tablet* judged that it formed 'a work of absorbing interest' (Meyers, 1975, p. 211), while Middleton Murry in *The Adelphi* placed Orwell alongside Cyril Connolly as one of 'the two most gifted critics of their generation' (ibid., p. 227). *Critical Essays* announced Orwell as an essayist of real quality while offering the largest representation of his work to a broad public. These selected essays stressed the cultural side of Orwell's output, as opposed to the more politically charged material that he had produced and would keep producing. Added to the short *Tribune* essays, the range of material Orwell considers in this period, the quality of material he writes and the variety of audiences he addresses are impressive. This first part of the decade can be understood as the great flourishing of Orwell's skills as an essayist, dramatically developing his command of the form, with *Critical Essays* one of the major achievements of the second half of his literary career.

By May 1946 an American edition of 5,000 copies with the more arresting title of *Dickens, Dali and Others: Studies in Popular Culture* had also appeared. Because of problems finding a publisher for *Animal Farm* in the United States, *Dickens, Dali and Others* came about before his allegory, making it the first book by him to be published in America since *A Clergyman's Daughter* more than a decade earlier. Orwell's 'London Letters' for *Partisan Review* had established a small beachhead among the anti-Stalinist section of American Left intellectuals in the United States, but given that neither *Wigan Pier* nor *Homage to Catalonia* had been published there (and *Down and Out in Paris and London* barely counts as documentary) John Rodden essentially is correct in arguing that *Dickens, Dali and Others* gained Orwell's non-fiction 'its first attention in America' (Rodden, p. 45). Rodden's more general point about the significance of *Dickens, Dali and Others* to Orwell's reputation in America holds true, the collection receiving mostly positive reviews: Edmund Wilson in the *New Yorker* labelled Orwell 'the only contemporary master' of the sociological study of literature (Meyers, 1975, p. 226) and Eric Bentley in the *Saturday Review of Literature* commented that the collection 'introduces to the American public a very talented English critic' (ibid., p. 219).

The success of *Dickens, Dali and Others*, is slightly harder to fathom than its British equivalent, especially as the collection's topics were predominantly British, or even restrictively 'English'. *Animal Farm* had been published months ahead of *Critical Essays* in Britain, its popularity thrusting Orwell's name firmly to the front of a potential readership's consciousness. But in the United States the novel was not published until after the essay collection. Even so, the New York firm of Reynal and Hitchcock printed 5,000 copies of *Dickens, Dali and Others*, a respectable number that in part reflected the larger North American market. Harcourt, Brace (which had taken over Reynal and Hitchcock) published *Animal Farm* in August 1946 in an initial run of 50,000 copies. No doubt the reputation building about *Animal Farm* in Britain fuelled American interest in the essay collection, the only other material by Orwell in print. Post-publication, positive reviews of both texts also helped, transforming Orwell's status in the United States. At the the beginning of 1945 he was a well-respected though still minor figure in British letters, with almost no American presence outside the pages of *Partisan Review*. By the end of 1946, on both sides of the Atlantic, Orwell was, in Crick's evaluation, 'famous' (Crick, pp. 473–509). One consequence of *Dickens, Dali and Others* was a request from an American agent asking if the essays from that collection had been put to any American magazines, and suggesting that *Harper's* and the *Atlantic Monthly* group might be suitable candidates. Orwell wrote to his agent, Leonard Moore, in September 1946, proposing that Moore put large articles to other magazines. One result was that a shortened version of 'The Prevention of Literature' appeared the following year in the venerable and widely read American magazine *The Atlantic Monthly*. Orwell later praised Moore for getting 'so good a price' for the article (*CO*, *XIX*, p. 30), which further enhanced Orwell's position in the American scene.

Most of the collection's essays had previously been published in periodicals, with 'Arthur Koestler' later appearing in the second number of the yearly miscellany, *Focus* (1945–50) edited by Balachandra Rajan and Andrew Pearse. (Rajan had previously sent Orwell a book of his poems to review when Orwell worked for the Indian Section of the BBC.) Despite the fact that Orwell and Koestler were friends who had similar though not identical political views, the essay provides a fairly critical survey of Koestler's work. Orwell rates Koestler's novel *The Gladiators* as 'in some ways an unsatisfactory work' (*CO*, *XVI*, p. 394) and *Arrival and Departure* similarly as 'not a satisfactory book' (ibid., p. 398). He judges that 'To take a rational decision one must have a picture of the future. At present Koestler seems to have none, or rather to have two that cancel out' (ibid., p. 399) – belief in an Earthly Paradise and a sense that the future will be tyrannical. What Koestler does possess, having been imprisoned in Spain and France, is experience of something approximating totalitarianism. Orwell begins the essay by noting the 'striking fact' that twentieth-century English literature 'has been dominated by foreigners' including Conrad, James, Joyce and Eliot, before focusing on 'the special class of literature that has arisen out of the European political struggle since the rise of Fascism' (ibid., p. 392). This literature had been produced by continental Europeans such as Koestler, Silone, Malraux and others, 'who are alike in that they are trying to write contemporary history, but *unofficial* history, the kind that is ignored in the text-books and lied about in the newspapers'. Orwell had made a similar point in 'Wells, Hitler and the World State'. His affinity with such writers should be obvious, especially as they seem to be writing the type of literature he had continued to advocate in essays such as 'The Prevention of Literature'. Having experienced totalitarianism 'from the inside' they are capable of writing what he categorizes as 'concentration-camp literature', a quasi-genre dealing with a 'special world created by secret-police forces, censorship of opinion, torture and frame-up trials' (ibid., p. 393). Orwell's fear that such a future loomed for Britain underscored the need for the type of writing Koestler was capable of producing at his best. But Orwell considered that despite the 'enormous spate of political literature [in Britain]' over the previous decade, British writers 'have produced nothing of aesthetic value and very little of political value' (ibid., p. 392).

Yet if British writers score lowly, Koestler himself is not without fault. The essay supplies a vigorous and unvarnished summary of his work, underpinned by Orwell's view that Koestler's main theme is 'the decadence of revolutions owing to the corrupting effects of power'. Having completed *Animal Farm* and started work on *Nineteen Eighty-Four*, it would seem likely if not obvious that Orwell would agree with Koestler, but instead he criticizes Koestler for avoiding the central 'problem of revolution', or not solving it. This shortcoming mars novels such as *The Gladiators, Arrival and Departure* and *Scum of the Earth* in Orwell's view, and threatens even *Darkness at Noon*. There, he contends, Rubashov's decision to confess crimes that he did not and could not have committed derives from Koestler's reading of the Moscow Show Trials: that innocent men 'were actuated by despair, mental bankruptcy and the habit of loyalty to the Party' (ibid., p. 396). The consequence for Koestler, an intensely and actively political creature by inclination, is that with the demise of the Russian Revolution as a Utopia, and from his sense that the future will be dire

> he draws the conclusion: This is what revolutions lead to. There is nothing for it except to be a 'short-term pessimist', i.e. to keep out of politics, make a sort of oasis within which you and your friends can remain sane. (ibid., p. 400)

In 'Notes on Nationalism' Orwell had argued forcefully against political quietism; here the metaphor of the oasis approximates the metaphor of 'Inside the Whale', with the worrying distinction that Henry Miller professed a genuine lack of interest in politics where Koestler has been aware and engaged. Orwell's own stance rejects both versions of disengagement. Instead he opposes Koestler's mix of hedonistic high hopes and disillusionment (which he describes as 'a blind alley') with a pragmatic, hard-nosed argument that 'perhaps' the Earthly Paradise is not possible.

> Perhaps some degree of suffering is ineradicable from human life . . . perhaps even the aim of Socialism is not to make the world perfect but to make it better. All revolutions are failures, but they are not all the same failure. (ibid., p. 400)

The repetition of 'perhaps' in some way indicates a level of tentativeness, but it also distinguishes Orwell's position from Miller's fatalistic refusal to act and Koestler's despairing withdrawal from action when the revolutionary ideals he held failed to materialize.

As with other pieces that later would be essential to Orwell's posthumous status as an essayist, 'Politics and the English Language', published in *Horizon* in April 1946, was prompted by a request. In this instance the commissioner was not Cyril Connolly, but someone Orwell had met while working at the BBC, George Weidenfeld. Weidenfeld was establishing a journal with the curious title *Contact: The Magazine of Pleasure*, and instructed his literary editor Phillip Toynbee to commission . . . articles by distinguished writers, keeping rigidly to the modes and canons of 'reportage'; what was wanted for this part of *Contact* were factual narratives and investigative articles. (*CO, XVII*, p. 431, n.1)

Amazingly, given its later acclaim, when 'Politics and the English Language' did not keep to this 'purist' brief Weidenfeld instructed Toynbee to reject it, something he later admitted to Peter Davison was a 'sacrilegious mistake' (ibid.). Instead, the essay was published by *Horizon*, which, given Orwell's long friendship with Connolly, his contributions, the nature of the essay's argument and its length, was an appropriate site. Ultimately, owing predominantly to the state of Orwell's health over the next four years, it would also prove to be his last major piece that the journal printed.

The essay's title bluntly advertises its concern with the sometimes problematic relationship between politics and language, and the examples he uses to demonstrate deficiencies are current, reflecting a recent deterioration. Because of the interactive relationship between language and politics, the decline of one indicates and simultaneously exacerbates that of the other. But while Orwell perceives a substantial and troubling problem, 'Politics and the English Language' attempts in its own small way to solve the problem:

> The point is that the process is reversible . . . If one gets rid of [bad] habits one can think more clearly, and to think clearly is a necessary first step towards political regeneration: so that the fight against bad English is not frivolous and is not the exclusive concern of professional writers. (*CO, XVII*, p. 421)

He makes the case for a social effort that would, were it carried out, amount to something approaching a political revolution, and certainly a massive revision of political practice. An important part of his target audience here is the general public. And while *Horizon*'s relatively small readership constituted a highly selective section of that public, in 1946 it was still one of the leading cultural journals in Britain. In fact, and unusually, the essay had an almost immediate afterlife, being reprinted by both *The Observer* and *The News of the World* papers for the benefit of their staff, and in The *New Republic* in the United States. The American journal had asked Orwell whether it could reprint some of his *Tribune* articles, and although he admitted to Dwight Macdonald, who edited the rival American journal *Politics*, that he knew those running the journal were 'Stalino-Liberals', he confided that since they had no control over what he wrote 'I rather like to have a foot in that camp'. By contrast, he told Macdonald that the *New Republic*'s 'opposite numbers over here, the "New Statesman", won't touch me with a stick' (*CO, XVIII*, p. 450). While certain sections of the British periodical culture were relatively open to him, Orwell's mutual antagonism with Kingsley Martin ensured that not all platforms were available.

'Politics and the English Language' makes the outwardly plausible though contestable case that language and thought are connected interactively, so that poor expression and poor thinking are symbiotically linked. Worse still, the decline resulting from this interaction necessarily has a negative effect on political discourse and political action. Orwell illustrates his claim by choosing five passages 'of the English language as it is now habitually written' (*CO*, *XVII*, p. 422). The selection is a reasonably eclectic sample from the political Left, although the topic is less important than the faulty expression revealed. Only two of the writers are named, and perhaps in order to give intellectuals a gentle cuff they are both Professors: the political theorist Harold Laski and the polymath Lancelot Hogben. The choices are more than chance. Laski had been one of the Left Book Club selectors who had aggressively criticized *Wigan Pier*, while Orwell had himself negatively reviewed Hogben's *Interglossa* in the *Manchester Evening News* (*CO*, *XVI*, 31–3), lampooning the same quote that he reprises here. Another example of poor political writing comes from a Communist pamphlet, but the final two extracts are from journals in which he had published, *Tribune* and *Politics*. The relatively broad catchment area defuses accusations of political bias, while the conscious focus on Leftist publications pitches the essay at *Horizon*'s readers.

Much of the first section of the essay gets taken up with a broad analysis of the defects on display: dying metaphors; verbal false limbs; pretentious diction; of meaningless words. Orwell sorts these into two general faults, staleness of imagery and lack of precision. Of the two, staleness of imagery would seem the least politically injurious, but it contributes to what he describes as the construction of ready-made and largely unconsidered '*phrases* tacked together like the sections of a pre-fabricated hen-house' (ibid., p. 423). Lack of precision can be a sign that the writer either does not really know what they think, or is using words with a conscious dishonesty. He then provides a parody translation of a section from the Bible into bureaucratese, noting how the modern version is less concrete, precise or vivid and that while it contains substantially more syllables it does not fully translate the meaning of the original. The descent into pre-fabricated phrase, Orwell argues, is attractive because it is easy, freeing the mind from grappling with or even acknowledging reality, one of the prevailing flaws of totalitarianism. His call for concrete language parallels his argument for an empiricist acceptance of a reality where two plus two always equals four. Overly abstract, hackneyed or imprecise language, he suggests, detaches the writer from reality.

While he asserts that '[i]n our time it is broadly true that political writing is bad writing', the qualifier 'broadly' indicates the possibility of good writing. Where good writing occurs, he continues, 'it will generally be found that the writer is some kind of rebel, expressing his private opinions, and not the "party line"' (CO, XVII, p. 427); a person, one might think, very much like Orwell. The essay aims not to valorize particular authors, but to bring about improvement in political expression. Part of this task involves exposing inexact, muddled, pretentious and dishonest political writing so that the essay's readers are alerted to the mistakes, the mannered style and the devious euphemism – Orwell uses current examples such as 'pacification' and 'the elimination of unreliable elements'. He supplies a catalogue of samples from which readers can detect the false and flawed, but the essay also gives them a set of memorable statements which are meant to be kept in mind: 'In our times, political speech and writing are largely the defence of he indefensible' (ibid.). 'The great enemy of clear language is insincerity' (ibid., p. 428); 'if thought corrupts language, language can also corrupt thought' (ibid.). If not quite principles, such statements sanction readers not merely to detect but also to challenge corrupt writing and writers. 'Politics and the English Language' provides a useful kitbag of rhetorical tools for readers (and potentially for writers). Primarily, it prompts readers to repair language by recognizing and then not accepting the pompous, the deceptive and the muddy. Despite the entrenched and pervasive flaws in political writing, Orwell remains optimistic that 'the decadence of our language is probably curable'. But the cure requires action from writers and from readers built on the basic premise that '[w]hat above all else is needed is to let the meaning choose the word, and not the other way about'. He provides a set of six 'rules that one can rely on when instinct fails', the last of which – 'Break any of these rules sooner than say anything outright barbarous' (ibid., p. 430) – stresses an active and energizing self-criticism. Essentially, writing that relies on pre-fabricated, stale and pretentious language remains writing without real thought.

The final thrust of 'Politics and the English Language' accentuates the need for active thinking, writing and reading. It rejects arguments by those who 'come near to claiming that all abstract words are meaningless' as a 'pretext for advocating a kind of political quietism'. In 'Notes on Nationalism' Orwell had opposed the view that all creeds and causes involve the same lies and therefore it was better to stay out of politics, and again he opts for engagement: 'If you simplify your English, you are freed from the worst follies of orthodoxy. You cannot speak any of the necessary dialects, and when you make a stupid remark its stupidity will be obvious, even to yourself' (ibid., p. 430). Clarity produces liberty. Arguing for liberating self-criticism, 'Politics and the English Language' ends with a call for readers to jeer loudly at worn-out and useless phrases so as to send them 'into the dustbin' where they belong. This almost gleefully riotous finale underlines the call to action the essay embodies and the directness of its personal address. An essay such as 'Notes on Nationalism' hectors its targets, with readers enjoying the blood sport from the sidelines. But although the title of 'Politics and the English Language' suggests something abstract or lofty, the essay itself repeatedly calls on readers to participate in the process it advocates. It persuades partly because the essay form creates an intimate relationship between writer and reader. Intimacy of itself is not enough to convince, but in this instance particularly the call to action requires reader commitment. The immediate reprinting of this essay in other journals and newspapers, as well as its enduring status, register that in the case of 'Politics and the English Language' the tactic succeeded.

Tribune continued to be the site for a set of shorter personal essays through 1946 that accentuated Orwell's mastery of different types of essay. These pieces, alongside his longer essays and short articles on popular culture for the *Evening Standard* (among them 'A Nice Cup of Tea' and 'The Moon under Water', in which Orwell respectively considers the perfect cup of tea and the perfect pub) and the *Manchester Evening News* (which ran a series of articles on 'The Intellectual Revolt') also signal his prolific output in this period. The *Tribune* essays also display Orwell's easy relationship with the paper's readers, so that 'The Decline of the English Murder' (February 1946), even begins in the second person:

> It is a Sunday afternoon before the war. The wife is already asleep in the armchair, and the children have been sent out for a nice long walk. You put your feet up on the sofa, settle your spectacles on your nose and open the *News of the World* . . . In these blissful circumstances, what is it you want to read about?
> Naturally, about a murder. (*CO, XVIII*, p. 108)

The compelling hook of nostalgia, domesticity and murder combined sets up what in some ways is a truncated companion piece to 'Raffles and Miss Blandish'. But where that earlier and more substantial essay explored the Americanization of crime fiction over the previous decades, 'The Decline of the English Murder' considers actual murders. Even so, Orwell explains that several of the most infamous local murders of the late nineteenth century – his 'high point' from which English murders have declined – have been made into books and melodramas, and that the literature surrounding them 'would make a considerable library'. These cases can be distilled into the 'perfect' murder for the tabloid *News of the World* reader: an affair involving a seemingly respectable citizen unsettled by a great passion, the weapon of choice being poison, with the case being solved because of a 'slip up over some tiny, unforeseeable detail'. By contrast, the most famous murder of the war just past was 'the so-called Cleft Chin Murder', now a booklet, which was committed in the anonymous world of the dancehall, and involved a male–female criminal partnership between two people who previously had been strangers and that embodies 'the false values of the American [gangster] film' (*CO, XVIII*, p. 109). Orwell's tone in describing the earlier murders had been one of wry amusement at the details, but he treats those of the Cleft Chin Murder with a slight disdain, wondering whether it 'is significant that the most talked-of murder of recent years should have been committed by an American and an English girl who had become Americanised'. He leaves the question dangling, ending on a note that echoes some of the argument in 'Raffles and Miss Blandish' that the crimes of an earlier England were the product of a stable, if hypocritical, society when crimes had 'strong emotions behind them' (ibid., p. 110). The decline of the English murder, then, comes not so much from the crime itself but partly from the way in which the process of Americanization generally is replacing depth with surface, real passion with imitation.

'Some Thoughts on the Common Toad' (April 1946) and 'A Good Word for the Vicar of Bray' (April 1946) argue for the counterbalancing force of nature. Being *Tribune* pieces they are short, but in 'Thoughts on the Common Toad' especially Orwell manages to pack in a lyrical ode to the nature's beauty, a defence of the particular delights of the eponymous toad, an argument that the love of nature is not sentimental but has vital political implications, and a rousing finale that pits nature against bureaucrats and dictators. His regular essays allowed him not only to respond to political events, but also to predictable events such as the change of seasons, which explains the April publication of 'Some Thoughts on the Common Toad'. It opens mock-lyrically – 'Before the swallow, before the daffodil, and not much later than the snowdrop,' – and then introduces the essay's hero, the common toad, who 'salutes the coming of spring after its own fashion, which is to emerge from a hole in the ground, where he has lain since the previous autumn, and crawl as rapidly as possible towards the nearest suitable patch of water' (*CO, XVIII*, p. 238). This consciously unromantic end to the opening sentence creates a dynamic between the celebration of spring, which the essay draws from but also investigates, and Orwell's delight at spring's onset. This essay is perhaps as close as Orwell gets to being a Romantic, but while his love of the common toad is genuine, he also wishes to ruffle those who champion the more overtly beautiful and inherently passive or inert elements of nature. Superficially unattractive, the toad benefits from Orwell's semi-comic description of it as having 'a very spiritual look, like a strict Anglo-Catholic towards the end of Lent'. But Orwell's description of the toad's eye shows his acute attention to crucial aspects beyond the obvious: 'It is like gold, or more exactly it is like the golden-coloured semi-precious stone which one sometimes sees in signet-rings, and which I think is called a chrysoberyl' (ibid.). This deft combination of sharp observation and arcane, if tentatively offered, personal knowledge could be read as the essay's rhetorical strategy distilled into a sentence. But Orwell also uses the toad for a far broader purpose, taking it as the most explicit sign of natural pleasures that 'are available to everybody and cost nothing' (ibid., p. 239). More significantly, these pleasures are not confined to 'natural settings', Orwell observing that 'it is remarkable how Nature goes on existing unofficially, as it were, in the heart of London' (ibid.). The term 'unofficially' is vital to the essay's argument, for its key dynamic is the relationship between nature and the notion of freedom.

In an obvious way the return of spring is physical and visible, but Orwell's sense that (especially in the grim days of the war) this is some kind of 'miracle' that transfigures 'the decaying slum in which I live' clearly has slightly metaphysical aspects as well. Despite the title, the second half of the essay largely dispenses with the common toad, instead examining the way in which nature, generally, and spring, more specifically, are conceived, linking these conceptions to a political outlook. Here Orwell initially attacks those whose concentration on the purely political detaches them from the natural world, by asking rhetorical questions: 'Is it wicked to take a pleasure in spring and other seasonal changes?' 'Is it "politically reprehensible" in a time of capitalist oppression to point out the delights of nature "which does not cost money and does not have what the editors of left-wing newspapers call a class angle?"' (ibid.). Where Orwell in several contemporaneous essays had argued vigorously against political quietism, he admits in 'Thoughts on the Common Toad' that his interest in nature has been decried by *Tribune* readers as an argument in favour of quietism: 'People, so the thought runs, ought to be discontented' in order to activate them. He contests this view, arguing that while political passivity should be rejected, 'if we kill all pleasure in the actual process of life, what sort of future are we preparing for ourselves? If a man cannot enjoy the return of spring, why should he be happy in a labour-saving Utopia?' (ibid., p. 240). This ties in with his long-held suspicion, going back to *Wigan Pier*, of a Socialism based on the worship of machines and technology, which he reiterates here in the comment that if 'nothing is to be admired but concrete and steel', humanity's 'surplus energy' will find an outlet in 'hatred and hero worship'. That idea feeds into *Nineteen Eighty-Four*.

The illicit enjoyment of nature also operates in that novel, and the essay concludes by turning away from contestation with others on the Left to a more general musing about the onset of spring and political control: 'spring is here, even in London N.1, and they can't stop you enjoying it. That is a satisfying reflection', prefiguring the rebellious conclusion:

> spring is still spring. The atom bombs are piling up in the factories, the police are prowling through the cities, the lies are screaming from the loudspeakers, but the earth is still going round the sun, and neither the dictators nor the bureaucrats, deeply as they disapprove of the process, can prevent it. (ibid.)

The first section of this final sentence presents a world closer to Airstrip One than to Britain in 1946, and one of the horrifying features of *Nineteen Eighty-Four* is that for most members of the Party nature has been eradicated as a positive concept. But even within the less totalitarian actuality of post-war Britain, there was the potential for something worse. The essay employed *Tribune* readers to simultaneously enjoy one of the few things that the war could not take away while remaining politically engaged.

'A Good Word for the Vicar of Bray' is a slighter piece, but again it links nature to personal and positive thoughts. In fact, though it begins by explaining the significance of various disreputable characters such as the vicar, its purpose is to argue that reprobates also perform acts that have public benefits beyond their own lives, whether they will them or not. The Vicar of Bray planted a yew tree in his churchyard, and whatever his own failings, the tree has given pleasure for generations. 'And it struck me as curious', Orwell reflects, 'that such a man should have left such a relic behind him'. This thought prompts him to consider that the planting of a tree 'is a gift you can make to posterity at almost no cost and with almost no trouble' (*CO, XVIII*, p. 260). This sparks to a summary of the flowers and trees Orwell has planted over the years at his cottage in Wallington. A *Tribune* reader had attacked an earlier column on roses on the basis 'that roses are bourgeois', Orwell replying here that he thinks the sixpence spent on a Woolworth's rose 'was better spent than if it had gone on cigarettes or even on one of the excellent Fabian Research Pamphlets'. This brief squirt of sarcasm does not upset the essay's thrust, and he populates its last section with the assortment of bushes, flowers and fruit trees that he has planted. These acts only gain retrospective significance by his realization that they will give pleasure for years to come, which prompts the comment

> I am not suggesting that one can discharge all one's obigations towards society by means of a private re-afforestation. Still, it might not be a bad idea, every time you commit an anti-social act, to make a note of it in your diary, and then, at the appropriate season, push an acorn into the ground. (*CO, XVIII*, p. 261)

The suggestion displays Orwell's wry comic side and his capacity to address *Tribune* readers with a positively critical affinity. 'A Good Word for the Vicar of Bray' and 'Thoughts on the Common Toad' respond to the interests and perceptions of readers who, if only in the abstract sense, Orwell interacted with through his regular contributions.

Orwell's third essay for *Polemic*, 'Second Thoughts on James Burnham', appeared in its third number in May 1946. He also wrote an unsigned editorial for that issue in which he defended *Polemic* energetically against the charges given that it was guilty of 'persistent attempts to confuse moral issues' (made in the British Marxist journal, *Modern Quarterly*). Periodicals are implicitly rivals in terms of attracting readers, but rarely do they come to open rhetorical blows. But given Orwell's keen advocacy of the moral dimension in literature and politics his counterblast is powerful, focusing on the *Modern Quarterly* writer, Marxist physicist and public intellectual J. D. Bernal. Orwell attacks what he sees as the political expedience of Bernal's moral position which (as he reads it) boils down to the notion that what is right is what serves the cause of progress and that since the Soviet Union is the embodiment of progress and must be supported, 'any thing is right which furthers the aim of Russian foreign policy' (*CO, XVIII*, p. 265). Given the argument Orwell presents in 'Politics and the English Language', an equally revealing failing in Bernal's case is that his views are conveyed in English that is 'at once pompous and slovenly . . . It is not pedantic to draw attention to this, because the connection between totalitarian thoughts and the corruption of language is an important subject which has not been sufficiently studied' (ibid.). 'Politics and the English Language' would count as a notable corrective, as would (in different ways) 'The Prevention of Literature', and this cross-hatching of arguments through different essays and journals meant the transmission of significant (though perhaps unrecognized) ideas to a broad assortment of readers.

'Second Thoughts on James Burnham' deals at length with the sometimes influential ideas of Burnham, an American political scientist who in works such as *The Managerial Revolution* and *The Machiavellians* set out his analysis of the political power and his predictions – at different times – for the organization of global power. As commentators (Newsinger, p. 106; Crick, p. 467) have noted, Burnham's belief that in the future the world will divide into warring managerial superstates, and his suggestion that power is always held by oligarchies in a process that requires force and fraud, influence *Nineteen Eighty-Four*. Crick notes, though, that Orwell's idea for oligarchical collectivism (the title of Goldstein's apparently subversive text in the novel) 'preceded his reading of Burnham, and was not derived from it' (Crick, p. 406). Orwell had critically reviewed both *The Managerial Revolution* and *The Machiavellians* in *Tribune* several years earlier (activating a peppery exchange with Burnham). One of Orwell's many accusations against Burnham in this essay is that Burnham himself has second thoughts, particularly when the predictions he had confidently made are proved false by events. Orwell claims that in 1940 Burnham based his speculations on the inevitable victory of Germany and the breakup of the Soviet Union, with the consequent argument that the emerging superstates will be centred around 'Japan, Germany and the United States' (*CO, XVIII*, p. 273). Later, Burnham sees the rise of the Soviet Union as an indication that it will achieve global dominance, and treats Stalin as a 'great man'. Orwell detects a disturbing but revealing pattern in these and other speculations by Burnham (e.g. that capitalism is terminally ill and will be succeeded by managerialism). In essence, Orwell considers that 'Burnham is predicting *a continuation of the thing that is happening*' (ibid., p. 278). For Orwell this approach 'is a major mental disease, and its roots lie partly in cowardice and partly in the worship of power' (ibid.). This sceptical reading of Burnham's work might be a standard tactic in Orwell's shorter essays, but the larger space offered by *Polemic* allowed Orwell to indulge in a more extended piece of political analysis. A polemical tone does emerge at times, but the extra length meant that telling criticism could be made in more measured fashion.

Not that Orwell disagrees with all of Burnham's conclusions or predictions. Clearly the notion of endlessly warring states (something Orwell had already used as the basis of his reading of the cold war future in 'You and the Atom Bomb') finds its way in modified form into *Nineteen Eighty-Four*, as does the notion of a post-capitalist slave state that worships a great man. Interestingly, Orwell contends that Burnham's general idea of a post-capitalism, post-socialism managerial society is not new, and lists a set of earlier dystopias that depict similar negative visions, including Jack London's *The Iron Heel* and Zamyatin's *We*. (Both of these can be seen as influences on Orwell's own dystopia.) But Burnham's repeated method of predicting some future state of political organization from current trends suggests to Orwell a belief in the efficacy of raw power and in the inevitability of its triumph. This amounts to what he describes as 'power-worship', indicated by Burnham's new-found respect for Stalin. Related to this is a moral relativism that excuses the crimes of whichever oligarchy rules, a defining element from 'Notes on Nationalism'. For Orwell, this betrays Burnham's wish 'to destroy the old equalitarian version of Socialism and usher in a hierarchical society where the intellectual can at last get his hands on the whip' (ibid., p. 282). Suitably modified, this finds its way into the analysis of the Party in *Nineteen Eighty-Four*. Burnham's vision of what he takes to be a better, and, importantly, an inevitable future, provides a form of negative blueprint from which Orwell selects elements that he incorporates into his own thoughts about where the world might be heading. That qualification is crucial to understanding the speculative nature of *Nineteen Eighty-Four*: it does not pretend, as Orwell thinks Burnham's work does, to know the future as a result of the intellectual's superior awareness. Burnham's certainty about the inevitable triumph of oligarchies, and his consequent respect for those oligarchies, reveals for Orwell the damage 'done to the sense of reality by the cultivation of what is now called "realism"' (ibid., p. 284). For Orwell, unlike Burnham, recent history reveals that oligarchies do not always triumph, and that when they do that triumph will only be temporary.

'Second Thoughts on James Burnham' had the distinction of later being published as a pamphlet, under the title *James Burnham and the Managerial Revolution*, by the Socialist Book Centre in London. Three thousand copies were printed, and sold for a shilling. Because the pamphlet's publisher was American, Orwell asked Leonard Moore whether an American edition might be possible, and in fact it was published in 'Chicago University's *University Observer: A Journal of Politics*' (*CO*, XVIII, p. 284). Orwell sent a copy to Dwight Macdonald, who complained that Orwell was not sending his own journal, *Politics*, any material (ibid., p. 357, n.1). But a more serious problem emerged back in London, when the Socialist Book Centre was taken over by the Communist-oriented Collets Bookshop. Orwell thought it 'simply calamitous if there isn't one large leftwing bookshop not under [Communist Party] control' (ibid., p. 410), and feared that Collets 'would certainly let my pamphlet drop' (ibid., p. 446). In the event no harm seems to have come to the pamphlet, although the incident reflects Orwell's continually hostile and suspicious relationship with communists generally.

Orwell maintained a prolific essay output through 1946. A month after 'Politics and the English Language', 'Second Thoughts on James Burnham' was published; the following month 'Why I Write' appeared. This essay gets placed first in several posthumous collections, as though it were a manifesto of intention, a template for Orwell's work. The declarative title can provoke this misreading, apparently introducing a statement similar to Orwell's 'Why I Join the I.L.P.' nearly a decade earlier. In fact, the essay was a mid-career assessment. And the impetus for it was not Orwell's need to state his position, but a request from an obscure journal, *Gangrel*, whose fleeting existence in 1945–6 went largely unnoticed. In his opening 'Editorial Letter', Thomas Sawyer observes that *Gangrel*'s editor, J. B. Pick, 'acknowledges the difficulty of starting a "small review" with the large number that already exist, but he argues that "literary reviews are in the front-line against the world-wide advance towards totalitarianism" ' (Sawyer, p. 191). In 1946 Pick and co-editor, Charles Neil, asked a variety of writers to comment on whether 'writing is a vocational task'. The request fitted Pick's belief, expressed in the journal's third number, that '[v]ocational work is the only salvation and happiness which an individual man who has honestly stripped himself of egoistic illusions can hope to discover in the modern world' (ibid.). The back cover of that number also proclaimed that the journal had persuaded 'Neil M. Gunn, Rayner Heppenstall, Claude Houghton, Henry Miller, George Orwell, Alfred Perles to give their views on Why I Write in the next Gangrel' (Marks, 1995, p. 272). In the event only Gunn, Heppenstall, Perles and Orwell were published, although Miller did publish essays in other numbers. The origins of 'Why I Write' and the fact that the topic was offered to Orwell and others undermine any sense of Orwell wishing to make a personal testament. The essay is personal in its content, but not as personally driven as often thought.

Orwell begins with an acknowledgement to the vocational aspect Pick foregrounded, recalling that

> From a very early age, perhaps the age of five or six, I knew that when I grew up I should be a writer. Between the ages of about seventeen and twenty-four I tried to abandon this idea, but I did so with the consciousness that I was outraging my true nature and that sooner or later I should have to settle down and write. (*CO*, *XVIII*, p. 316)

The first half of 'Why I Write' conforms to *Gangrel's* brief, elaborating on Orwell's childhood thoughts and experiences as they relate to his literary development, with its strong sense of an aesthetic vocation. Most of these early memories record naïve hopes, clumsy efforts and stifled ambitions, offering a nostalgic account of his youth, ending with the recollection that at 16 he had wanted to write 'enormous naturalistic novels with unhappy endings, full of detailed descriptions and arresting similes' (ibid., p. 317). This aspiration, he suggests, is manifest in his first novel, *Burmese Days*. Naturally the degree of selection here involves some creative editing of his literary life (how does *Down and Out in Paris and London* fit this pattern?) but its more general purpose lies in supplying background information without which, Orwell argues, 'I do not think you can assess a writer's motives' (ibid., p. 318). As with the notion of a vocation, the question of motives highlights character, but despite the highly personalized account to this point, the 'four great motives for writing' he lists – 'sheer egoism'; 'aesthetic enthusiasm'; 'historical impulse'; 'political purpose' (ibid.) – are those he considers common to writers.

That generalizing prompts the assertion that the 'various impulses must war against each other . . . [fluctuating] from person to person and from time to time' (ibid.). The specific circumstances for individual writers, then, also have a determining effect on the type of writing they produce, mediating the degree to which one or other impulse dominates. 'I am a person', Orwell writes, 'in whom the first three motives would outweigh the fourth. In a peaceful age I might have written ornate or merely descriptive books, and might have remained unaware of my political loyalties' (ibid., pp. 318–19). Experiences in Burma and life and among the down and out, however, recalibrated the effect of each motive. Crucially, though,

> The Spanish war and other events in 1936-7 turned the scale and thereafter I knew where I stood. Every line of serious work that I have written since 1936 has been written, directly or indirectly, *against* totalitarianism and *for* democratic Socialism, as I understand it. (ibid., p. 319)

Context matters, its impact being both difficult to resist and consequential; the ongoing interplay between motivating factors and circumstance in Orwell's case creating a dominating aspiration: 'What I have most wanted to do throughout the past ten years is to make political writing into an art' (ibid.). The undoubted centrality of politics had not eradicated other impulses, but he indicates that his starting point for writing 'is always a feeling of partisanship, a sense of injustice', that there is 'some lie I want to expose, some fact to which I want to draw attention' (ibid.). These qualities and impulses energize his non-fiction especially, but he also indicates that the act of writing could not be completed if it were not also 'an aesthetic experience'. The essay ends with a reconsideration of egoism and its relation to aesthetics and politics.

'All writers are vain, selfish and lazy', he declares – 'And yet it is also true that one can write nothing readable unless one constantly struggles to efface one's own personality.' This almost contradictory dynamic between motive, circumstance and the effacing of personality prefaces a sentence that in time would be closely associated with Orwell's writing and his personality: 'Good prose is like a windowpane' (ibid., p. 320). Commentators and critics have repeatedly pointed out both the problems with this statement and the fact that while Orwell's prose often can be a model of lucidity it can also be generalized and hyperbolic. The overriding point in terms of the essay, though, lies in the statement's setting up of a stylistic model that in some way resolves the tensions between motives and context, enabling writers to expose lies and to publicize facts. These aspirations and the attention to the relationship between style and some notion of truthfulness links 'Why I Write' to 'Politics and the English Language' and to 'The Prevention of Literature'. But where the former essay had ended on the exhortation to write and think clearly and jeer formulaic and mindlessly orthodox phrases out of existence, 'Why I Write' concludes on the self-critical and retrospective note that

> looking back through my work, I see that it is invariably when I lacked a *political* purpose that I wrote lifeless books and was betrayed into purple passages, sentences without meaning, decorative adjectives and humbug generally. (*CO, XVIII*, p. 320)

For an essay that begins with the rather romantic evocation of childhood as an apprenticeship for a literary vocation, 'Why I Write' concludes not on the triumphal fulfilment of an aspiration but on the rather more sombre admission of failure. As Pick suggested, vocations demand the honest stripping away of egoistic illusions, and the essay is both Orwell's declaration and a piece of considered self-criticism.

Polemic provided Orwell with sufficient latitude to write at length on topics that interested him, one result being 'Politics vs. Literature: An Examination of *Gulliver's Travels*' in the journal's September-October 1946 number. In some ways an essay on a 200-year-old text can be seen as something of an indulgence, even if that text is a classic piece of political literature. But the essay figures as one of the few works by Orwell to carry out something approaching an extended piece of literary criticism. He had written hundreds of reviews and considered writers such as Dickens, Shakespeare and Kipling at length (and it is telling that Dickens, Shakespeare and Swift would be among the writers whose work was still being translated into Newspeak in *Nineteen Eighty-Four*; *CO, XVIII*, p. 325) though rarely had an essay focused primarily on a single text. 'Politics vs. Literature' also exhibits *Polemic*'s own eclecticism, and by implication the range of interests readers might have of a journal whose subtitle only included philosophy, psychology and ethics.

While concentrating on *Gulliver's Travels* Orwell links it to contemporary concerns about totalitarian control, as well as to more general questions about the complicated relationship between literary merit and enjoyment. This sometimes leads him to equate Swift with Gulliver too easily (although he does recognize the complex and uneasy relationship between the author and his creation) and the essay to a degree is an examination of Swift as much as his book.

Orwell leaps into the text, arguing in the opening sentence that '[i]n *Gulliver's Travels* humanity is attacked, or criticized, from at least three different angles, and the implied character of Gulliver himself necessarily changes somewhat in the process' (*CO, XIX*, p. 417). The term 'implied character' is rather odd, as Gulliver narrates the various tales in the first person – they are 'his' travels, after all – but this introductory statement sets up the later proposition 'that in his shrewder moments Gulliver is Swift himself' (ibid.). This position allows Orwell to ascribe opinions to Swift – as in, '[t]he Houyhnhnms, Swift's ideal beings' (ibid., p. 420) – that are properly Gulliver's. Since, after an initial degree of association with the tale's narrator readers are likely to be put off by Gulliver's arrogance and lack of awareness, and alienated by his descent into horse-adoring madness, the distinctions between the author and his increasingly risible creation are worth retaining. The absence of any extended consideration of Gulliver as a device indicates that Orwell's interest lies less in the purely literary aspects of the text than in the ideas that animate it and the pertinence of those ideas to the modern world. Swift's name appears far more than Gulliver's, and it is Swift's rancorously pessimistic mind and political thought that Orwell is interested in. Intriguingly, he characterizes Swift as being a 'Tory anarchist', the term he used to describe himself to the staff at *The Adelphi* in the early 1930s. But this coincidence should not be seen as a conscious sign of Orwell's identification with Swift, for Swift's 'animus . . . against *England*' (ibid., p. 418) his ambivalence to democracy (ibid., p. 419), his desire for 'a static, incurious civilzation'(ibid., p. 421) and his 'inability to think that life – ordinary life on the solid earth, and not some rationalized, deodorized version of it – could be made worth living' (ibid., p. 425) stand in outright opposition to Orwell's own views. Where Swift sees no chance for a better world, and therefore remains disdainful of progressive ideas, Orwell repeatedly makes the case for political engagement that takes account of actual conditions, real possibilities and dangers.

Yet Orwell dismisses neither Swift nor *Gulliver's Travels*, understanding the writer as 'a rebel and an iconoclast' who cannot, however, 'be labeled "Left". He is a Tory anarchist, despising authority while disbelieving in liberty, and preserving the aristocratic outlook while clearly seeing that the aristocracy is contemptible' (ibid.). And he argues for Swift's current pertinence by declaring that his 'greatest contribution to political thought' is his attack in Part III of *Gulliver's Travels* on what would now be called totalitarianism. He has the extraordinarily clear prevision of the spy-haunted 'police State', with the endless heresy-hunts and treason trials, all designed to neutralize popular discontent by changing it into war hysteria. (ibid., p. 423)

Orwell links this into another illuminating idea from Swift's satire, that 'one of the aims of totalitarianism is not merely to make sure that people will think the right thoughts, but actually to make them *less conscious*' (ibid., p. 424). He was composing the first draft of *Nineteen Eighty-Four* when he wrote the essay. The interchange between the works is interesting to speculate on without it necessarily being possible to establish actual links. Certainly the concerns overlap and partly explain the choice of Swift as a subject. As well as making the rather anachronistic connection between *Gulliver's Travels* and totalitarianism, Orwell idiosyncratically fuses the ideology with anarchism and pacifism, as he had done in his 1942 'London Letter' which excoriated the anarchist journal *Now* and some of its staff. For Orwell, the anarchist half of the 'Tory anarchist' epithet has totalitarian aspects, for in a world with no laws 'the only arbiter of behaviour is public opinion' (ibid.) and since in the land of Houyhnhnm's rationality has done away with disagreement, '[t]hey had reached, in fact, the highest state of totalitarian organization, the stage when conformity has become so general that there is no need for a police force' (ibid., p. 425). This take on anarchism would draw a strong response from *Now*'s editor George Woodcock, eventually published in the journal *Freedom – Through Anarchism*, who argued that Orwell had misunderstood anarchism, in that it advocated private judgement not public opinion, and that he had wrongly conflated anarchism and pacifism. ('Many anarchists', retorted Woodcock, 'believe in violence' [*CO, XVIII*, p. 431].)

For all his criticism of Swift and his ideas, Orwell admits that he is 'one of the writers that I admire with least reserve' (ibid., p. 428) a comment that prompts the essay's concluding discussion of the relationship between literary merit, enjoyment, and the reader's agreement with the ideas or world view the writer puts forward. In different ways the associations and tensions between the ability to appreciate ideas that a reader does not agree with reappear through Orwell's work, both in relation to his own views and to his broader sense of how various orthodoxies require readers to prejudge a book's merits on the basis of its perceived or preconceived 'position'. For Orwell this approach is inherently corrupting of the individual's response and of the cultural climate generally. Swift provides something of a test case for considering how the reader can appreciate a writer with whom in many respects they disagree profoundly. He thinks it insufficient that some form of aesthetic merit can be invoked, excusing Swift his views because 'he was a good writer' (ibid., p. 429). Even accepting this as true is not sufficient, and Orwell declares that while Swift's pessimism is 'diseased' he also states some unappealing truisms about humans and the human condition. What he does not do is consider the whole, but is 'leaving something out'. So while '[h]uman behaviour . . . especially in politics, is as he describes it . . . it contains more important factors which he refuses to admit' (ibid., p. 430). Despite the deficiency (and perhaps, one might add to Orwell, because of it) while 'Swift did not possess ordinary wisdom . . . he did possess a terrible intensity of vision, capable of picking out a single hidden truth and then magnifying and distorting it' (ibid.). For some, this assessment would also count as valid for *Nineteen Eighty-Four* and its author.

In the post-war period Orwell was consciously trying to get his essays and articles published in the United States, but he noted later that his American agents failed to find a publisher for 'Politics vs. Literature' (*CO, XIX*, p. 127). He had better luck in Britain with 'How the Poor Die', published in the November 1946 issue of *Now*, surprising given that *Now*'s editor George Woodcock had recently attacked Orwell over his misrepresentation of anarchism. If nothing else the essay shows Orwell's habit of befriending people he had previously abused. (Woodcock, in fact, would later write the highly appreciative book, *The Crystal Spirit: A Study of George Orwell* (1966).) The essay gives an autobiographical account of the time Orwell spent in a Parisian hospital in 1929 (when he was still the would-be writer Eric Blair) and Peter Davison speculates that initial drafts of the essay might have been written between 1931 and 1936 and then set aside (ibid., p. 456). What does appear certain is that *Horizon* rejected the essay, perhaps under advice that the rendition of conditions in the hospital was exaggerated. When Woodcock asked him for material Orwell retrieved 'How the Poor Die' and sent it to *Now*. Woodcock would later recall that Orwell also sent him 'quite a large donation . . . to help in keeping the magazine alive' (ibid., p. 459, n.1). Margaret Baker Graham indicates the importance of such generosity in noting that '[f]rom the beginning, *Now* failed to have the necessary financial backing to appear consistently. Seven issues were published in 1940 and 1941; in the new series nine issues appeared between 1943 and mid-1947' (Graham, p. 316). Within a year of Orwell's contribution *Now* would be gone.

'How the Poor Dies' gives a bleak account of a short stay in the 'Hospital X, in the fifteenth Arrondissement of Paris', but as Davison explains, several differences between the portrait painted here and Blair's actual time in the Hôpital Cochin reveal that the essay, 'though based on experience, is not strictly autobiographical' (*CO, XVIII*, p. 466, n. 1). The same was true of many other works from the period before Blair became Orwell, accounts that draw from experience but are edited to present the facts in a striking way. This essay produces a nightmare picture of terrible conditions and indifference to the suffering of the poor from a sympathetic rather than a merely sociological perspective. Orwell had written before from the eyewitness position, that of someone who ventures in dangerous places and is reporting back to those who might otherwise have no awareness of the hidden reality. But here the journey is involuntary, the result, he writes, of being ill with pneumonia (Davison indicates that it was influenza; *CO, XVIII*, p. 466, n.2) and without funds. There follows an extended rendering of his own harsh treatment, before he begins to consider the position of one of the patients packed into the crowded ward, where they are treated as specimens by medical students and with degrees of indifference by other staff. The hospital context, its attitudes and practices are at least as important as the sketched-in lives of the other patients, who are distinguished Dickens-like by catchphrases and repeated actions, or, in the case of Numero 57, by a number. While his experience took place in Paris, this anonymous and amorphous group of suffering poor are treated as symbolic of a whole class of people still likely to receive substandard treatment in Britain. Orwell understood, though, that local conditions and practices were far better.

While it moves easily from personal experience to a broader awareness of the plight of the Parisian poor, the essay ends not in the world of 1929 but in Orwell's childhood memories. Given the grim report of conditions this is odd, but throughout the essay Orwell weaves documentary with a feel for the invisible but powerful mood of the hospital, the atmosphere that overrides the physicality of the place. 'The dread of hospitals still survives among the very poor', he concludes, 'and in all of us it has only recently disappeared. It is a dark patch not far beneath the surface of the mind' (ibid., p. 466). Orwell broods on the 'strange feeling of familiarity' activated by his time in the hospital, finding a source in a poem read to him by a sick-nurse as a child: Tennyson's *The Children's Hospital*. 'We had shuddered over the poem together', he remembers, 'and then seemingly I had forgotten it'. But the Hospital X 'suddenly roused the train of thought to which it belonged . . . and I found myself remembering the whole story and atmosphere of the poem, with many of its lines complete' (ibid.). This somewhat gothic ending, with its worrying return of an apparently forgotten memory, demonstrates Orwell's capacity in 'How the Poor Dies' to integrate an array of modes, moods and perspectives: documentary and personal revelation; the public and private worlds; literary portrait and social analysis; fear, disgust and horror. It reprises the world in which he began as a writer, but does so with a more complex and sophisticated understanding of social forces.

In February 1947 Orwell commented in a letter to Dwight Macdonald that he had joined the editorial board of *Polemic* and thought the 'paper [was] now taking shape a bit, and is doing fairly well from the point of view of circulation, though hampered by the usual organizational difficulties' (*CO, XIX*, p. 50). He also made some suggestions about 'Lear, Tolstoy and the Fool', an essay *Polemic* was publishing and that Macdonald had indicated he might print in truncated form in *Politics*. The trigger for the essay was Tolstoy's obscure pamphlet attacking Shakespeare, and in an earlier letter Orwell accepted that here was 'something in what you [Macdonald] say about Tolstoy's denunciation of

Shakespeare not being worth answering' (ibid., p. 28). In the event Macdonald did not publish 'Lear, Tolstoy and the Fool', and his comment and the idea of truncating the essay suggest a certain justified reluctance; the subject matter was more literary than political in any case, and the essay seems a rather odd exercise in exhuming Tolstoy's 1906 pamphlet *Shakespeare and the Drama* only to bury it again and stamp on the grave. The first pages of 'Lear, Tolstoy and the Fool' require a capitulation of the pamphlet's argument, since most *Polemic* readers would not have read it. Orwell considers the play that Tolstoy focuses on in the pamphlet, *King Lear*, briefly examining Tolstoy's analysis, which he takes to be partial and 'a prolonged exercise in misrepresentation' (ibid., p. 57). More important for Orwell's argument, though, are parallels between the play and Tolstoy's own life, and the essay's main interest lies not so much in the pamphlet, or *Lear*, than in what the pamphlet tells us about Tolstoy's philosophy. Rather as 'Politics vs. Literature' concentrated more on Swift than on *Gulliver's Travels*, 'Lear, Tolstoy and the Fool' addresses itself primarily, once the purely literary aspects are taken care of, with the dangers of Tolstoy's desire to be a saint.

Tolstoy has a brief walk-on part in 'Politics vs. Literature', judged as someone who, like Swift and William Blake, 'hates the very idea of studying the processes of Nature' (*CO*, XVIII, p. 421). While Swift does not get mentioned in 'Lear, Tolstoy and the Fool' it is possible to connect the two writers in their disdain for humanist struggle. Swift, in Orwell's reading, disavows the idea that life can be made worth living and also denies the possibility of a better world beyond. Tolstoy, in his attempt to live a saintly life

> is not trying to work an improvement in earthly life: he is trying to bring it to an end and put something different in its place . . . If only, Tolstoy says in effect, we could stop breeding, fighting, struggling and enjoying . . . then the whole painful process would be over and the Kingdom of Heaven would arrive. (*CO*, XIX, pp. 63–4)

Swift does not give himself the comfort of Tolstoy's afterlife, but both reject the earthly struggle. And for Orwell this disdain for the messy tussle with life as it is lived and for humans as they are reveals why Tolstoy despises *King Lear*. There are, he suggests, parallels between the Russian writer and the Shakespearean character (both are powerful men who in old age must confront their failing powers). But there are more fundamental differences, particularly that while Tolstoy renounces the world, *King Lear*, like all of Shakespeare's tragedies starts 'out with the humanist assumption that life, although full of sorrow, is worth living, and that Man is a noble animal'. Lear the character comes to recognize this too late through his own suffering and the death of Cordelia, but this is 'a belief that Tolstoy in his old age did not share' (ibid., p. 63).

What Tolstoy does possess, in Orwell's interpretation, is a desire for power. This reading of him also connects Tolstoy to the analysis presented in 'Politics vs. Literature' in which – counter-intuitively at best and incorrectly at worst – Orwell equates pacifism and anarchy to totalitarianism. Despite Woodcock's challenge to that account of anarchism, Orwell lays a similar charge here: that Tolstoy fervently believes he is right and therefore tries to

> get inside [the reader's] brain and dictate his thoughts for him in the minutest particulars. Creeds like pacifism and anarchism, which seem on the surface to be a complete renunciation of power, rather encourage this habit of mind. For if you have embraced a creed which appears to be free from the ordinary dirtiness of politics . . . surely that proves that you are in the right? And the more that you are in the right, the more natural that everyone else should be bullied into thinking likewise. (ibid., p. 66)

Clearly Orwell did not take Woodcock's views on board in making this sweeping and unsubstantiated connection between anarchy, pacifism and power lust. In any case, that attack is a passing blow compared to Orwell's more substantial assault on Tolstoy's attempt to denounce Shakespeare. He ends the essay by noting with satisfaction that in the contest between the saintly but quasi-totalitarian novelist and the messy humanist the plays have survived far better than the 'yellowing pages of a pamphlet that hardly anyone has read' (ibid.).

Despite Orwell's hope for the future of *Polemic* it ceased abruptly after this issue. Although a new member of its Editorial Board, this took him by surprise, and in a puzzled letter to his friend Celia Kirwan, who helped produce the journal, he asked did she 'know the inner story of what happened to *Polemic*? I merely had a line from Humphrey [Slater] saying they were packing up. Did [*Polemic*'s financial 'angel'] Rodney Phillips get sick of spending money on it, or was there a quarrel?' (*CO, XIX*, p. 223). As Davison explains, the former interpretation was correct: 'When Phillips tired of giving it financial support, it folded. Slater then moved to Spain. There was no quarrel' (ibid., n.4). Orwell later described this to Julian Symons as a 'calamity' (ibid., p. 237), but as we have seen repeatedly, *Polemic*'s demise was anything but rare.

One journal that continued to flourish was *Partisan Review*, for which Orwell continued to write occasional 'London Letters'. He noted in an 'As I Please' column that it was to be published in London from February 1947, describing it as 'one of the best highbrow magazines – rather like a synthesis of *Horizon* and *Polemic*' (*CO, XIX*, p. 26). Davison reveals that the journal 'invited a number of well-known authors to contribute to a series called "The Future of Socialism". Orwell's essay was the fourth' (ibid., p. 161). The journal's editors, he continues, asked contributors to consider whether in the uncertain post-war world the relative failure of European nations to install

Socialism was a 'temporary setback or a more permanent check to its progress' (ibid., p. 162). More than most requested essays, Orwell's response – 'Toward European Unity' – adheres to *Partisan Review*'s brief. He adopts a schematic approach; after the literary flourish of the opening, where he represents a socialist as a 'doctor treating an all but hopeless case', Orwell lists three possibilities ahead: that the Americans use the atom bomb while only they have it; that the 'cold war' continues until more nations are nuclear armed, after which a more widespread nuclear war ravages the population; that no such war occurs and that three superstates would emerge, ruled over by elites, with the 'crushing out of liberty' exceeding 'anything that the world has yet seen' (ibid., p. 163). The last of these, roughly approximating the one he was fashioning in *Nineteen Eighty-Four*, was the worst. The only means of avoiding such futures would be 'a socialist United States of Europe' something he judges 'the only worth-while political objective today' (ibid., p. 164). The relatively confined space of this essay (just over 2,000 words) ensures that Orwell has no time to sketch what that union might look like; instead he lists the difficulties facing such a plan, the greatest being the 'apathy and conservatism of people everywhere' (ibid.).

Against this inertia he lists four 'active malignant forces working against European unity' (ibid.): Russian hostility; American hostility; Imperialism; The Catholic Church. The first three are relatively unsurprising in themselves, while the fourth sets up one of Orwell's most consistently vilified targets along with the Soviet Union and left-wing intellectuals. The Russians have obvious reasons to be hostile to a Socialist European union, but he complicates the relationship by adding that for Socialism to attract sufficient support the 'Russian myth' that it somehow embodies Socialism needs to be rejected. From another ideological perspective American hostility to any Socialist Europe also seems obvious, Orwell speculating whether the United States might try to draw Britain away as a means of neutralizing the threat. He counters, though, that Britain can only overcome its dependence on the United States by joining Europe. He repeats his claim from as far back as 'Not Counting Niggers' that British workers are the beneficiaries of imperialism because they receive the fruits of colonial exploitation, adjusting this only by including all European peoples. But he suggests that in order to compete with the Soviet Union and the United States, a European federation would need to include Africa and the Middle East, and that this in turn would lead to tensions that would 'not likely be settled without bloodshed' (ibid., p. 165). Clearly, this projection never became a reality. His sense that if the Catholic Church remains powerful 'true socialism' would be 'impossible' rests on the conviction that the institution is 'against freedom of thought and speech, against human equality, and against any form of society tending to promote earthly happiness' (ibid., p. 166). Whether or not (even in 1947) its influence in Europe was sufficient to warrant this level of antagonism remains questionable, but more surprising perhaps is

Orwell's failure to take up the suggestion in the *Partisan Review* brief that 'narrow nationalism' has also retarded the broader spread of Socialism. Whatever the reason for this, 'Toward European Unity' offers speculations rather than expectations, including the projection that 'there may by 1960 be millions of young Russians who are bored by dictatorship and loyalty parades, eager for more freedom, and friendly in their attitude toward the West' (ibid., p. 167). History would record this as a false prediction but it remains an intriguing reading of political potential. The essay ends on a suitably ambiguous thought that even if the world devolved into superstates, the liberal tradition might survive and hold out

> some hope of progress. But all this is speculation. The actual outlook, so far as I can calculate, is very dark, and any serious thought should start out from that fact.

The superficially negative take on Socialism's future hides complexities and possibilities. While the hope of progress is speculation and the outlook is dark, the qualification that that reading is subjective immediately exposes it to questioning. Even while prosecuting a hardheaded argument, 'Toward European Unity' advertises its limitations, and as with so many other essays the apparent 'conclusion' acts to primarily prompt responses.

Orwell completed the first stage of a far more extended and bleaker speculation in November 1947 with the draft of *Nineteen Eighty-Four*, but by December was so ill with tuberculosis that he was advised to enter a sanatorium the following month. He stayed at Hairmyes Hospital in Glasgow from December 1947 until May 1948, restricted by doctors' orders to light work. There he wrote 'Writers and Leviathan' for the fledgling journal *Politics and Letters,* part of its series 'Critic and Leviathan', commenting to Julian Symons that he

> was quite well impressed by the magazine, which I hadn't seen before, & it may well develop into the sort of thing we need so badly. The trouble is you must have an angel or you can't keep the magazine alive. 'Politics' is evidently tottering badly – it's become a quarterly which is usually a very bad symptom. (*CO, XIX*, p. 287)

Orwell's ignorance of *Politics and Letters* was understandable. It had been founded in 1947 by Wolf Mankowitz, Clifford Collins and Raymond Williams, the trio that had also edited the two issues of *The Critic: A Quarterly Review of Criticism*, before it was incorporated into *Politics and Letters.* Williams was later a massively influential figure in cultural studies, but in 1947 was a postgraduate tutoring at Oxford. His highly complex, changing and ultimately antagonistic reading of Orwell need not concern us here, but the overlap between these two influential figures from different generations re-emphasizes how journals

established and maintained networks and associations of the like-minded –
and sometimes of the opposed. Certainly Orwell was a major catch for the
new journal, although it also published work by Jean-Paul Sartre, the Marxist
historian Christopher Hill and the critic F. R. Leavis, *Scrutiny*'s editor. Williams
later recalled that the journal aimed to

> unite a radical left politics with Leavisite criticism. We were to be to the left
> of the Labour Party, but a distance from the [Communist Party]. Our affili-
> ation to *Scrutiny* was guarded, but it was none the less quite a strong one.
> (Williams, p. 65)

Orwell's own political position might be assessed in comparable terms at this
stage, partly explaining the fit between author and journal. In his study of
Williams, John Higgins situates *Politics and Letters*

> in opposition to three currents of thought . . . the failed Marxist theory
> of the 1930s . . . the (a)political stance of Leavis's *Scrutiny*, by now the key
> journal of [British academic] literary studies . . . and what was seen as the
> self-conscious metropolitanism and self-indulgent aestheticism of Cyril
> Connolly's *Horizon*. (Higgins, p. 10)

We might see Orwell similarly (though not identically) situated. His contribution to the 'Critic and Leviathan' series partly reworks ideas about the dangers
of political orthodoxy on the independence of the writer going back to the
mid-1930s, particularly the idea that because of ideological positions and divisions, reviewed books 'are judged before they are read, and in effect before
they are written. One knows in advance what reception they will get in what
papers' (*CO, XIX*, p. 288). This general attack upon the intellectual dishonesty of reviewers nests within a larger argument that the overwhelming political imperatives of the age have led to the 'invasion of literature by politics'
(ibid.). The devotion to aestheticism of a Joyce or a James is now impossible, he
writes, but there is a worrying consequence: 'to accept political responsibility
now means yielding oneself over to orthodoxies and "party lines", with all the
timidity and dishonesty that that implies' (ibid., p. 289).

What has changed substantially since Victorian times, and especially since
the beginning of the 1930s, is that 'the dominant ideology, especially among
the young, has been "left" ' (ibid.). While he accepts this as better than the
preceding conservative orthodoxy, for Orwell, as it has been at least as far
back as the essay 'Charles Dickens', orthodoxy itself inherently requires
adherence to a set of beliefs despite the evidence of reality. Orwell would
depict orthodoxy at its farthest point in *Nineteen Eighty-Four*, where Syme
explains to Winston Smith: 'Orthodoxy means not thinking, not needing to
think. Orthodoxy is unconsciousness' (*CO, IX*, p. 56). But, in the actual world

of 1948 orthodoxy still involved a conscious act and, in Orwell's eyes, should be resisted. Part of the aim of 'Writers and Leviathan' was to expose the realities an orthodox left-wing supporter needed to ignore: that the Soviet Union was not Socialist in any meaningful sense, and that Britain's empire made even the British workers exploiters of the colonized peoples. While these problems affect all those who accept orthodox positions, the essay's title indicates Orwell's particular concern with writers and the impact of orthodoxy on what they produce. The 'acceptance of any political discipline', he argues, 'seems to be incompatible with literary integrity' (*CO, XIX,* p. 291). His own association with the ILP in the late 1930s perhaps provides a personal point of reference. 'As soon as [group loyalties] are allowed to have any influence' he continues, 'the result is not only falsification but often the actual drying up of the inventive faculties' (ibid.). The writer can work for a political party, but must retain the freedom to 'completely [reject] official ideology. He should never turn his back on a train of thought because it may lead to heresy' (ibid., p. 292). Political engagement should not entail the sacrifice of intellectual independence.

What about the activity of writing itself? 'Do we have to conclude', he asks rhetorically, that 'it is the duty of every writer to "keep out of politics"?' As in 'Notes on Nationalism' and 'The Prevention of Literature' the response is clear and emphatic: 'Certainly not!' (ibid., p. 291). Instead, Orwell distinguishes between involvement in politics in the more everyday sense and writing, a distinction that needs to be maintained: 'When a writer engages in politics he should do so as a citizen . . . but not *as a writer*'. Does this proposition also require that the writer should stop writing about politics? 'Once again, certainly not!' he replies, noting that 'to lock oneself in the ivory tower is impossible' in an overtly political age. But the capacity to engage in politics while writing creative and independent-minded literature means that writers move beyond a simplistic Manichean view of good and evil ideologies to a more subtle and empirically based sense that in 'politics one can never do more than decide which of two evils is the less' (ibid., p. 292). By 1948 the reality of a Labour government supplies the most obvious and consequential difference to the political dynamic and outlook: 'At this moment we see our own government, in its desperate economic straits, fighting in effect against its own past propaganda' (ibid., p. 290). Yet this acceptance of the 'dirty, degrading business' (ibid., p. 292) of politics does not mean that writers should succumb to the call by political parties to write, in effect, for them. The writer can

act resolutely . . . violently if need be . . . But his writings, in so far as they have any value, will always be the product of his saner self that stands aside, records the things that are done and admits their necessity, but refuses to be deceived as to their true nature. (ibid.)

Political engagement did not release writers from the key duty to tell the truth, nor, in advance of that, to relinquish the sceptical assessment of political arguments against reality's yardstick.

The essay was published in the fourth number of *Politics and Letters*, which would be its last. It also appeared in the New York-based independent journal *The New Leader* (not to be confused with the ILP's paper of the same name), for which Orwell had previously written a review. This reaching out to new periodicals in both Britain and the United States emphasizes his sustained effort to publish his views in as wide a range of journals as possible. It also indicates his developing status in America. But his comment about the 'tottering' *Politics* and the actual demise of *Politics and Letters* after only four issues (despite publishing Orwell and Sartre) starkly exposes the pressured environment most journals operated in – *Polemic*, too, by this stage had already folded. Financial imperatives, paper shortages (especially in Britain), the undulating enthusiasms of staff and the need continually to attract quality material, as well as the competition from other journals (and other media) ensured that individual journals lived by their wits. One positive aspect of this pressure was that in order to survive journals needed to publish good writing, and in offering themselves to writers they also provided vital encouragement, creating an immense effect on what was produced. Another general plus, although not always appreciated by editors, contributors or readers, was that the rise and fall of journals ensured a regularly renewed periodical culture generally. Obviously this turnover need not in itself be a good thing – excellent, if edgy, journals sometimes floundered while more careful and mediocre periodicals stayed afloat. But the absence of the ideal periodical culture need not completely devalue the reality that did exist, one that supplied outlets for innumerable writers and intellectual sustenance for a far greater number of readers.

Illness continued to have a devastating effect upon his writing through 1948 and 1949. Having left Hairmyes Hosptial in July 1948 Orwell returned to his home on the Scottish island of Jura where he completed *Nineteen Eighty-Four*, which he sent to Secker and Warburg in December 1948. He did manage a small amount of other writing, most notably an essay for *Partisan Review*, 'Reflections on Gandhi', published in January 1949. Its opening sentence, 'Saints should always be judged guilty until they are proved innocent' carries echoes of Orwell's verdict on Tolstoy and in fact the two men are linked in 'Lear, Tolstoy and the Fool': 'A sort of doubt has always hung around the character of Tolstoy, as around the character of Gandhi' (*CO, XIX*, p. 65). Tolstoy gets criticized for his love of power, but Orwell does not comment on Gandhi there, by implication distinguishing the two. Here, though, Orwell uses a recently translated edition of Gandhi's *The Story of My Experiments with Truth* along with his own reading of Gandhi's actions to test the case for Gandhi's saintliness. As we might expect from his assessment of Tolstoy, Orwell by nature remains antagonistically sceptical of such claims or beliefs, but his first view of the opening chapters of the autobiography that he had read in an Indian newspaper

> made a good impression of me, while Gandhi himself, at the time, did not. The things that one associated with him – homespun cloth, 'soul forces' and vegetarianism – were unappealing, and his medievalist program was obviously not viable in a backward, starving overpopulated country. (*CO, XX*, p. 5)

Orwell, though, acknowledges Gandhi's moral strength: that he was not corrupt or vulgarly ambitious; did nothing because of fear or malice; was courageous; treated all people equally. 'Almost from childhood onwards', Orwell writes, 'he had a deep earnestness, and attitude ethical rather than religious' (ibid., p. 7). Whereas Tolstoy's saintliness in Orwell's eyes remains egocentric and oppressive to others, Gandhi's thought and action have an actively social component that because of his refusal to compromise instigated massive change.

That said, Orwell tries to distinguish Gandhi from left-wing Westerners who would claim him for pacifism and anarchism, criticizing these groups for ignoring that Gandhi 'was opposed to centralism and State violence and ignoring the otherwordly, anti-humanist tendency of his doctrine' (ibid.). Orwell's own championing of humanism in pieces such as 'Politics vs. Literature' and 'Lear, Tolstoy and the Fool' might produce a level of disdain for Gandhi, but in this instance the fact that 'Gandhi's teachings cannot be squared with the [humanist] belief that Man is the measure of all things, and that our job is to make life worth living on this earth, which is the only earth we have' (ibid., p. 6) is used not against him but against Western Leftists. Orwell wishes also to distinguish between the pacifism of such Leftists and Gandhi's own programme of *Satyagraha*, which he explains translates not as 'passive resistance' but as 'firmness in truth'. Thus *Satyagraha*, evolved in South Africa where Gandhi as a young lawyer had led action against local racism, involved 'a sort of non-violent warfare' (ibid., p. 8). This active programme understands the need for struggle, and for the preference for one arrangement over another, so that Gandhi did not 'take the sterile and dishonest line of pretending that in every war both sides are exactly the same and it makes no difference who wins' (ibid., p. 9). Orwell does not admire Gandhi's inhuman abstinence, but does respect his capacity to make moral decisions based on a programme of political change. And Gandhi's moral courage makes him able to face up to the potentially terrible implications of his philosophy, such as when he was asked what should German Jews have done in the late 1930s. Gandhi's answer was 'collective suicide, which "would have roused the world and the people of Germany to Hitler's violence"' (ibid.). While dubious that this would have worked, Orwell nonetheless applauds its bold and resolute acceptance of consequences. Even so, he suggests that Gandhi does not really understand the reality of totalitarianism and that 'firmness in truth' only works when one's opponent believes in truth. As *Nineteen Eighty-Four* and many essays show, for Orwell totalitarianism meant the cynical disregard for truth. Ultimately, Orwell judges Gandhi favourably, perhaps because he fulfils the brief not of a saint but of a unique combination of political idealism and realism. 'One feels there is much that he did not understand', Orwell writes, 'but not that there was anything that he was frightened of saying or thinking' (ibid., p. 10). Better still, Gandhi achieved his main political aim of the peaceful ending of British rule. And because of his tactics and 'by keeping up his struggle obstinately and without hatred, [Gandhi] disinfected the air'. Where Swift's idealized Houyhnhmns achieve a static inhumane perfection and Tolstoy's saintliness masks a repressive disdain for this world, Gandhi (who, Orwell comments, never claimed to be a saint) presents a far more complex and compelling figure, one whose personal rectitude – excessive and otherworldly though it was to Orwell – underpinned a shrewd and successful operator. He had immense effect while retaining his integrity: 'regarded purely as a politician', Orwell concludes, 'and compared with the other leading political figures of our time, how clean a smell he has managed to leave behind!' (ibid.). For a writer as sensitive to smelly little orthodoxies as Orwell, that metaphor carries significant personal freight.

'Reflections on Gandhi' was the last of Orwell's essays published in his lifetime. He had no reason to know this, of course, and the essay bears no trace of the valedictory. Through 1949, much of which was spent at the Cotswold Sanatorium in Gloucestershire, he wrote occasionally when his health allowed it. Davison notes that '[i]n the last nine months of his life Orwell had in mind four major pieces of writing: long essays on Waugh and Conrad, and two novels, one short, set in Burma earlier in the century, and one long, set in 1945' (*CO, XX*, p. 188). His last notebook had notes for one of the novels, and he also managed to type part of the essay on Waugh. Writing to Warburg in August 1949 Orwell talks of a proposed essay collection that would include a representative selection of his work: 'Lear, Tolstoy and the Fool', Politics vs. Literature', 'Reflections on Gandhi', 'Politics and the English Language', 'Shooting an Elephant' and 'How the Poor Die', along with essays on Conrad and George Gissing. He lists the periodical origins of all the published essays, which includes work from *Polemic, Partisan Review, Horizon, New Writing* and *Now*. Neither the Waugh nor the Conrad essay was completed, however, by the time he died in January 1950, nor had the collection been published. But work on the Waugh essay and plans for one on Conrad, as well as the early draft of part of the novel 'A Smoking Room Story', suggest that Orwell was projecting a writing life beyond *Nineteen Eighty-Four*. He knew, of course, that he was seriously ill, but was planning a visit to a Swiss sanatorium for further treatment of his tuberculosis. That he died when he did had a warping effect on the interpretation of *Nineteen Eighty-Four*, so that some commentators misconstrued it as a despairing final testament, a work that reflected despair and political defeatism. But as the contemporary essays in which Orwell road-tested ideas for the novel repeatedly show, he continued to argue for engagement, sceptical inquiry and forthright debate in which people were not afraid to say or think anything. The essays themselves were active contributions to the type of open and ongoing debate Orwell thought vital to the staving off of totalitarianism and to the creation of democratic socialism. Publishing them across a range of journals helped seed discussion among diverse readerships. Orwell never travelled to the United States, but the fact that the last essay to appear in his lifetime – on a pseudo-saintly Indian's lasting impact on British imperialism and on India – was published in a New York-based periodical, exemplifies the sorts of political and cultural cross-fertilization periodicals made possible.

Graham Good's comment 'that the effect of the war years and their imme-diate aftermath was clearly to make the essay his main form of expression' (Good, p. 152) has a certain contentious truth. The post-war period proved a particularly challenging one for Orwell, his anxiety about the uncertain future menaced by the cold war, atom bombs and the potential for totali-tarianism underpinned by substantial health problems. But the early post-war years when he was reasonably healthy were ones of tremendous and varied output, ranging from defences of naïve comic writers through quirky compar-isons of book and cigarette buying, forceful analyses of nationalism and the decline of political language, personal accounts of the motivations for writ-ing and sustained examinations of literary classics. Variety also manifested itself in approach, so that different essays could critically examine pieces of inept prose, work from personal anecdotes, offer schematic breakdowns of different forms of nationalism, produce sociological analyses of literature or popular culture, or present bleak documentary-style accounts of Parisian hospitals. Necessarily, different subject matter and approach required a wide tonal range: quizzical; polemical; ironic; affectionate; exhortatory; admon-ishing; intimate. And although the number of essays he produced after 1946 was small by comparison, he still managed to write on Tolstoy's attack on Shakepeare, the prospects of European unity, the need for political writers to maintain their independence and the qualities that made Gandhi unique. In total, these post-war essays constituted an impressive body of work across a range of interrelated interests in literature, politics and popular culture, underlining the flexibility and utility of the essay as a means of entertaining, arguing, criticizing and illuminating.

The periodical culture in which the individual essays appeared was crucial to the types of argument and analyses they mounted and to their initial reach among the readerships of distinct journals. The post-war period created its own cultural and intellectual climate, some of it a continuation of earlier trends and compulsions, others peculiar to the age. Many of the essays Orwell wrote in this period were published in journals established post-war, such as *Gangrel*,

Windmill, Polemic, Politics and Letters, while *Horizon* and *Now* had been started at the outset of the decade. But even this relatively short list reveals an assortment of motivations and attitudes, from the 'deliberately bookish' and 'old-fashioned' *Windmill* through the grab bag of *Gangrel,* the politically detached aestheticism and cosmopolitanism of *Horizon,* the avowed anarchism of *Now,* the intellectualism of *Polemic* or *Politics and Letters'* Left Leavisism. The different alignments and imperatives of this sample hints at the diversity of opinion being produced by the British periodical culture, to which can be added the American journals such as *Atlantic Monthly* and *Partisan Review* that published Orwell's work. The distinct constituencies that made up the readership of these journals also underline their importance to intellectual and cultural diversity and vitality. That said, *Windmill, Polemic, Gangrel, Now* and *Politics and Letters* would all be defunct by the time Orwell died, while Cyril Connolly would wind up the decade-old *Horizon* later in 1950. All was not gloom: *Partisan Review* flourished in the United States, becoming one of the most respected cultural and political journals of the following decades, and the British periodical culture would continue to be replenished by new enthusiasms, new writers and new readers. Later that year those readers could read the first posthumous collection of Orwell's essays, *Shooting an Elephant and Other Essays,* which included all the essays Orwell had suggested to Warburg in August 1949. Secker and Warburg printed 7,530 copies that were released in October 1950, along with a smaller though respectable American run of 4,000. The afterlife of the essays, and their contribution to Orwell's reputation, had begun.

There were still two completed essays unpublished when Orwell died: 'George Gissing', written for *Politics and Letters,* and 'Such, Such Were the Joys'; both would appear posthumously. 'George Gissing' is a standard piece of review criticism, with the obvious qualification that the choice of Gissing, one of the most respected Victorian writers but highly unfashionable in the late 1940s, seems a characteristically idiosyncratic subject. This is part of the problem that Orwell discusses in what is a very slight piece: that Gissing, though one of the major British novelists of the nineteenth century and, in Orwell's opinion, one of its 'better novelists' (*CO, XIX,* p. 350) is largely out of print. The essay was prompted by the publication of two Gissing novels, but Orwell suggests that they were the wrong two, and that *New Grub Street* and *The Odd Women* are far superior. He had been unable to buy a copy of the former and the latter is 'about as thoroughly out of print as a book can be' (ibid., p. 347), so he gives quick plot summaries and assessments of the novels, available or not, built around the central idea that 'Gissing's novels are a protest against that form of self-torture that goes by the name of respectability' (ibid.). Gissing novels are grimly realistic evocations of lower-middle class misery underpinned by a rigid class structure and risible social taboos. Orwell indicates that, putting the atom bomb to one side, these works are among the many reasons 'for thinking that the present age is a good deal better than the last' (ibid.). The essay had been written for *Politics and Letters*, but when that periodical wound up it was lost, only being rediscovered by one of the editors in 1959, and published in 1960 in the *London Magazine* (*CO, XIX*, p. 346).

'Such, Such Were the Joys' was a far more serious and substantial essay. Orwell had completed it in 1947, but knew that its almost gothic account of his schooldays at St Cyprian's potentially was libellous (*CO, XIX*, p. 149). He told Warburg that he had not sent it to *Horizon* (Connolly's *Enemies of Promise* [1938] had contained a more benign account of St Cyprian's) because it was too long for a periodical, but that 'it should be printed sooner or later when the people most concerned are dead' (*CO, XIX*, p. 149). Ironically, he would be the first to die. 'Such, Such Were the Joys' is one of Orwell's most extended and emotionally intense essays, and while other examples such as 'Shooting an Elephant' and 'How the Poor Die' deal with memories of personal humiliation and different forms of shame, the salient and lasting difference here is that Orwell's reported degradation takes place from the age of 8 when he arrives at St Cyprian's and soon after starts wetting his bed. This extraordinarily intimate revelation sets up the basic dynamic of the whole essay, one in which the young Orwell (or Eric Blair, as he was) finds himself regularly in a state of apprehension and abasement: humiliated by the headmaster and (especially) the headmaster's wife, nicknamed Sambo and Flip respectively; degraded by teachers; bullied and sneered at by those of a supposedly superior class; forced to endure mindless teaching, physical privations and filth. The general atmosphere and some of the narrative recall Dickens' portraits of distressed childhoods in *Great Expectations* and *David Copperfield*, where a largely innocent young boy is terrorized by grotesque adults and malignant children. Structurally the essay comprises six parts, recording the initial bedwetting and its comi-tragic consequences, the school's snobbery and intellectual corruption, a brief interlude of happy memories undermined by the depiction of a grim and painful routine, sexual humiliations, the consideration of the fact that the 'religious, moral, social and intellectual codes' promoted by the school 'contradicted one another if you worked out their implications' (*CO, XIX*, p. 375), some thoughts about whether the present system is as bad, and concluding with a final and unforgiving repudiation of St Cyprian's. The essay's emotional palette remains an almost totally negative array of bitterness, disgust, sarcasm, indignation and hatred. 'I hated Sambo and Flip,' Orwell writes 'with a sort of shamefaced, remorseful hatred, but it did not occur to me to doubt their judgement' (ibid., p. 366). 'Such, Such Were the Joys' must rate as one of the most sustained attacks on a British public school from the perspective of a non-fictional autobiographical account, and Orwell's sense that it should not and probably could not be published in Britain while the principals were alive seems well-founded.

Orwell admitted to Fredric Warburg that 'Such, Such Were the Joys' was libellous and 'too long for a periodical', describing it as 'a long autobiographical sketch' (*CO, XIX*, p. 149). That label does not exclude the piece from being an essay, but the Dickensian touches point to it being closer to a personal account than a detached documentary. Connolly's rosier interpretation of St Cyprian's indicates that contemporaries could have different memories of the same environment, without this invalidating either or both portraits. The degree of subjectivity on display in Orwell's sketch has much to do with the fact that, in contrast to essays such as 'A Hanging' and 'Shooting an Elephant', the narrator is a child, powerless and endlessly put upon. Rather than an engaged and aware adult eyewitness reporting back to readers on the largely ignored social underbelly or from a misreported battle zone, here the perspective is that of an adult looking back with undisguised horror on a prolonged period of what had seemed endless oppression, trying to convey the child's experiences and (crucially) the emotions of that period. The essay offers readers a series of vignettes that present extended representations of different forms and instances of abuse, hypocrisy, snobbery and corrupt attitudes and practices. The length and vividness with which each scene is rendered reinforces the effect of what, for a young boy, was a type of torture. The relatively long account gathers some of its persuasive power simply from the quantity of detail supplied, itself a tactic Orwell uses to substantiate the veracity of his testimony. And yet, as he also acknowledges in his description to Warburg, 'Such Such Were the Joys' was a sketch, incorporating forms of selection and artful emphasis. All the same, the harrowing quality of the essay is undeniable, underlined by the consequent impression from his time at the school that

> I did know that the future was dark. Failure, failure, failure – failure behind me, failure ahead of me – that was by far the deepest conviction that I carried away. (Ibid., p. 382)

The clear sense of damage done by St Cyprian's gets registered in the sardonic final statement that 'I now have not enough animosity left to make me hope that Flip and Sambo are dead or that the story of the school being burnt down was true' (ibid., p. 386). 'Such, Such Were the Joys' counts in Orwell's work as a whole as perhaps the most personal of personal essays, yet another illustration of the essay form's flexibility and utility. Given the provocation that so many of his essays sought to ignite, and Orwell's almost instinctive compulsion to reveal the unpleasant or dangerous fact, the reality that the essay could not be published in his lifetime speaks to the power of libel laws in controlling what is and is not published. The truth or otherwise of its unforgiving portrait would become a staple of Orwell commentators and especially his biographers in the decades beyond his death.

Chapter 5

The Posthumous Orwell and the Afterlife of the Essays

Had Orwell not written *Nineteen Eighty-Four*, he might now be largely forgotten, a minor writer remembered chiefly for one best-selling though anomalous post-war animal allegory, 1930s novels of varying distinction, and some idiosyncratic non-fiction. His writing would then be treated with the type of respect given to that of Cyril Connolly or Stevie Smith, appreciated by a loyal but relatively tiny coterie of supporters, and occasionally exhumed and examined by academics. While *Animal Farm* brought him acclaim, it was the necessary but not sufficient condition of the astounding posthumous status he would achieve. In this non-*Nineteen Eighty-Four* scenario *The Road to Wigan Pier* would be treated as an historical curiosity, while the 700 copies of *Homage to Catalonia* sold would probably be largely forgotten curios. Only 1,000 volumes of *Inside the Whale* had ever been printed, and while more copies existed of *Critical Essays* and *Dickens, Dali and Others*, by 1950 these collections were both long out of print. Even then, they contained less than a dozen essays, and a list of those *not* included would today make up a volume of classic essays: 'A Hanging', 'Shooting an Elephant', 'The Lion and the Unicorn', 'Politics and the English Language', 'Why I Write', 'Some Thoughts on The Common Toad' and 'Reflections on Gandhi'. Dozens more lay hidden in the periodicals that originally published them. Many of those journals had folded years before and in most cases only their readers remembered their contents. But Orwell did write *Nineteen Eighty-Four*, and literary salvage crews began to search those periodicals for more of the 'lost' essays that, until 1950, had often only been read by a few thousand subscribers of *The Adelphi*, *Gangrel* or *Horizon*. That situation would change remarkably as new collections and selections of essays appeared – seven in the 1950s alone, along with translations in Danish and a Japanese edition in English. By the end of the decade far more people in more places had read a wider sampling of Orwell's essays than at any time during his life.

These posthumous collections added substantially to public awareness of the essays individually and collectively, revealing the breadth and variety of his cultural and political interests. *Shooting an Elephant and Other Essays* resurrected examples from as far back as 'A Hanging', first published in *The Adelphi* in 1931, as well as the title essay (published 20 years earlier), short pieces from *Tribune* and more substantial and ultimately lauded essays such as 'Politics and the English Language'. For readers more familiar with *Animal Farm* and the rising literary phenomenon of *Nineteen Eighty-Four*, the essays offered a sense of Orwell as a writer with extremely wide cultural and political concerns. Essays as different as 'How the Poor Die', 'Lear, Tolstoy and the Fool', 'The Prevention of Literature' and 'Some Thoughts on the Common Toad' displayed a powerful assortment of ideas and attitudes, and the success of the British volume led to it being reprinted less than six months after initial publication. But the collection (no doubt unconsciously) began the posthumous fashioning of Orwell's image. The essays in the collection were not placed in chronological order, and there was no indication of the periodical origins from which most of them came. We need see nothing sinister in this, but the effect of decoupling the essays from their initial context necessarily blurred the reality that they might have addressed pressing issues of the moment, or illustrated a development of change in Orwell's ideas, been written with a particular audience or journal in mind, or been prompted by editors. It was not vital to understand these things in order to enjoy the essays, but not knowing that the young writer who described a hanging in imperial Burma was nearly two decades younger and far less politically aware than the one who considered Gandhi's effect on the British Empire created a more 'homogenous' Orwell. This unified figure was at odds with the actual writer who repeatedly responded to new conditions, who sometimes radically revised his positions where appropriate, who developed substantially over time, and who often wrote to small but specific readerships. In the unifying process that took place in the selection and placement of the essays, something of Orwell's prickly individuality was lost.

At the same time, the essay collections presented Orwell as a writer with interests beyond the overtly political ones manifest in either *Animal Farm* or *Nineteen Eighty-Four*, and widened and deepened reader awareness of what constituted the 'political'. 'Politics vs. Literature' and 'Politics and the English Language' clearly addressed that topic, but each took them into the cultural realm, assessing fiction and non-fiction for signs of ideological content and applicability to the contemporary world. The analysis of *Gulliver's Travels* in 'Politics vs. Literature' examined what Swift's masterpiece might illustrate about the nature of totalitarianism while arguing against its dangerously stultifying anti-humanism. 'Politics and the English Language' provided readers with a checklist of faulty writing, empowering them to critically assess the political arguments presented to them by supposed intellectuals and experts, but just as importantly it encouraged – indeed implored – them to become active thinkers, readers and writers. Essays such as 'Shooting an Elephant', 'A Hanging' or 'How the Poor Die' offered glimpses of worlds beyond the experience of most readers, calling them to attend to the ethical aspects of political power, and to their only connection to the domination of others. 'Reflections on Gandhi' and 'Second Thoughts on James Burnham' provided astute if contestable interpretations of very different political actors, one an activist whose ideas and practices potentially had wider applicability, the other a theoretician attempting to analyse global power relations and predict the future. These pieces explored politics at the national and international level through a critical engagement with the ideas of provocative individuals. Collected together, they reflected a multifaceted, multidimensional and flexible understanding of what constituted (the political) in a cold war environment that threatened to reduce politics to dangerously simplistic binaries. But Orwell's essays also opened up the area of everyday culture to active and fine-grained scrutiny by ordinary readers, making the seemingly mundane or ephemeral worth considering, or reconsidering from an inquisitive perspective. When the choice of purchasing either books or cigarettes, the activities of toads in the spring, or the planting of trees were considered for their sociological implications, the everyday could be seen alive with previously unrecognized richness and social relevance.

Undoubtedly part of the success of these collections, and what continued to generate more of them, was Orwell's engaging and readable style. Or, rather, styles, because as this study has repeatedly shown, Orwell's distinctive voice is no monotone, stretching instead over several octaves and capable of tonal shading from amused to querulous to polemical. The contentious proposition in 'Why I Write' that 'good prose is like a window pane' wrongly suggests that such prose is invisible, contributing nothing except in the negative sense of not obscuring what is being observed. The metaphor of 'voice' is more instructive, for any reading of Orwell's essays immediately picks up modulations: the tonal differences between 'A Hanging' and 'Shooting an Elephant' (one guilt-ridden, the other ultimately morose) are apparent even though the setting and the general subject matter are similar. These again are distinct from the defiant vitality of 'Some Thoughts on the Common Toad' or the forthright challenge and critical mocking discernable in 'Politics and the English Language'. The essay form encourages this variety by allowing that any subject matter can be gathered up and examined and that no approach is promoted or prohibited. So Orwell can investigate Tolstoy's animus towards Shakespeare, or how writers need to maintain their independence in the face of totalitarianism, the notion that English murders have been Americanized, or why 'good bad' books survive. In taking on this and other material he acts as occasionally as amateur sociologist, polemicist, literary critic, sceptic. His capacity to adopt these approaches and adapt them to diverse material while still writing in a way that can engage the average reader requires a literary voice of substantial clarity, range and subtlety.

Another pair of collections, one British, the other American, was published in 1953, but while for the most part their contents were identical, their respective titles, *England Your England* and *Such, Such Were the Joys* advertise a significant difference: the American volume contains the title essay, Orwell reminiscences of his days at the prep school St Cyprian's. Fredric Warburg in Britain had decided for legal reasons not to publish the essay, but the American publishers Harcourt Brace felt under no constraints. Ironically, because the essay was published in the second posthumous American collection and not in its British counterpart, those best placed to assess its validity were denied immediate access to it. This is not to say, of course, that 'Such, Such Were the Joys' could not be read by British readers with access to the American edition, but it would not be published in a British collection until *The Collected, Essays, Journalism and Letters of George Orwell* of 1968. Two slightly different 'Orwells' were produced by the different contents, *England Your England* replacing 'Such, Such Were the Joys' with documentary pieces about conditions in Britain, 'North and South' and 'Down the Mine'. The subtle fashioning of Orwell's image was augmented by both collections placing 'Why I Write' first, so that that essay acted as an introduction to the rest of the work. This placement concealed the reality that most of the essays had been published before 'Why I Write', not in response to the argument about motives Orwell presents there. The remaining essays in both collections were not placed in any chronological order, so that again a rather more indistinct impression was created of Orwell's development. These collections continued the process begun in *Shooting an Elephant* of disconnecting the essays from their initial periodical contexts. They also presented the less politically radical components of Orwell's work, so that there were no essays from the late 1930s, for example, or his calls for Socialist revolution in the early part of the Second World War – no 'Spilling the Spanish Beans', no 'Lion and the Unicorn' with its call that '[b]y revolution we become more ourselves, not less'. The plausible argument could be made that these essays have lost their relevance in the face of actual events, and that the sheer number of essays meant that no collection could be definitive. Both propositions are valid, but the consequence was that the Orwell who responded actively to political circumstances (and perhaps later revised his interpretations or arguments) was lost. This effacing of Orwell's political radicalism and emphasis instead on his cultural side would remain a feature of many future anthologies.

Two American collections were published in the mid-1950s: *A Collection of Essays* (1954) and *The Orwell Reader: Fiction, Essays and Reportage* (1956). The fact that there were no British equivalents confirms John Rodden's view that by the mid-1950s in the United States the 'Orwell ascension had become the Orwell cult, and then the Orwell industry' (Rodden, p. 46). Obviously, *Animal Farm* and *Nineteen Eighty-Four* were critical to the cult and the industry, especially given that Orwell's perceived anti-Communism fitted the cold war mood in America. In Britain, where the foundations of the welfare state were being set, both these texts were seen more in terms of the British Socialist tradition, quirky but understandable in that context. Not that American essay collections were in any way anti-Communist gatherings; indeed, with the opening essays being 'Such, Such Were the Joys', 'Charles Dickens', 'The Art of Donald McGill' and 'Rudyard Kipling', *A Collection of Essays* (1954) was decidedly Anglocentric. *The Orwell Reader: Fiction, Essays and Reportage* (1956) was a more substantial collection, primarily because while it offered an impressive range of essays it also carried, as it subtitle advertises, extracts from Orwell's novels and non-fiction. None of Orwell's 1930s novels and non-fiction after *A Clergyman's Daughter* had been published in the United States during his lifetime, so *The Orwell Reader* greatly expanded the offerings available to American readers. It also gave a rough historical shape to the collection (although the popular 'Shooting an Elephant' led off the collection ahead of 'A Hanging' and 'How the Poor Die' was resituated next to an extract from *Down and Out in Paris and London*) giving the most comprehensive selection of Orwell's works in one volume then available. A paperback reissue by Harvest in 1956 indicates the collection's popular success and the growing readership for Orwell's work beyond his last two pieces of fiction. Two more British collections published in the late 1950s, *Selected Essays* (1957), a Penguin paperback, and *Selected Writings* (1958), reinforced the popularity of his essays. And the publication of *Elefanten og Andre Essays* (1952) in Danish created a foreign language readership as well (Fenwick, pp. 271, 275). Within eight years of his death audiences that far exceeded anything he enjoyed during his life were reading his essays on both sides of the Atlantic and beyond.

Looking back over the publication and popularity of Orwell's essays in the 1950s, the most obvious thing to observe is that they depended entirely on the success of *Animal Farm* and especially of *Nineteen Eighty-Four*, which with amazing rapidity transformed Orwell from a marginal British writer into a global literary figure. The fact that he was dead and therefore would not write any new material threw attention back on works already published but long out of print or, as was the case with most of his essays, 'lost' in yellowing periodicals. Gathering these pieces together in posthumous collections displayed the diversity and quality of his essays in ways that were unprecedented and that probably would have not even been attempted but for the phenomenon of *Nineteen Eighty-Four*, which by the end of the 1950s had already sold in the millions, and which was seen by many as the defining text of the Cold War. Because he died soon after its publication, the book's apparently unleavened bleakness was misinterpreted as a testament of personal despair. This was especially true in the United States, where the anti-Communist mood of the decade, or at least the mood promoted by some government agencies, prompted the wilful misreading of Orwell's antagonism to Soviet-style Communism as a repudiation of Socialism generally. Orwell repeatedly and explicitly argued this in the last months of his life – 'My recent novel is *not* intended as an attack on socialism or on the British Labour Party (of which I am a supporter)' (*CO*, *XX*, p. 135), being only one of several instances – but Frances Stonor Saunders has argued that in the United States Orwell's work as well as its distribution and reception were manipulated by the CIA as part of the 'cultural cold war' (Saunders, pp. 293–8). The same climate did not apply in Britain, and *Nineteen Eighty-Four* was recognized as a text with a broader attack on totalitarianism. As with *Animal Farm*, the fact that the action took place in Britain itself argued against a purely anti-Soviet or anti-Communist critique, especially with a leftist Labour government in power.

Relating *Nineteen Eighty-Four* to the early cold war context and the real or imagined manipulation of the text and its writer raises the question of how Orwell's reputation changed after his death and how the essays collectively and individually fed into and affected those changes. John Rodden has provided an immensely detailed and intelligently considered study of that reputation, at one point giving a brief overview of the changes from 1927 through to the late 1980s (Rodden, pp. 41–50; as should be obvious, much of my argument draws from Rodden's definitive work). Rodden notes several highpoints in the period up until the late 1950s in terms of Orwell's essays and his status as an essayist, including that his essays in *Inside the Whale* and 'throughout the war years . . . established him as an essayist of distinction and made clear his serious interest in popular culture' (Rodden, p. 43). Simon During would later acknowledge Orwell as an important 'precursor' of the more systematic study of popular culture at universities, recognizing how Orwell had exposed 'the invisibility of the working class in dominant British . . . culture' and demonstrated that popular culture expressed a 'stoic yet boisterous defiance' (During, p. 35). Rodden suggests that together *Animal Farm* and *Critical Essays* 'occasioned comparisons of Orwell as political writer and critic with past masters and notable contemporaries, including Swift, Voltaire, Hazlitt, Anatole France, Chesterton, Koestler and [Edmund] Wilson' (Rodden, p. 45). The essays presented a more rounded, humane figure than that suggested by either of the last two fictions. In the 1950s they began to feed into new thinking about the value and popular or mass culture and

> exerted enormous influence on the direction and tone of post-war Anglo-American culture criticism. Indeed *Inside the Whale* and *Critical Essays* could be interpreted in retrospect as the opening salvos of the culture debates about 'midcult' and 'masscult' that raged in the 1950s and '60s. (Rodden, p. 1989)

Ironically, the essays began to have a much larger influence long after their initial moment, outside the original circumstances that some of them specifically addressed, and beyond Orwell himself.

Again, the use of Orwell's essays on different sides of the Atlantic spoke to different priorities and situations. Dwight Mcdonald used the terms 'midcult' and 'masscult' to distinguish faux high culture and homogenized and commodified mass culture in the United States in an emerging age of rampant consumerism. In Britain, the rising academic interest in popular culture through the 1950s in the work of Raymond Williams and Richard Hoggart drew in part from Orwell's essays, but also reflected Williams' and Hoggart's concern with the working class in a nation still pinched by post-war austerity. In his groundbreaking 1957 study *The Uses of Literacy*, Hoggart acknowledges 'a general debt' to 'Raffles and Miss Blandish' in the 'Sex-and-Violence Novels' section (Hoggart, pp. 256–72). The subtitle of his book, *Aspects of working-class life with specific reference to publications and entertainments* shows an affiliation with Orwell's essays and interests. Williams, originally a great supporter of Orwell's (his periodical had published 'Writer and Leviathan') eventually became antagonistic to Orwell's work. But in Williams' breakthrough study, *Culture and Society 1780-1950* (1963), he remains wary rather than wholly dismissive, accepting that Orwell is 'a fine observer of detail' and adding that detail 'is the great merit of that group of essays of which "The Art of Donald McGill" is typical'. But the quality of the detail, Williams contends, is undermined by an 'unusual amount of plausible yet specious generalization' (Williams, 1963, p. 277). He uses quotations from 'Rudyard Kipling' and 'Wells, Hitler and the World State' to substantiate the claim, declaring that in the distance from assertion to generalization Orwell 'moved very easily into the propagandist's kind of emotive abuse' (ibid., p. 278). While an entirely valid criticism, Williams' attack ignores the possibility that as essays 'Rudyard Kipling' and 'Wells, Hitler and the World State' might be using generalization tactically, and that the *Horizon* audience which both address might be sophisticated enough to decode the propaganda and ignore the abuse.

This is not to say that Williams is wrong, but the situation of Orwell's essays in the 1950s and later uncovers an irony that can be exemplified by a more general and later criticism from Williams. Interviewed several decades after *Culture and Society* by the editors of the journal *New Left Review*, Williams addressed the question of Orwell's influence on his own thinking. By the time the interview took place, Williams was openly dismissive of Orwell, but at one point he reflects on Orwell's cultural impact:

> In the Britain of the Fifties, along almost every road that you moved, the figure of Orwell seemed to be waiting. If you tried to develop a new kind of cultural analysis, there was Orwell; if you wanted to report on work or ordinary life, there was Orwell; if you engaged in any kind of socialist argument, there was the enormously inflated statue of Orwell warning you to go back. (Williams, 1979, p. 384)

Williams' clear sense of Orwell's negative presence is apparent, and just as clearly Orwell's essays contribute to his capacity to stifle new work. But in the 'Britain of the Fifties' Orwell literally was dead, even while the posthumous influence of his work was rising dramatically. This recalibrating of Orwell's importance after his death produced the enormously inflated statue that warned-off Williams, although the fundamental change in Orwell's import-ance did not make his influence any less inhibiting or prohibiting. Essays that originally had been written perhaps two decades earlier and published in obscure journals absorbed the cultural power that *Animal Farm* and *Nineteen Eighty-Four* retrospectively conferred on all of Orwell's writing. Eric Blair's 'A Hanging', for example, initially published to no fanfare in *The Adelphi*, would in time not only be seen as a classic essay, but be examined for what it explained about the experience of imperialism or the morality of capital punishment. This would never have occurred had Orwell not written *Nineteen Eighty-Four*. As for 'A Hanging' so too for Orwell's other essays, such as 'Inside the Whale'. Because of what the Marxist historian E. P. Thompson claimed in 1960 was its quietist message, 'the aspirations of a generation were buried' by 'Inside the Whale'; 'not only was a political movement, which embodied much that was honorable buried, but also the notion of disinterested dedication to a cause'. This seems an extraordinary burden to place on an essay that when it was published in 1940 addressed the temporary situation that obtained at the beginning of the Second World War, and sold less than 1,000 copies in a col-lection that also championed Charles Dickens 'as a man always fighting about something'. It had not been published again in Orwell's life. Whatever cultural influence it held over the 1950s generation was activated by its inclusion in posthumous collections that were the consequence of *Nineteen Eighty-Four*.

Detached from their original settings, then, particular essays or sets of essays began to take on greater authority and new resonances. Whereas those on the political Left in Britain were struggling with Orwell's ambigu-ous legacy, Deborah Cameron suggests that the so-called 'Movement' writers, more inclined to the Centre-Right (and moving ever rightward) appreciated Orwell's attention to clear, unpretentious prose as an antidote to the self-advertising sloganeering of the 1930s and the arcane jargon and references of 1920s Modernism. 'There seems little doubt', Cameron comments 'that the Movement writers were influenced by Orwell's views on language' expressed in essays such as 'Why I Write', with its windowpane metaphor, and 'Politics and the English Language' (Cameron, p. 149). In the United States of the 1950s this connection between Orwell's essays and good prose was given a different inflection by their inclusion in university composition courses. Rodden sup-plies crucial information once again, explaining that 'Politics and the English Language' and 'Shooting an Elephant' were the most frequently included in anthologies, and that following the publication of '*The Orwell Reader* compo-sition anthologies also began to include some of the selections from *Down and Out*, *The Road to Wigan Pier* and *Nineteen Eighty-Four*' (Rodden, p. 390). The cumulative impact of this over the following decades, when the essays cemented themselves in composition courses, is incalculable, and Rodden makes the fascinating supposition that more Americans might have read

Orwell's essays in college than have read 'either *Animal Farm* or *Nineteen Eighty-Four* in high school' (ibid.). He also notes that because British universities do not have those courses, the effect there was far less.

By the 1960s Orwell was a well-established literary figure whose posthumous status had peaked as the insecurities of the first full decade of the Cold War gave way to accommodation with the superpower standoff. *Nineteen Eighty-Four* and *Animal Farm* were established school texts in the Anglophone world, and still sold phenomenally for works now over a decade old. Orwell's essay collections also continued to attract a public readership, one or other of Penguin's *Inside the Whale and Other Essays* and *Decline of the English Murder and Other Essays* – with a cover by artist Peter Blake, the artist who would design the cover for The Beatles' *Sgt Pepper* album – being reissued through the 1960s (Fenwick, pp. 255–9). Along with the public popularity the essays had come to generate more interest as the 'image of a depoliticised "cultural" Orwell . . . replaced the Cold War image of an "ideological" Orwell' (Rodden, p. 48).

The series of single-volume collections was arrested temporarily in 1968 when the four-volume *Collected Essays, Journalism and Letters of George Orwell* was published to significant acclaim. While not comprehensive, the set brought together in almost chronological order – 'Why I Write' was placed anachronistically at the beginning of the first volume – a mass of new material that had been out of print for at least two decades, alongside the essays that had populated the earlier posthumous collections. This compilation massively enhanced Orwell's stature as a writer, prompting the influential American critic Irving Howe to proclaim:

> He was neither a first-rank literary critic nor a major novelist, and certainly not an original thinker; but he was, I now believe, the greatest English essayist since Hazlitt, maybe since Dr Johnson. He was the greatest moral force in English letters during the last several decades. (Howe, p. 98)

The stringent critic George Steiner approvingly noted in *New Yorker*: 'These four volumes are a place of renewal for the moral imagination' (Meyers, 1975, p. 363). The variety and quality of work brought together in the collection propelled Orwell to the forefront of public intellectuals whose ideas were worth quoting and discussing, significantly broadening his public and scholarly appeal. The essays' readability, variety of tone and diversity of topic had much to do with this attractiveness, and their often highly personal take on literary, cultural and political subjects deepened an awareness of Orwell the man. No authorized biography had appeared by 1968, and Orwell's widow Sonia seemed to think that the collection was a sufficient substitute. Rodden comments that the four volumes ' "revived" Orwell – who had become something of a dated figure – as a subject of ideological dispute on the Left' (Rodden, p. 149). Not all those on the Left approved of the collection. Peter Sedgwick in the *Socialist*

Worker acknowledged Orwell's 'honesty and courage in an age of suffocating political illusion' while decrying his 'Cold War tendencies' (Sedgwick, p. 3), while Mary McCarthy attacked so hard in the *New York Review of Books* that Sonia Orwell wrote an article in his defence. Conor Cruise O'Brien, although praising Orwell, described the collection 'as a contribution to a cult' (Meyers, 1975, p. 345). And he made the perceptive comment that 'the present time [1968] is so different from 1948-50 that he should no more be presented as fixed at that point than he should remain forever associated with his position of 1938-9' (ibid., p. 348). The four volumes placed most of the material in order ('Why I Write' a conspicuous but not unique exception) and recorded the journals and collections in which the essays appeared, but critics tended to ignore this information or not to make anything of it. The reality was, of course, that most of the journals were long gone in 1968 – *The New Statesman and Nation* and *Partisan Review* being two notable survivors – as was the periodical culture in which so many of the essays had first appeared. Orwell's lofty status reinforced a sense that the essays were in some way 'classics' existing outside their originating moment. The collection also elevated the essays' status in Orwell's body of work. He was now considered a major essayist who had also written two important political fictions. And as *Animal Farm* became a respected but little-considered text, the essays as a group began to rival *Nineteen Eighty-Four* as Orwell's greatest achievement; in time, for some commentators, they would eclipse the novel.

The Collected Essays, Journalism and Letters gained Orwell a place at literature's top table of essayists, the set brilliantly promoting his qualities as an essayist while simultaneously displaying the form's flexibility and reach. Yet for all the newly recovered material, the four volumes did little to change substantially established opinions on Orwell the man and his thinking. Rather, they tended to confirm assessments, as Howe acknowledged in admitting that he had hesitated over the volumes, worried that a writer he had considered 'an intellectual hero' might disappoint. Instead, the collection 'has convinced me that Orwell was an even better writer than I had supposed' (Meyers, 1975, p. 349). Howe's positive take on the essays is less instructive than his admiration for Orwell as an intellectual, ironically because of what would appear to be Orwell's almost pathological antagonism towards intellectuals. Howe was not alone in thinking of Orwell in this way, the American critic Lionel Trilling being only one of many who saw Orwell in this light. The term 'intellectual' has many nuances, some of them associated with highbrow thinking, but Orwell's claim, something underpinned by the breadth of topics of his essays and their readability and popularity, was to the position of 'public intellectual'. This fuzzily defined subgroup encompasses individuals who employ their superior insight or knowledge in the public sphere, contributing to general discourse on topics of the day, or presenting innovative or provocative interpretations or proposals on topics of public interest. One oddity about treating Orwell in this way is that he was long-dead by the time he was granted this position; Orwell the public intellectual is almost entirely a posthumous creation. While *Nineteen Eighty-Four* still generates some of the weight behind his status as a public intellectual, much of his most provocative and enduring work ('Politics and the English Language', 'A Hanging', 'Inside the Whale' 'Why I Write', 'Shooting an Elephant') resided in his essays. Their variety provided multiple sources for 'channelling' Orwell and bringing him into the public conversation. Some essays are more equal than others in this regard.

Howe's response might also reflect the tendency for readers to find in the great variety of Orwell's essays the Orwell of one's choice or preconceptions. Conservative readers such as John Major could discover a conservative Orwell evoking the delights of England, while contrarians such as Christopher Hitchens could find a contrarian who was right on 'the three great subjects of the twentieth century . . . imperialism, fascism and Stalinism' (Hitchens, p. 4). But that variety, and Orwell's own liking for the hyperbolic and the polemic, coupled with his capacity to change his opinions and his increasing cultural standing, meant not only that a politician like Major might try to 'cash in' on those elements of Orwell that he agreed with (conveniently ignoring Orwell's Socialist convictions), but that Orwell's opponents might feel the urge to bring him down in some ways. Raymond Williams had argued that in the 1950s Orwell blocked alternative ways of seeing, and in the decades beyond the publication of *The Collected Essays, Journalism and Letters*, that cultural power increased rather than diminished. An obvious target among these in this regard from the Left was 'Inside the Whale', which Salman Rusdhie would argue (while being under a fatwah at the time) presented an argument for quietism that he wished to repudiate. For Orwell's supporters, the same essay offers a perceptive take on ill-considered, self-advertising and ultimately ineffectual political engagement, and is counterbalanced by Orwell's continuing political writing. The point here is not to make the case for one or other side but to note how Orwell's mostly posthumous international status as a writer whom the general public also read gave some of his pronouncements (even after 50 years) a significance they had not had when written. The essay form itself allows for these opposed readings, its openness and incompleteness encouraging readers to interact more flexibly and personally with it than with a more extended or fully worked-through thesis. If the essay does not welcome the passive reader it encourages and requires the engaged, interactive variety, but in creating an open intellectual space for readers, essays do not and cannot mandate any one interpretation.

The critical and popular success of the *Collected Essays, Journalism and Letters* proved a major event in the posthumous fashioning of Orwell's reputation. By a circular dynamic his heightened status gave what might have been very slight essays a surprising and perhaps unwarranted importance. The variety of topics addressed meant that they could be consulted as a reliable guide to what a now-important political and cultural figure like Orwell might have thought on major political topics of the day such as Vietnam, or the Soviet Union, or the state of political language. Over the 1970s Orwell's star faded somewhat as the threat suggested in *Nineteen Eighty-Four* seemed neutralized, although regular reprinting of essay collections showed that the interest in this aspect of his writing remained firm. In the lead-up to 1984 massive global interest in the novel projected it back into the bestseller list, and it and *Animal Farm* continued to sell well into the twenty-first century, cementing their position as the two most read political fictions in the last half century. Yet repeated reprints of essay anthologies indicate that they also remain popular, and although it is hard to quantify, it seems likely that Orwell is the most widely read English essayist in the same period.

Some essays also fed back into the biographies of Orwell, that began with Bernard Crick's politically oriented study in 1980 and continued on into the new century. Individual pieces – 'A Hanging', 'Shooting an Elephant' and 'Such, Such Were the Joys' especially – tested generic boundaries; were they sketches, autobiography thinly- or heavily-veiled, or merely essays that drew from Orwell's life but fashioned more open, tentative thoughts? Crick had questioned whether Orwell had seen a hanging or shot an elephant, something other biographers (and his second wife, Sonia) were adamant he had. Michael Shelden relied heavily on 'Such, Such Were the Joys' for *Orwell: The Official Biography* (1991) something Crick took him to task over in the Appendix to his revised biography of 1992 (Crick, pp. 585–6). Whether Orwell as the schoolboy Eric Blair had or had not experienced the horrors depicted in the essay remains beyond the scope of this study, but this academic skirmish says something about how Orwell continued to be thought worth tussling over, and the importance that initially obscure essays came to play in those tussles. Intertwined with the 'reality quotient' in these and similar essays were notions of Orwell as someone aiming to tell the truth. As we have seen, at times he had consciously and actively invoked the position and status of the eyewitness to argue a case or correct what he took to be a faulty fact or a lie. The complexities of the relationship between fact and fiction were addressed by the academic and writer David Lodge in his analysis of 'A Hanging' next to a newspaper account of a hanging. Having contrasted their various literary and non-literary aspects, Lodge comes to the judicious (if, for some, frustrating) conclusion that '[w]hether or not Orwell's "A Hanging" is axiomatically a literary text is . . . problematical and the answer probably depends upon the context in which it is read, and the expectations of the individual reader' (Lodge, p. 16). From the original *Adelphi* readers on, this has likely to have been the case.

The degree to which Orwell's essays have come to transcend their moment was illustrated with the publication of *What Orwell Didn't Know: Propaganda and the New Face of American Politics* (2007), a collection of essays that gave American intellectuals the chance to consider Orwell's 'Politics and the

English Language' in terms of contemporary political discourse in the United States in the run-up to the campaign that led eventually to Barack Obama's election. Contributors included important academics from several disciplines, internationally acclaimed journalists and the financier George Soros, who gave differing takes on the relevance of Orwell's 1946 examination of political language to twenty-first century North America. Some argued that it still contained perceptions worth considering, lessons worth learning, others thought its conclusions dated or – in the idea that thought and language are causally related – simply wrong. Nevertheless, the majority praised qualities of 'Politics and the English Language', though the balance of opinion is less important than the fact that an essay first published in *Horizon* (after being rejected by *Contact*) when Clement Atlee was British Prime Minister formed the centre-piece of a book of essays published on the cusp of Barack Obama's presidency. This speaks to sustaining qualities in 'Politics and the English Language' itself in terms of approach and argument. It also reinforces Orwell's continuing cultural presence, suggests the importance of the essays as a whole to the ongoing construction and assessment of his reputation.

Orwell's status as the most read and referenced political writer in English of the last century means that he has been well worth claiming by both political wings. The invocation of Orwell, sometimes in the crude 'What would Orwell think?' formulation, almost invariably involves 'him' confirming the position of the writer. His essays often provide evidence for such self-serving exercises, partly because the variety of his pronouncements over two decades and in various contexts offers an assortment of pithily, clearly or memorably written views and observations that can be used to validate any number of arguments. Orwell's ideas in these instances are far less important than his cachet. That Orwell can be and is employed as a largely unanswerable authority remains immensely frustrating to those critical of his views, most obviously those on the Left who see him as essentially reactionary, are suspicious of how easily he can be co-opted by the Right, and remain resentful that his scathing attacks on the British Left from more than half a century ago were still used as a stick to beat the modern Left. They have worked to topple the regressive and stifling cultural and political monument they feel that Orwell has become. Peter Davison's 20-volume *Complete Works of George Orwell*, finally published in 1998 after heroic efforts over two decades, was one measure of the degree to which the attempt to 'deconstruct' the monument or destroy the 'myth' of Orwell has so far failed.

Ironically, in the twenty-first century the mythical or monumental 'Orwell' continues to enjoy a critical and popular acclaim and an international influence that the actual Orwell never experienced. The status of individual essays and his essay output as a whole in 1950 was infinitesimal compared to that in 2000. Millions of people in scores of countries and in a dozen languages have read 'A Hanging', 'Shooting an Elephant' and 'Politics and the English Language' since his death, while when they were first published the primarily British readership of any one of *The Adelphi*, *New Writing* or *Horizon* was no more than 10,000. For the twenty-first century reader the name 'George Orwell' would leap from the contents page were they to come across a copy of *New Writing* or *Horizon* (remembering that he was 'Eric Blair' when *The Adelphi* printed 'A Hanging') but in 1933 he was unknown and in 1936 still little known. Even in 1946, when 'Politics and the English Language' was published, Orwell would not have been rated equal to contemporaries such as W. H. Auden, Evelyn Waugh, Graham Greene or Christopher Isherwood. Those same essays in the twenty-first century, however, come bolstered by Orwell's commanding international presence. While this frustrates those who see his modern canonical position as masking the contradictions, inconsistencies, hyperbole, unsubstantiated claims and damaging accusations that run through many of his essays, the reality is that when the essays were written Orwell was a marginal figure trying to unmask the contradictions, inconsistencies, polemic and hyperbole of his opponents. As he wrote in 'Why I Write':

> My starting point is always a feeling of partisanship, a sense of injustice. When I sit down to write a book, I do not say to myself, 'I am going to produce a work of art'. I write it because there is some lie I want to expose, some fact to which I want to draw attention, and my initial concern is to get a hearing. (*CO*, *XVIII*, p. 319)

This admission, written four years before he died, is not that of a writer with a commanding international presence, but of someone used to being read by thousands of people at best, not millions, and whose work had been refused publication when it challenged preferred orthodoxies. It is the admission of a writer very much part of a rich, sometimes unstable but often enabling periodical culture, where work could appear in a journal that would only last four issues. The Orwell of 'Why I Write' is one whose literary career has mostly been that of a relatively peripheral figure within the British literary scene. Not by any means the most peripheral – Orwell by dint of his background could activate connections within the subsection of the periodical and publishing culture which he inhabited, and his political and cultural views in most cases could find a home, even if in an obscure journal. His relative marginality does not excuse hyperbole, generalization and unsubstantiated claims and accusations, but to some extent it explains their use as part of his intention to get a hearing in an often crammed and noisy public sphere. That intention also explains the use of periodicals, reviews and newspapers to convey a message quickly and effectively to a potentially informed and interested audience. Orwell was an engaged writer with something to say, and periodicals provided the necessary and best available platforms for his views – sometimes the only available platforms. They also offered space and opportunity for less 'current' topics, for more considered thoughts on Dickens, boys' magazines, or common toads. Essays supplied the flexible medium through which to present his views, observations and arguments.

The monumental 20-volume *Complete Works of George Orwell* registered and contributed to Orwell's in many ways surprising place in twenty-first century cultural and political life. Yet the meticulous and fine-grained research that went into the extensive footnotes accompanying the essays, the inclusion of material such as letters recording requests for essays, Orwell's judgements on journals and editors, lists of the periodicals he wrote for and the topics he covered in those essays registered as never before the contexts in which Orwell's essays first appeared. The inclusion of as much material as was available made plain by its sheer bulk the amount of time and energy Orwell invested in essays, articles and reviews and the impressive array of journals in which he wrote. Admittedly, some of this material was ephemera, but collected together and organized chronologically it gave an unprecedented view of Orwell's literary life as it developed, some of it planned but much of it in response to events, requests, commitments, friendships and antagonisms, the acceptance or rejection of material, the arguments of others – essentially, in response to the established but ever-changing literary, political and cultural environment in which Orwell found himself. While no life can be recreated from documents, the *Complete Orwell* revealed a writer fundamentally, willingly and actively embedded in his time, not a literary colossus surveying the terrain and making colossal judgements from on high. The changes of directions and revisions displayed in the material indicated a committed, inquisitive writer who was also self-critical, willing to respond and adapt, to admit errors even as he remained resolute. Resolution can sometimes harden into obsession, and there is something obsessive, for example, in his relentless attacks on members of the Left. But that same relentlessness also energized his sustained criticism of the totalitarian nature of the Soviet Union, a view not universally held by the British Left in the 1930s especially, but one vindicated by time. The obsessive are not necessarily deluded. Orwell did not always acknowledge the misjudgements and faulty predictions, the hyperbolic statements and unsubstantiated attacks, and perhaps did not recognize them, but the *Complete Orwell* provides unparalleled material for fresh appraisals of his work by general readers and scholars, although, naturally enough, the massive size of the collection inhibits it being read in anything like its entirety by most people. The Orwell that emerges from Davison's monumental enterprise paradoxically is less unified and homogenous, more varied in his opinions and interests, and more tentative, inquisitive and open-ended. These qualities might also function as a checklist for the essay form. And Orwell is also more obviously connected to the vast interactive and mutable periodical culture that did so much to foster and shape his essays and his thinking, providing him with support, friendship and validation, topics to consider, the opinions of others to assess and where necessary, attack. It also gifted him, assortments of audiences willing to attend to and sometimes respond to his arguments and observations. Those particular periodicals and that specific periodical culture are now gone, along with the editors, writers and readers that created such a vigorous and multifaceted public sphere. Orwell the man has long gone too, of course, replaced in part by a monumental and mythical figure that in the twenty-first century continues to attract public attention. Whether that will remain so is impossible to predict (think of the decline in public esteem and recognition of Bernard Shaw, H. G. Wells and Jean-Paul Sartre). But if we fail to take account of the actual man we risk losing sight of the variety and challenge of his writing. We become passive readers, lazy promoters of the Orwell myth, inattentive admirers of the Orwell monument, or drearily automatic naysayers. His essays remain the best examples of the variety of his interests and arguments as they developed and the complex qualities of his prose style. Individually and collectively, especially when we pay attention to the context in which they first appeared and for which they were written, they offer an immensely informative and endlessly stimulating record of his writing and thinking, with all its flaws and flashes of illumination, its excesses and its excellence.

Bibliography

Adorno, T. 1984. 'The Essay as Form'. *New German Critique*, no. 32, 151–71.

Anand, M. R. 1936 (September). 'Towards a New Indian Literature'. *Left Review*, vol. 2, no. 12, 612–23.

Auden, W. H. 1986. *The English Auden: Poems, Essays and Dramatic Writings 1927-1939*. Mendelson, E. (ed.). London: Faber and Faber.

Ayer, A. J. 1977. *Part of My Life*. London: Collins.

Bloom, H. 1984. 'Introduction', in Bloom, H. (ed.) *George Orwell's 1984: Modern Critical Interpretations*. New York: Chelsea House.

Bond, R. 1971. *The Tatler: The Making of a Literary Journal*. Cambridge, MA: Harvard University Press.

Bort, F. 2009. 'A New Prose: John Lehmann's *New Writing* (1936-40)', in Brooker, P. and Thacker, A. (eds), *The Oxford Critical and Cultural History of Modernist Magazines, Volume 1, Britain and Northern Ireland 1880-1935*. Oxford: Oxford University Press, pp. 669–87.

Brockway, F. 1936. 'Communism and the Thieves' Kitchen: An Answer to a "Daily Worker" Challenge'. *New Leader*, 12 June, p. 2.

—1937. 'The Test of Spain: "The Communists Are on the Wrong Side of the Barriades"'. *New Leader*, 28 May, 3.

—1938a. 'Has Hitler Anything to Teach our Ruling Class?'. *New Leader*, 29 April, iv–v.

—1938b. 'India in the Coming War'. *New Leader*, July, 3.

Cain, W. E. 2004. 'Orwell's Perversity: An Approach to the Collected Essays', in Cushman, T. and Rodden, J. (eds), *George Orwell into the Twenty-First Century*. Boulder, CO: Paradigm.

—2007. 'Orwell's Essays as a Literary Experience', in Rodden, J. (ed.) *The Cambridge Companion to George Orwell*. Cambridge: Cambridge University Press.

Cameron, D. 2009. 'The Virtues of Good Prose: Verbal Hygiene and the Movement', in Leader, Z. (ed.) *The Movement Reconsidered: Essays on Larkin, Amis, Gunn, Davie, and Their Contemporaries*. Oxford: Oxford University Press.

Cole, M. 1941. Review of *The Lion and the Unicorn*. *Tribune*, 21 March, 14–15.

Collini, S. 2006. *Absent Minds: Intellectuals in Britain*. Oxford: Oxford University Press.

Connolly, C. 1935. 'Review of *Burmese Days*'. *The New Statesman and Nation*, July 6.

—1940. Comment. *Horizon*, 1, 5.

—1973. 'Little Magazines', in Connolly, C. (ed.) *The Evening Colonnade*. London: David Bruce and Watson.

Cooney, T. A. 1986. *The Rise of the New York Intellectuals: Partisan Review and Its Circle, 1934-1945*. Madison: University of Wisconsin Press.

Coppard, A. and Crick, B. 1984. *Orwell Remembered*. London: Ariel Books.

Cornford, J. 1933–4. 'Left?'. *Cambridge Left*, Winter 1933–4, 25–9.

Crick, B. 1980. *George Orwell: A Life*. Harmondsworth: Penguin Books.

—1992. *George Orwell: A Life* (revised edition). London: Penguin.

—1994. 'Introduction: An Essay', in *The Penguin Essays of George Orwell*, pp.vii–xxv. London: Penguin Books.

Cuddon, J. A. 1976. *A Dictionary of Literary Terms*. Harmondsworth: Penguin.

Cunningham, V. 1988. *British Writers of the Thirties*. Oxford: Clarendon Press.

de Obaldia, C. 1995. *The Essayistic Spirit: Literature, Modern Criticism, and the Essay*. Oxford: Clarendon Press.

Davison, P., Angus, I. and Davison, S. (eds), 1998. *The Complete Works of George Orwell*. (London: Secker and Warburg).

Dowson, J. 2009. 'Interventions in the Public Sphere: *Time and Tide* (1920-30) and the Bermondsey Book (1923-30)', in Brooker, P. and Thacker, A. (eds), *The Oxford Critical and Cultural History of Modernist Magazines, Volume 1: Britain And Ireland 1880–1935*. Oxford: Oxford University Press.

During, S. 2005. *Cultural Studies: A Critical Introduction*. Oxford: Routledge.

Eatwell, R. 1996. *Fascism: A History*. London: Vintage.

Edwards, R. D. 1987. *Victor Gollancz: A Biography*. London: Victor Gollancz.

Evans, J. 1936 (November). 'The Moscow Trials'. *Controversy*, 4–5.

Fenby, C. 1937. 'British Public Opinion on Spain'. *The Political Quarterly*, iii, 248–58.

Fenwick, G. 1998. *George Orwell: A Bibliography*. Winchester: St Paul's Bibliographies.

Fish, S. 1972. *Self-Consuming Artifacts: The Experience of Seventeenth Century Literature*. Berkeley: University of California Press.

Fisher, C. 1996. *Cyril Connolly: A Nostalgic Life*. London: Papermac.

Fox, P. 1994. *Class Divisions: Shame and Resistance in the British Working Class Novel, 1890-1945*. Durham, NC: Duke University Press.

Fox, R. 1933. *The Colonial Policy of British Imperialism*. London: Martin Lawrence.

Fyvel, T. 1982. *George Orwell: A Personal Memoir*. London: Weidenfeld and Nicolson.

Gollancz, V. 1936 (May). 'Editorial: The Left Book Club'. *Left News*, no. 1, 2–4.

—1938 (January). 'Editorial'. *Left News*, no. 21, 636–7.

—1941. *The Betrayal of the Left: An Examination and Refutation of Communist Policy from October 1939 to January 1941: With Suggestions for an Alternative and an Epilogue on Political Morality*. London: Gollancz.

Good, G. 1988. *The Observing Self: Rediscovering the Essay*. London: Routledge.

Gortschacher, W. 1993. 'Interview with Malcolm Bradbury', in Gortschacher, W. (ed.) *Little Magazine Profiles: The Little Magazines in Great Britain 1939-1993*. Salzburg: University of Salzburg Press.

Graham, M. A. B. 1986. 'Now', in Sullivan, A. (ed.) *British Literary Magazines: The Modern Age, 1914-1984*. Westport, CT: Greenwood Press.

Grigson, G. 1933. 'Why'. *New Verse*, January, 1–2.

Guessler, N. 1976. 'Henri Barbusse and His *Monde*: Progeny of the Clarte Movement and *Review Clarte*'. *Journal of Contemporary History*, 11, 173–97.

Habermas, J. 1974. 'The Public Sphere: An Encyclopedia Article (1964)'. *New German Critique*, 3, 49–55.

—1989. *The Structural Transformation of the Public Sphere.* Cambridge, MA: M.I.T. Press.

Hahn, E. L. E. 1992. *The Philosophy of A.J. Ayer.* La Salle, IL: Open Court.

Hammond, J. 1982. *A George Orwell Companion: A Guide to the Novels, Documentaries and Essays.* London: Macmillan.

Hewison, R. 1988. *Under Siege: Literary Life in London 1939-45.* London: Methuen.

Higgins, J. 1999. *Raymond Williams: Literature, Marxism and Cultural Materialism.* London: Routledge.

Hitchens, C. 2002. *Orwell's Victory.* London: Penguin.

Hoggart, R. 1958. *The Uses of Literacy: Aspects of Working Class Life with Special Reference to Publications and Entertainments.* Harmondsworth: Penguin.

Hollis, C. 1956. *George Orwell: The Man and His Works.* London: Hollis and Carter.

Horrabin, W. 1941 (April). Review of *The Lion and the Unicorn. The Plebs,* 64–5.

Howe, I. 1969 (January). 'George Orwell: "As The Bones Know" '. *Harper's Magazine,* 98–103.

Hunter, J. 1986. 'The Windmill', in Sullivan, A. (ed.) *British Literary Magazines, the Modern Age, 1914-1984.* Westport, CT: Greenwood Press.

Hynes, S. 1992. *The Auden Generation: Literature and Politics in England in the 1930s.* London: Pimlico.

Joeres, R. and A. Mittman. 1993. 'An Introductory Essay', in Joeres, R. and Mittman, A. (eds) *The Politics of the Essay: Feminist Perspectives.* Bloomington: Indiana University Press.

Johnson, S. 1963. *Johnson's Dictionary: A Modern Selection,* edited by McAdam, E. and Milne, G. London: Pantheon Books.

Kent, C. 1984. 'Introduction', in Sullivan, A. (ed.) *British Literary Magazines: The Victorian and Edwardian Age 1837-1914.* Westport, CT: Greenwood.

Klaus, C. 1991. 'Essay', in Scholes, R., Klaus, C., Comley, N. and Silverman, M. (eds), *Elements of Literature.* New York: Oxford University Press.

Kurzweil, E. 1996. 'Introduction', in Kurzweil, E. (ed.) *A Partisan Century: Political Writings from* Partisan Review. New York: Columbia University Press.

Koss, Stephen. 1981. *The Rise and Fall of the British Political Press in Britain. Volume Two: The Twentieth Century.* London: Hamish Hamilton.

Laski, H. 1937 (March). 'Review of *The Road to Wigan Pier*'. *Left News,* no. 11, 275–6.

Latham, S. 2009. 'Cyril Connolly's *Horizon* (1940-1950) and the End of Modernism', in Brooker, P. and Thacker, A. (eds), *The Oxford Critical and Cultural History of Modernist Magazines.* Oxford: Oxford University Press.

Law, M. H. 1934. *The English Familiar Essay in the Early Nineteenth Century.* New York: Russell and Russell.

Leavis, Q. D. 1975. 'Review of *Inside the Whale*', in Meyers, J. (ed.) *George Orwell: The Critical Heritage.* London: Routledge and Kegan Paul.

Lehmann, J. 1936. 'Manifesto'. *New Writing,* 1, v.

—1940. 'Dear Reader'. *Folios of New Writing,* 5–6.

—1957. *The Whispering Gallery.* London: Longmans, Green.

—1960. *I Am My Brother: Autobiography I.* London: Longmans.

Lodge, D. 1977. *The Modes of Modern Writing: Metaphor, Metonymy, and the Typology of Modern Literature.* London: Edward Arnold.

Lucas, S. 2004. *The Betrayal of Dissent: Beyond Orwell, Hitchens and the New American Century.* London: Pluto Press.

Lyon, J. 1999. *Manifestos: Provocations of the Modern.* Ithaca, NY: Cornell University Press.

Macdonald, D. 1942 (March). Review of *The Lion and the Unicorn. Partisan Review,* 116–19, included in Meyers, J. (ed.) *George Orwell: The Critical Heritage.* London: Routledge and Kegan Paul, 1975, pp. 191–4.

Mairet, P. 1938. Review of *Homage to Catalonia. New English Weekly,* 26 May, 129–30, included in Meyers, J. (ed.) *George Orwell: The Critical Heritage.* London: Routledge and Kegan Paul, 1975, pp. 127–30.

Marks, P. 1997. 'Illusion and Reality: The Spectre of Socialist Realism in Thirties Literature', in Williams, K. and Matthews, S. (eds), *Rewriting the Thirties: Modernism and After.* London: Longman.

—1999. 'Reputations: George Orwell'. *The Political Quarterly,* 70, 83–90.

—2004. 'Making the New: Literary Periodicals and the Construction of Modernism'. *Precursors and Aftermaths: Literature in English 1914-1945,* 2, 24–39.

Martin, A. 1996. *The New Statesman: Portrait of a Political Weekly 1913-31.* London: Frank Cass.

Martin, K. 1936. 'Spain and British Public Opinion'. *The Political Quarterly,* vii, 573–87.

—1968. *Editor: A Second Volume of Autobiography 1931-45.* Harmondsworth: Penguin.

Maxton, J. 1938 (19 August). 'So This Is Empire'. *New Leader,* 4–5.

McGovern, J. 1936 (January). 'Socialism without Compromise'. *New Leader,* 2.

McNair, J. 1937. 'Night Attack on the Aragon Front'. *New Leader,* no. 30, 3.

Mellown, E. 1986. 'The Adelphi', in Sullivan, A. (ed.) *British Literary Magazines, the Modern Age, 1918-1984.* Westport, CT: Greenwood Press.

Meyers, J. 1975. *George Orwell: The Critical Heritage.* London, Routledge and Kegan Paul.

—2000. *Orwell: Wintry Conscience of a Generation.* New York: W.W. Norton and Company.

Montagu, I. 1936. 'The U.S.S.R. Month by Month: The Trial'. *Left News,* 123–8.

Montaigne, M. 1927. *The Essays of Montaigne,* translated by E. J. Trechmann, with an introduction by J. M. Robertson.

Morpurgo, J. E. 1979. *Alan Lane, King Penguin: A Biography.* London: Hutchinson.

Morrisson, M. 2001. *The Public Face of Modernism: Little Magazines, Audiences, and Recption 1905-1920.* Madison: University of Wisconsin Press.

Mulhern, F. 1978. *The Moment of 'Scrutiny'.* London: New Left Books.

Murry, J. M. 1923 (June). 'The Cause of It All'. *The Adelphi,* vol. 1, no. 1, 8.

—1933 (January). 'Communism and Art: Or Bolshevism and Ballyhoo'. *The Adelphi,* vol. 5, no. 4, 263–70.

Newsinger, J. 1999. *Orwell's Politics.* London: Macmillan Press.

O'Neill, J. 1982. *Essaying Montaigne: A Study of the Renaissance Institution of Writing and Reading.* London: Routledge.

Orwell, G. et al. 1938 (October). 'S. O. S.'. *Controversy,* vol. 1, no. 25, 250–1.

Phillips, W. 1976. 'How Partisan Review Began'. *Commentary,* no. 62, 43.

Pimlott, B. 1977. *Labour and the Left in the 1930s.* Cambridge: Cambridge University Press.

Plowman, M. 1931 (October). 'Notes and Comments'. *The Adelphi*, vol. 3, no.1, 1–3.

—1941 (April). Review of *The Lion and the Unicorn*. *The Adelphi*, 248–50.

Pugh, M. 2006. *'Hurrah for the Blackshirts!' Fascists and Fascism in Britain between the Wars*. London: Pimlico.

Rees, R. 1961. *George Orwell: Fugitive from the Camp of Victory*. London: Secker and Warburg.

Rodden, J. 1989. *George Orwell: The Politics of Literary Reputation*. New York: Oxford University Press.

Rolph, C. R. E. 1973. *Kingsley: The Life, Letters and Diaries of Kingsley Martin*. London: Victor Gollancz.

Rushdie, S. 1991. *Outside the Whale. Imaginary Homelands: Essays and Criticism 1981-1991*. London: Granta.

Rust, W. 1949. *The Story of the* Daily Worker. London: People's Press Printing Society.

Ryan, Mary P. 1992. 'Gender and Public Access: Women's Politics in Nineteenth-Century America', in Calhoun, C. (ed.). *Habermas and the Public Sphere*. Cambridge, MA: MIT Press, pp. 259–88.

Saunders, F. S. 1999. *Who Paid the Piper: The CIA and the Cultural Cold War*. London: Granta.

Sawyer, T. A. 1986. 'Gangrel', in Sullivan, A. (ed.) *British Literary Magazines, the Modern Age, 1914-84*. Westport, CT: Greenwood Press.

Sayce, R. 1972. *The Essays of Montaigne: A Critical Exploration*. London: Weidenfeld and Nicolson.

Screech, M. A. (ed.). 1993. *Michel de Montaigne: The Complete Essays*. Harmondsworth: Penguin.

Scruton, R. 2006. *England: An Elegy*. London: Continuum.

Sedgwick, P. 1968 (November). Review of *Collected Essays, Letters and Journalism of George Orwell*. *Socialist Worker*, 3.

Shelden, M. 1989. *Friends of Promise: Cyril Connolly and the World of Horizon*. London: Hamish Hamilton.

—1991. *Orwell: The Authorised Biography*. London: William Heinemann.

Sloan, P. 1936 (October). 'They *Were* Guilty'. *Controversy*, 6.

Smith, A. 1996. *The* New Statesman*: Portrait of a Political Weekly 1913-1931*. London: Frank Cass.

Smith, C. A. 1936 (October). 'Through Discussion to Unity'. *Controversy*, vol. 1, no. 1, 1.

Stannard, M. 1992. *Evelyn Waugh*. London: J. M. Dent.

Stansky, P. and W. Abrahams. 1972. *The Unknown Orwell*. London: Constable.

Szántó, A. 2007. 'Editor's Note', in Szántó, A. (ed.) *What Orwell Didn't Know: Propaganda and the New Face of American Politics*. New York: Public Affairs.

Taylor, D. J. 2003. *Orwell: The Life*. New York: Henry Holt.

Thompson, E. P. 1960. 'Outside the Whale'. *Out of Apathy*. London: Stevens and Sons.

Unsigned. 1932. 'Scrutiny: A Manifesto'. *Scrutiny*, 1, 2–7.

—1934. 'Communists Take the Wrong Turning'. *New Leader*, 13 April, 2.

—1935. 'Open Letter to Harry Pollitt: Where Does the Community Party Stand?'. *New Leader*, 13 December, 2.

—1936. Editorial on Spanish Civil War. *Time and Tide*, vol. 12, 1 August, 1090.

—1936. Editorial. *New Leader*, 28 August, 3.

—1937 (January). 'How's This "Daily Mail"? An Eye Witness Story of an ILP'er in Madrid'. *New Leader*, 29 January, 3.

—1937 (May). 'Spain's New Government'. *Time and Tide*, 22 May, 680–1.

—1939. Statement from the General Secretary of the Workers' Education Association. *The Highway*, April, 198.

Walker, H. 1915. *The English Essay and Essayists*. London: J. M. Dent and Sons.

Warburg, F. 1959. *An Occupation for Gentleman*. London: Hutchinson.

West, R. 1936. 'Rudyard Kipling'. *New Statesman and Nation*, 25 January, 112–14.

Whitworth, M. 2009. 'Enemies of Cant: *The Athenaeum* (1919-21) and *The Adelphi* (1923-48)', in Brooker, P. and Thacker, A. (eds) *The Oxford Critical and Cultural History of Modernist Magazines*. Oxford: Oxford Univesity Press.

Wilford, H. 1995. *The New York Intellectuals: From Vanguard to Institution*. Manchester: Manchester University Press.

Williams, R. 1963. *Culture and Society 1780-1950*. Harmondsworth: Penguin.

—1979. *Politics and Letters*. London: New Left Books.

Writers' International (British Section) Statement. 1934 (October). *Left Review*, 37.

Index

Abrahams, William 31
Ackland, Valentine 13
Acland, Richard
    Unser Kampf 112
Action 52
Addison, Joseph 3, 29
Adelphi, The (and *The New Adelphi*) 2, 5,
    14, 16, 20, 22–39, 50, 72, 76–7, 84,
    98, 109, 116, 154, 170, 187, 194,
    198, 200
Adorno, Theodor
    'The Essay As Form' 8, 80
American Revolution 115
Americanization 128–9, 137, 161–2,
    189
Ami du Peuple 20, 93
Anand, Mulk Raj 39, 42, 125
Anarchism 171–2, 175, 181, 184
Anderson, Sherwood 19
Anti-Comintern Pact 49
Anti-Communism 141, 190–2
Anti-Fascism 41, 54, 60, 64, 69–70, 74,
    76, 96, 113, 141
Anti-Semitism 85, 129–32, 142, 144
Anti-Stalinism 73–4, 108, 139, 155,
    192
Athenaeum, The 32
Atlantic Monthly, The 156, 184
Atlee, Clement 199
Auden, W. H. 1, 13, 21, 66, 72–3, 82,
    85, 95, 117, 200
    'Consider this and in our time' 21
    'Spain' 72–3
Austen, Jane 45
*Authors Take Sides on the Spanish Civil
    War* 66
Ayer, A. J. 140–2, 153
    'Deistic Fallacies' 141

Bacon, Francis 3–4, 6–10
BBC 44, 83–4, 108, 117, 121–6, 131–2,
    137, 139, 156–7
Bagnold, Enid
    National Velvet 37
Bailey, L. I. 18
Barbusse, Henri 19, 50
Barthes, Roland 33
Beatles, The
    Sgt Pepper's 195
Beaverbrook, Lord 38, 59, 139
Beecher Stowe, Harriet 124, 147
    Uncle Tom's Cabin 124, 147
Bernal, J. D. 164–5
Betrayal of the Left, The 4, 104–5, 111,
    131–2
Bevan, Aneurin 62, 127
Blackshirt, The 52
Blair, Eileen (nee O'Shaughnessy) 42,
    53, 71, 75, 135
Blair, Eric 18–37, 52, 54, 84, 99, 172,
    185, 194, 198, 200 *see also* George
    Orwell
Blake, Peter 195
Blake, William 174
Bloom, Harold 3
Blunden, Edmund 23
Bodley Head, The 85
Bolshevism 31, 120
Book-of-the-Month Club 1
Borges, Jorge Luis 3
Borkenau, Franz 121
    Spanish Cockpit, The 55, 61, 67
Bort, Françoise 40–1, 85
Bradbury, Malcolm 14
Brereton, Geoffrey 54
British Empire 18, 31, 36, 38–9, 42–3,
    76–9, 89, 102, 110, 114, 179, 188

Briton, The 10
Brittain, Vera 71
Brockway, Fenner 62, 71, 77
    'Truth About Barcelona, The' 62
Brooker, Peter 14–15
Browne, Sir Thomas 7
Buchenwald 143
Burma 18, 22, 28, 43, 168, 182, 188
Burnham, James 126, 148
    Machiavellians, The 165
    Managerial Revolution, The 126,
      147–8, 165–7
Byron, Lord 142

Calder-Marshall, Arthur 98
Cambridge Left 15, 22, 34, 40, 102
Cameron, Deborah 194
Carlyle, Thomas 147
Catholics and Catholicism 20, 47, 73,
    88–9, 119, 142–3, 147, 154, 162,
    176
Caudwell, Christopher 117
Causerie 127
Chamberlain, Neville 71
Champion 92
Chapayev 93
Chase, James Hadley
    No Orchids For Miss Blandish 128–9
Chaucer, Geoffrey 130
Chesteron, G. K. 88, 143, 146, 192
Churchill, Winston 77
Cockburn, Claud
    The Week 15
Cocteau, Jean 99
Cold War 2, 135, 147–8, 166, 176, 183,
    189–96
Cole, Margaret 116
Collected Essays, Journalism and Letters
    of George Orwell, The 5, 148, 190,
    195–7
A Collection of Essays 190
Collets Bookshop 167
Collini, Stefan 141, 145, 153
Collins, Clifford 177
Collins, Norman 54
Comfort, Alex 109

Comintern 49
Commentary 129, 134
    see also Contemporary Jewish Record
Common, Jack 22, 24, 34, 50
Communists and Communism 31–2,
    47, 50–64, 68–9, 73–5, 77, 90, 95–6,
    103, 110–1, 126, 140–4, 153–4, 159,
    167, 191
Communist Party of Great Britain
    (CPGB) 52, 55–6, 61–2, 69, 75, 78,
    85, 103–4, 107, 143, 178
Communist Party of the USA
    (CPUSA) 107
Complete Works of George Orwell, The 5,
    80, 199, 201
Congress of Revolutionary Writers 19
Connolly, Cyril 14–15, 23, 36, 39, 41,
    53–4, 83, 94–5, 98–9, 122–5, 131,
    141, 154, 157–8, 178, 184–7
    Enemies of Promise 185
Conrad, Joseph 156, 182
Conservative Party 21, 93, 106, 197
Conservatives and Conservatism 20, 68,
    91–4, 102, 116, 125, 137, 176, 178
Contact: The Magazine of Pleasure 157–8,
    199
Contemporary Jewish Record 84, 129–32,
    134 *see also Commentary*
Contemporary Poetry and Prose 15, 22
Controversy 60–1, 66, 78 *see also Left*
    Forum
Cornford, John 34, 102–3, 105
    'Before the Storming of Huesca' 103
    'Left?' 34
Cornhill Magazine 83
Cowley, Abraham 7
Crick, Bernard 3, 21, 29, 52, 68, 115,
    127, 155, 165, 198
Criterion, The 14, 40–1, 46, 83, 108–9,
    135
Cunningham, Valentine 66

Dachau 143
DADA 24
Daily Express 59, 84
Daily Mail 56, 59, 63

Daily Mirror 115
Daily Worker 40, 54, 56, 59, 61–3, 67–8, 72, 110
  'Where Does the I.L.P. Stand?' 62
Dali, Salvador 154
Davies, W. H.
  Autobiography of a Supertramp 36
Davison, Peter 18, 54, 75, 126, 158, 172–3, 175, 182, 199, 201
Day-Lewis, Cecil 13, 31–2, 36
  'The Poet And Revolution' 32
De la Mare, Walter 23
Decline of the English Murder and Other Essays 195
Dick, Kay 136, 139
Dickens, Charles 1, 25, 45, 85, 87–93, 120, 130, 152, 169, 173, 185–6, 194–201
  David Copperfield 185
  Great Expectations 185
  Oliver Twist 130
Don Quixote and Sancho Panza 123
During, Simon 2, 192
Durrell, Lawrence 99

Eagleton, Terry 12
Edwards, Bob 54
Edwards, Ruth Dudley 51, 75
Ehrenburg, Ilya 153
Einstein, Albert 19
Elefanten og Andre Essays (Danish translation) 191
Eliot, T. S. 3–4, 23, 34, 66, 95, 117, 124–5, 130, 156
Ellis, Havelock 71
Emerson, Ralph Waldo 3–4
Empson, William 125, 139
England Your England (British edition) 189–90
England Your England (Japanese edition) 191
English Digest 84
Eton 13–14, 23, 26, 99, 140–1
Evans, Jon 60
Evening Standard 161
Experiment 15

Faber & Faber 84
Fabian Society 32
  Fabian Research Pamphlets 164
Fact 83
Fascists and Fascism 2, 34–6, 40–1, 49–77, 92, 96–7, 101–2, 109–11, 114–17, 121, 124–8, 134, 137–9, 156, 197
Fenby, Charles 49–50
Fenwick, Gillian 84, 136
Fish, Stanley 8–9
Fisher, Clive 124
Focus 4, 156
Folios of New Writing 2, 83–4, 100, 105
Fontaine 127
Fortnightly Review 5, 44
Forward 84
Fox, Patricia 13
Fox, Ralph 36
  The Colonial Policy of British Imperialism 36
France, Anatole 192
Franco, Gen. Francisco 49, 54, 58, 60, 63, 66, 68, 74–5
Frank, Waldo 98
Frankford, Frank 67
Freedom–Through Anarchism 171
French Revolution 115
Freud, Sigmund 24, 129
Fyvel, Tosco 112, 133

G. K.'s Weekly 18, 20–1
Galsworthy, John 18
Gandhi, Mahatma 1, 136, 180–3, 188
  Story of My Experiments With Truth, The 180–1
Gangrel 5, 15, 135, 167–8, 183–4, 187
Gem 87, 91–2
Gibbon, Lewis Grassic 35
Gide, Andre 164
Gissing, George 184
  New Grub Street 184
  Odd Women, The 184
Goebbels, Josef 55
Gollancz, Victor (and Victor Gollancz Ltd) 34, 47, 51–4, 61, 75, 78, 84, 87–8, 97, 103–4, 111–2, 154

'The CP, Revolutionary Defeatism, and the "People's Convention"' 104
'Thoughts After Munich' 104
'Victory Books' 112
Good, Graham 3, 9, 29, 136, 183
Goodbye To Berlin 42 *see also* Christopher Isherwood
Gorer, Geoffrey 59, 67–8, 88
Gorki, Maxim 19
Gow 141
Graham, Margaret Baker 172
Greenberg, Clement 108
Greene, Graham 1, 200
Grigson, Geoffrey 15, 22, 35
Guilty Men 112, 116
Gulliver's Travels 169–71, 174, 188
Gunn, Neil M. 167

Habermas, Jurgen 10–2, 61
Hall, Radclyffe
    The Well of Loneliness 45
Hammond, John 3, 41, 127
Harcourt, Brace 155, 190
Harper's 155
Hartley, L. P. 37
Hawkins, Desmond 108
Hazlitt, William 3, 29, 192, 195
Heinemann 136
Henderson, Philip
    The Novel Today 47, 117
Heppenstall, Rayner 167
Hewison, Robert 83, 132
Higgins, John 178
Highway, The 5, 74–5
Hill, Christopher 178
Hilliard, Christopher 13
Hitchens, Christopher 197
Hitler, Adolf 49, 51, 60, 76–9, 84, 96, 101, 105–6, 111, 113, 120, 126, 131, 143, 181
Hoffman, Frederick 12
Hogarth Press 40, 85 *see also* Leonard *and* Virginia Woolf
Hogben, Lancelot 159
Hoggart, Richard
    The Uses of Literacy 193

Home Guard 105, 123
Hopkins, Gerard Manley
    'Felix Randal' 118–19
Horizon 14–16, 84–5, 94, 99, 108–9, 120–5, 132, 140–1, 146, 149, 154, 157–9, 172, 175, 178, 182, 184–5, 187, 193, 199–200
Hornung, E. W. 128
Horrabin, Winfred 116–17
Houghton, Claude 167
Howe, Irving 3, 195–7
Hunter, Jefferson 136
Hutchinsons 4
Huxley, Aldous 95, 130
Hynes, Samuel 40–1

Imperialism 30, 35–9, 42–4, 69–72, 76–80, 84, 87, 114, 124–5, 131, 176, 183, 194, 197
Independent Labour Party (I. L. P.) 16, 23, 31, 52–5, 60–3, 67, 69–72, 75, 77, 79–81, 84, 101, 104, 109, 137, 179–80
Intellectuals and the Intellgentsia 1, 16, 19, 24, 39, 47, 50–1, 70, 72–4, 84, 91, 94, 96–7, 102, 108–10, 114, 120, 122, 130, 132, 134, 140–5, 152–5, 159, 161, 164–6, 176–80, 184–5, 188, 195–8
Intelligentsia of Great Britain 47
    see also D. M. Mirsky
Isherwood, Christopher 1, 42, 85, 200
    see also Goodbye to Berlin
    'The Nowaks' 42

Jackson, T. A. 88
James, Henry 156, 178
Jellinek, Frank 65
Joad, C. E. M. 71, 141
Joeres, Ruth-Ellen Boetcher 9
Johnson, Dr Samuel 3–4, 195
    Dictionary 6
Jonathan Cape 84
Joyce, James 23, 34, 37, 95, 97, 117, 156, 178
    Ulysses 19, 37, 95

Kent, Christopher 12–13
Keynes, John Maynard 32
Kipling, Rudyard 36–9, 45, 92, 124–5,
    137, 146, 169
    A Choice of Kipling's Verse (edited by
    T.S. Eliot) 124
Kirwan, Celia 175
Klaus, Carl 29, 362
Koestler, Arthur 67, 121, 123, 141, 154,
    156–7, 192
    Arrival and Departure 156–7
    Darkness at Noon 157
    Gladiators, The 156–7
    Scum of the Earth 157
Koss, Stephen 15

Labour Party 76, 78, 84, 112, 125, 127,
    134, 178–9, 191–2
Lamb, Charles 3, 7
Larkin, Philip 119
Laski, Harold 51–2, 104, 159
Law, Marie Hamilton 7–8
Lawrence, D. H. 22–3, 95
Lawrence and Wishart 85
Le Monde 19
Le Progrès Civique 18, 20, 25
Leavis, F. R. 22, 178 *see also Scrutiny*
    Leavisism 178, 184
Leavis, Q. D. 98–9, 133
Lee, Jennie 54
Left Book Club (LBC) 16, 51, 55, 60,
    67, 69, 72, 75, 78, 103–4, 111–2,
    125, 159 *see also Left News*
Left Forum 145, 146
Left News 16, 51–2, 60, 84, 104–5,
    110–2, 132 *see also* Left Book Club
Left Review 13, 15, 22, 34–5, 39–40, 66,
    107
Lehmann, John 15, 22, 40–2, 44, 83,
    85, 100, 109 *see also New Writing*
Lewis, Wyndham 95, 147
Life and Letters 84
Listener, The 68, 84, 117–19
Locke, John
    *Essay Concerning Human
    Understanding* 6

Lodge, David 2, 198
London, Jack
    The Iron Heel 166
London Magazine 185
London Mercury 83
Lucas, Scott 2
Lukács, Georg
    'On the Nature and Form of the
    Essay' 8
Lyon, Janet 13

McCarthy, Mary 108, 196
Macdonald, Dwight 116–17, 127, 135,
    141, 158, 166, 173–4
MacDonald, Ramsay 21
McGovern, John 54
McNair, John 54
MacNeice, Louis 94, 117
Magnet 87, 91–3
Mairet, Philip 65, 68–9
Major, John 2, 197
Malraux, Andre 156
Manchester Evening News 84, 134, 159, 161
Manifestoes 5, 12–13, 35, 40, 71, 123–4,
    167
Mankowitz, Wolf 177
Mannin, Ethel 71
Mansfield, Katherine 23
Martin, Kingsley 15, 32, 49–50, 54–5,
    61, 82, 159
Marx, Karl 40, 89
Marxists and Marxism 19, 24, 31, 47,
    88–91, 94, 107, 117, 141, 144, 164,
    178, 194
Maugham, Somerset 28
Maxton, James 62, 71, 77
Mellown, Elgin 31
Mellown, Muriel 14
Melville, Herman
    Moby Dick 24
Mendes, Alfred 42
Merrick, Leonard 146
Meyers, Jeffrey 29, 31
Miller, Henry 87–8, 94–9, 123, 131,
    141, 157, 167
    Tropic of Cancer 94–5

Miller, Max 123
Milton, John 150–2
  Areopagitica 150
Mirsky, D. S.
  Intelligentsia of Great Britain 47, 93
Mitchison, Naomi 62
Mittman, Elizabeth 9
Modern Boy 92
Modern Essays 44
Modern Quarterly 164
Modern Scot, The 35
Modernism 13, 15, 23, 40, 194
Monde 18–21
Montagu, Ivor 60
Montaigne, Michel de 3–9, 29, 88
Moore, George 147
Moore, Leonard 52–5, 87, 136, 156, 166
Morris, William 50
Morrisson, Mark 12
Mortimer, Raymond 67
Moscow Show Trials 60, 157
Mosley, Oswald 49, 51
Movement, The 194
Muggeridge, Malcolm 1
Mumford, Lewis 24
Munich Crisis 71–2, 75, 104
Murry, John Middleton 22–3, 31–2, 72, 154
  'Communism and Art: or, Bolshevism and Ballyhoo' 31–2
Mussolini, Benito 51, 113
  The Trial of Mussolini 112

Nationalism 2, 35, 88–9, 120, 131, 142–5, 177, 183
Nazi-Soviet Pact 78, 120, 151
Nazism 14, 105, 121, 129, 138, 147
Nehru, Jawaharlal 77
Neil, Charles 167
New Age 32
New Directions in Prose and Poetry 99
New English Weekly 5, 16, 22, 33–4, 37–8, 45–7, 55–7, 65–8, 84, 94, 98, 137
New Leader 16, 53–5, 62–3, 67, 69, 71, 77
  'Communists Take Wrong Turning' 118
  'Empire Special' 143

'Eye-witness Story by an I.L.P.er in Madrid' 119
'If War Comes, We Shall Resist' 133
'We Are Proud of P.O.U.M.' 63
'Why Communists Attack P. O. U. M.' 63
New Leader, The (New York) 180
New Left Review 193
New Masses 107
New Republic 84, 158
New Saxon Pamphlets 84
New Statesman and Nation (including *The Nation*) 14–15, 32–9, 53–5, 61–7, 72, 76–7, 83–4, 99, 109, 158, 196
New Stories 83
New Verse 15, 22, 35, 40, 83
  'An Enquiry' 35
New Writing 15–16, 22, 40–2, 44, 81, 83–5, 141, 182, 200 *see also* John Lehmann
New York Review of Books 196
New Yorker 155, 195
Newbolt, Sir Henry 102–3, 105
  'There's a breathless hush in the Close tonight' 103
News Chronicle 56–7, 59, 61, 72, 80
News of the World 158, 161
Newsinger 31, 140–1
North Briton, The 31
Now 171–2, 182, 184
Now and Then 84

O'Brien, Conor Cruise 196
O'Casey, Sean 66
O'Neill, John 9
Oak, Liston 54
Obaldia, Claire de 3, 29
Obama, Barack 2, 199
Observer, The 37, 84, 121, 134, 158
OED 2, 148
Old Moore's Almanac 126
Orage, Alfred 22, 32, 37
Orwell, George *see also* Eric Blair
  Animal Farm 1, 3, 17, 39, 51–2, 84–5, 111, 121, 123, 126, 134–5, 139–40, 154–7, 187–8, 190–8
  'Anti-Semitism in Britain' 129–31

'Art of Donald McGill, The' 4, 16, 122, 128, 154, 191, 193
'Arthur Koestler' 156–7
'As I Please' 84, 126–7, 132, 145, 175
'Barcelona Tragedy' 55
'Benefit of Clergy' 4
'Books vs Cigarettes' 149–50
'Bookshop Memories' 4, 44–5, 90
'Boys' Weeklies' 2, 4, 16, 88–94, 99, 122, 128, 137
Burmese Days 31, 34–8, 99, 168
'Charles Dickens' 3–4, 91, 94–5, 99, 130–1, 152, 178, 191
'Charles Reade' 99–100
A Clergyman's Daughter 31, 37, 39, 155, 191
Coming Up for Air 75, 85, 98, 122
'Common Lodging Houses' 33
Critical Essays 3–4, 99, 136, 154–5, 187, 192
'Decline of the English Murder' 4, 161–2
'Democracy in the British Army' 78–80, 89, 101, 103
Dickens, Dali and Others: Studies in Popular Culture 4, 155, 187
Down and Out in Paris and London, Lady Poverty, The (rejected title) 18, 21–2, 31, 34–6, 48, 51, 155, 168, 191, 194
'Down the Mine' 190
'England Your England' 113–16
English People, The 4
'Eye-Witness In Barcelona' 55, 61–6, 78, 82
'A Farthing Newspaper' 18, 20
'Fascism and Democracy' 110–1
'Frontiers of Art and Propaganda, The' 117–18
'George Gissing' 182, 184–5
'Good Bad Books' 145–7
'A Good Word for the Vicar of Bray' 162–4
'A Hanging' 2–4, 16–17, 28–31, 36, 38, 42–4, 48, 81, 86–7, 186–9, 191, 194, 197–200
Homage To Catalonia 53–5, 59, 65–8, 81–2, 139, 155, 188

'Hop Picking' 32–3
'Hop-Picking Diary' 32
'How the Poor Die' 172–3, 182, 185, 188, 191
'In Defence of P. G. Wodehouse' 4, 136–9, 154
'In Defence of the Novel' 45–6, 57
Inside The Whale and Other Essays 3–4, 75, 87–99, 108, 131–2, 154, 187, 192, 195
'Inside the Whale' 2, 88, 94–9, 102, 117–18, 131, 139, 152, 157, 194, 197
'Intellectual Revolt, The' 161
Keep The Aspidistra Flying 39–40, 98–9
'La Censure en Angleterre' 18–19
'Lear, Tolstoy and the Fool' 173–5, 180–2
Lion and the Unicorn, The 4, 116
'Lion and the Unicorn, The' 2–3, 107, 111–17, 131–2, 138, 142, 187, 190
'Literature and Totalitarianism' 119
'London Letter' 16, 84, 107–9, 140, 155, 171, 175
'Marrakech' 85–7, 100, 132
'Meaning of a Poem, The' 118–19
'Moon Under Water, The' 161
'My Country Right or Left' 2, 100–3, 105, 107, 113–14, 116, 131, 142
'A Nice Cup of Tea' 161
'Night Attack on the Aragon Front' 54
Nineteen Eighty-Four 1–3, 52, 120, 135–6, 139, 142, 144, 148, 150–3, 163, 165–6, 169, 171–2, 176, 178–82, 187–8, 190–8
'North and South' 190
'Not Counting Niggers' 75–80, 85–7, 89, 101, 103, 176
'Notes on Nationalism' 136, 140–5, 150–1, 157, 160, 166, 179
'Our Opportunity' 104–7, 111
'Pacifism and the War: A "Controversy"' 109–10
'Paper is Precious' 83
'Patriots and Revolutionaries' 104–5
'Political Reflections on the Crisis' 72–3

'Politics and the English
  Language' 136, 152, 157–61, 165,
  167, 169, 182, 187–9, 194, 197–200
'Politics vs. Literature' 169–72,
  174–5, 181–2, 188
'Prevention of Literature, The' 136,
  150–6, 165, 169, 179, 194
'Raffles and Miss Blandish' 4, 127,
  132, 137, 154, 161–2, 193
'Reflections on Gandhi' 4, 136,
  180–2, 187–9
'Revenge is Sour' 145, 147
Road To Wigan Pier, The 39, 47,
  50–3, 56–7, 69–71, 79, 86, 106,
  122, 140, 149, 155, 159, 163,
  187, 194
'Rudyard Kipling' (1936) 38, 124
'Rudyard Kipling' (1942) 4, 124–5,
  137, 154, 191, 193
'Second Thoughts on James
  Burnham' 164–7, 189
'Shooting an Elephant' 2, 29, 40–4,
  48, 77, 81, 86–7, 100, 147, 182,
  185–9, 191, 194, 197–9
'Shopkeepers at War' 113–14
'A Smoking Room Story' 182
'Socialism and War' 75
'Spike, The' 25–9, 32–3, 35–6
'Spilling the Spanish Beans' 16,
  55–68, 74, 147
'Such, Such Were the Joys' 184–6,
  190–1, 198
'That Mysterious Cart' 54, 67
'Tolstoy and Shakespeare' 118
'Toward European Unity' 176–7
'W. B. Yeats' 4, 154
'Wells, Hitler and the World State' 4,
  120–2, 154, 156, 193
'Why I Join the I. L. P.' 69–71, 97,
  102, 167
'Why I Write' 2, 4, 136, 167–9, 187,
  189–90, 194–7, 200
'You and the Atom Bomb' 2, 135,
  145, 147–8, 150, 166
Orwell Reader, The 190–1
Orwell, Sonia 195–6, 198

Pacifism 14, 62, 72, 77, 100, 109, 125,
  142, 144, 171, 175, 181
Padmore, George 71
Partisan Review 5, 16, 84, 107–9, 116,
  121–2, 127, 129, 132, 140, 146, 155,
  175–7, 180, 182, 184, 196
  'The Future of Socialism' 175–8
Patriotism 14, 149, 153, 169, 175, 185,
  187, 188, 190, 191, 192, 193, 194,
  205, 206, 207, 208, 210, 235, 247,
  253
Pearse, Andrew 156
PEN 150
Penguin Books 41, 51, 112, 191, 195
  Penguin New Writing 44
People's Front 49, 52, 58, 70
  see also Popular Front and United
  Front
Perles, Alfred 167
Persuasion (periodical) 84
Phillips, Rodney 175
Phillips, William 107
Pick, J. B. 167, 169
Picture Post 84
Pimlott, Ben 51
Pitcairn, Frank 54
Plebs, The 116
Plomer, William 39, 100
Plowman, Max 20, 23–5, 28, 34, 116
Poetry (London) 84
Poetry and the People 13, 15
Polemic 15–16, 135, 140–2, 144–6,
  149–50, 153–4, 164, 166, 169,
  173–5, 180, 182, 184
Politics 4, 84, 127, 132, 158–9, 166,
  173–4, 180
Politics and Letters 15, 135, 177–8, 180,
  184–5
  'Critic and Leviathan' 177–8
Pollitt, Harry 62, 75
Pope, Alexander
  Moral Essays 6
Popular Front 49, 51, 58–9, 69, 72, 84,
  103, 125 *see also* People's Front and
  United Front
P. O. U. M. 51–3, 63–8

Pound, Ezra 34, 66, 95, 117
Pritchett, V. S. 37, 100
Pritt, D. N. 112
Propaganda 11, 20, 41, 47, 50, 52, 55, 59, 61, 67, 79, 90–3, 106, 109–10, 115, 118, 138, 179, 193, 198
Public sphere 10–15, 40, 51–2, 61, 99, 104, 109, 112, 141, 196, 200, 202
Purpose 83

Quennell, Peter, 37

Raffles 128–9, 146
Rahv, Philip 107, 122, 125–6, 140
Rajan, Balachandra 156
Rauschning, Hermann 121
Read, Herbert 73
Rees, Richard 16–17, 23, 27, 31, 34, 39–40, 50, 72
Revolt 73–4
Reynal and Hitchcock 155
Richardson, Dorothy 23
Rodden, John 3, 155, 190, 192, 194–5
Roditi, Edouard 24
Rolland, Romain 19
Rosenberg, Alfred 121
Rothermere, Lord 59
Rushdie, Salman 2
Russell, Bertrand 141, 153
Russian Revolution 115, 157
Rutherford, Mark 126
Ryan, Mary 12

Sartre, Jean-Paul 178, 180, 202
Saturday Book 4
Saunders, Frances Stonor 191–2
Savage, D. S. 109
Sawyer, Thomas 167
Sayce, Richard 8
Sceats, John 69
Scott, A. F. 44
Screech, M. A. 6
Scrutiny 22, 35, 40, 46, 83, 98, 178
    see also F. R. Leavis
Searchlight Books 112, 117, 123, 133, 190, 194

Second World War 15, 34, 78, 80, 100–1, 134, 137, 139, 148
Sedgwick, Peter 195–6
Selected Essays 191
Selected Writings 191
Seven 83
Shakespeare, Wiliam 118, 130, 169, 173–5, 189
    King Lear 174
Shaw, George Bernard 50, 125–6, 130, 202
Shelden, Michael 24, 29, 31, 123, 127, 198
Shooting an Elephant and Other Essays 184, 187
Silone, Ignazio 121, 156
Sinclair, Upton 19, 50
Slater, Humphrey 140, 175
Sloan, Pat
    'They *Were* Guilty' 114
Smillie, Bob 104
Smith, Adrian 32
Smollett, Tobias 10, 30
Social Credit 37–8
Socialist Book Centre 166
Socialist League 125
Socialist Realism 72, 364
Socialists and Socialism 2–3, 30–1, 35, 40, 47, 49–52, 59–63, 70–6, 78–80, 83–5, 90, 95, 100–17, 125, 131–2, 134, 157, 163, 166–8, 175–9, 183, 190–3, 197
Sommerfield, John
    Volunteer in Spain 67
Soros, George 199
Soviet Union 14, 34–5, 47, 50–1, 58–60, 69, 72, 78–9, 80, 90, 103, 107–12, 120–1, 134–5, 139–40, 144, 151–4, 165, 176, 179, 191–2, 198, 201
Spanish Civil War 16, 35, 47, 49–75, 79, 99–100, 110, 143, 147, 168, 190
Spectator, The 10, 12, 15, 37, 39
Spender, Stephen 35, 66–7, 82, 85, 95, 98, 117, 123, 141

Stalin, Josef 50, 96, 165–6
Stansky, Peter 31
Steele, Richard 3, 29
Stein, Gertude 99
Steiner, George 195
Strachey, John 36, 51, 104, 107
   Coming Struggle for Power, The 36
   'Literature and Dialectical
     Materialism' 107
Strand Magazine 4
Streit, Clarence K.
   Union Now 75–6
Surrealism 53
Swift, Jonathan 3, 169–71, 174, 182,
   188, 192
Swingler, Randall 154
Symons, Julian 175, 177
Synopsis 84

Tambimuttu 125
Tatler, The 10, 12, 29
Taylor, D. J. 21, 29
Tennyson, Alfred, Lord
   The Children's Hospital 173
Thacker, Andrew 14–15
Thackeray, William Makepeace 45, 89,
   130
Thomas, Dylan 99
Thompson, E. P. 194
Time and Tide 14–16, 35, 54, 61, 63,
   67–8, 84, 98
   'Men and Books', 72
Times, The 54
Times Literary Supplement 36, 37, 39–40
Tolstoy, Alexei 153
Tolstoy, Leo 118, 173–5, 180–3, 189
   Shakespeare and the Drama 174
Totalitarianism, 1, 16, 58, 73, 81, 91,
   93, 95–7, 107, 110–14, 119–29,
   134, 138–40, 144, 150–6, 159,
   163–70, 175, 182–3, 188–9, 192,
   201
Toynbee, Phillip 157–8
Trechmann, E. J. 9
Tribune 84, 116, 121, 125–7, 131–2, 134,
   145–9, 153–4, 158–65, 188

Trilling, Lionel 108, 196
Trollope, Anthony 44–5, 147
Trotsky, Leon 50
Trotskyists and Trotskyism 60–2, 69, 73,
   105, 121, 142–4
Twentieth Century Verse 15, 84

United Front 51 *see also* People's Front
   and Popular Front
Upward, Edward 94, 117

Venture 15
Victory or Vested Interest? 4
Voice of Scotland 83
Voltaire, François 192

Wales 153, 206
Walker, Hugh 7–10
War Commentary–For Anarchism 84
Warburg, Fredric (including
   Martin Secker & Warburg and
   Secker & Warburg) 53–5, 85, 112,
   116, 136, 154, 180, 182, 184–6,
   190
Waugh, Evelyn 1, 66, 124, 154, 182,
   200
W. E. A. (Workers' Educational
   Association) 74–5
Week, The 15
Weidenfeld, George 157–8
Wellington, Duke of 78
Wells, H. G. 89, 120–2, 202
Welsh Review 83
West, Rebecca 39
Westrope, Francis and Myfanwy 37
Whitworth, Michael 22–3, 32
Williams, Raymond 177–8, 193–4, 197
   Culture and Society 1780–1950 193
Williams, William Carlos 99
Wilson, Edmund 108, 155, 192
Windmill, The 4, 15, 136, 139, 184
Wingate, S. D. 147–8
Wizard 92
Wodehouse, P. G. 136–9
   My Man Jeeves 137
Woodcock, George 109, 171–2, 175

Woolf, Leonard 40, 85 *see also* Hogarth
    Press
Woolf, Virginia 3, 23, 40, 147
    see also Hogarth Press
World Digest 84

Writer's International Statement 34–5

Zamyatin, Yevgeny
    We 166
Zionism 142, 144